INFOCOMP 2016

The Sixth International Conference on Advanced Communications and Computation

MODOPT 2016

The International Symposium on Modeling and Optimization

May 22 - 26, 2016

Valencia, Spain

INFOCOMP 2016 Editors

Claus-Peter Rückemann, Westfälische Wilhelms-Universität Münster / Leibniz Universität Hannover / North-German Supercomputing Alliance, Germany
Malgorzata Pankowska, University of Economics, Katowice, Poland

Printed from e-media with permission by:

Curran Associates, Inc.
57 Morehouse Lane
Red Hook, NY 12571

Some format issues inherent in the e-media version may also appear in this print version.

Printed by Curran Associates, Inc. (2016)

International Academy, Research, and Industry Association (IARIA)
412 Derby Way
Wilmington, DE 19810

Phone: (408) 893-6407
Fax: (408) 527-6351

petre@iaria.org

Additional copies of this publication are available from:

Curran Associates, Inc.
57 Morehouse Lane
Red Hook, NY 12571 USA
Phone: 845-758-0400
Fax: 845-758-2633
Email: curran@proceedings.com
Web: www.proceedings.com

TABLE OF CONTENTS

INFOCOMP 2016

Foreword

The Sixth International Conference on Advanced Communications and Computation (INFOCOMP 2016), held between May 22-26, 2016, in Valencia, Spain, continued a series of events dedicated to advanced communications and computing aspects, covering academic and industrial achievements and visions.

The diversity of semantics of data, context gathering and processing led to complex mechanisms for applications requiring special communication and computation support in terms of volume of data, processing speed, context variety, etc. The new computation paradigms and communications technologies are now driven by the needs for fast processing and requirements from data-intensive applications and domain-oriented applications (medicine, geo-informatics, climatology, remote learning, education, large scale digital libraries, social networks, etc.). Mobility, ubiquity, multicast, multi-access networks, data centers, cloud computing are now forming the spectrum of de factor approaches in response to the diversity of user demands and applications. In parallel, measurements control and management (self-management) of such environments evolved to deal with new complex situations.

INFOCOMP 2016 also featured the following Symposium

- MODOPT 2016: The International Symposium on Modeling and Optimization

We take here the opportunity to warmly thank all the members of the INFOCOMP 2016 Technical Program Committee, as well as the numerous reviewers. The creation of such a broad and high quality conference program would not have been possible without their involvement. We also kindly thank all the authors who dedicated much of their time and efforts to contribute to INFOCOMP 2016. We truly believe that, thanks to all these efforts, the final conference program consisted of top quality contributions.

Also, this event could not have been a reality without the support of many individuals, organizations, and sponsors. We are grateful to the members of the INFOCOMP 2016 organizing committee for their help in handling the logistics and for their work to make this professional meeting a success.

We hope that INFOCOMP 2016 was a successful international forum for the exchange of ideas and results between academia and industry and for the promotion of progress in the areas of communications and computations.

We are convinced that the participants found the event useful and communications very open. We hope that Valencia provided a pleasant environment during the conference and everyone saved some time to enjoy the charm of the city.

INFOCOMP 2016 Chairs:

INFOCOMP General Chair

Claus-Peter Rückemann, Westfälische Wilhelms-Universität Münster / Leibniz Universität Hannover / North-German Supercomputing Alliance, Germany

MODOPT 2016 Advisory Chairs

Ian Flood, University of Florida, USA
Claus-Peter Rückemann, Westfälische Wilhelms-Universität Münster / Leibniz Universität Hannover / North-German Supercomputing Alliance, Germany
Mauro Iacono, Seconda Universita' degli Studi di Napoli, Italy

INFOCOMP 2016

COMMITTEE

INFOCOMP General Chair

Claus-Peter Rückemann, Westfälische Wilhelms-Universität Münster / Leibniz Universität Hannover / North-German Supercomputing Alliance, Germany

INFOCOMP Advisory Committee

Hans-Joachim Bungartz, Technische Universität München (TUM) - Garching, Germany
Petre Dini, Concordia University - Montreal, Canada / China Space Agency Center - Beijing, China
Sik Lee, Supercomputing Center / Korea Institute of Science and Technology Information (KISTI), Korea
Subhash Saini, NASA, USA
Manfred Krafczyk, Institute for Computational Modeling in Civil Engineering (iRMB) - Braunschweig, Germany

INFOCOMP Academia Chairs

Alexander Knapp, Universität Augsburg, Germany
Malgorzata Pankowska, University of Economics, Katowice, Poland

INFOCOMP Research Institute Liaison Chairs

Kei Davis, Los Alamos National Laboratory, USA
Edgar A. Leon, Lawrence Livermore National Laboratory, USA
Ivor Spence, School of Electronics, Electrical Engineering and Computer Science, Queen's University Belfast, Northern Ireland, Research for High Performance and Distributed Computing / Queen's University Belfast, UK

INFOCOMP Industry Chairs

Alfred Geiger, T-Systems Solutions for Research GmbH, Germany
Hans-Günther Müller, Cray, Germany

INFOCOMP Special Area Chairs on Large Scale and Fast Computation

José Gracia, High Performance Computing Center Stuttgart (HLRS), University of Stuttgart, Germany
Björn Hagemeier, Juelich Supercomputing Centre, Forschungszentrum Juelich GmbH, Germany
Walter Lioen, SURFsara, Netherlands
Lutz Schubert, Institute of Information Resource Management, University of Ulm, Germany

INFOCOMP Special Area Chairs on Networks and Communications

Noelia Correia, University of the Algarve, Portugal
Wolfgang Hommel, Leibniz Supercomputing Centre - Munich, Germany

INFOCOMP Special Area Chairs on Advanced Applications

Bernhard Bandow, Max Planck Institute for Solar System Research (MPS), Göttingen, Germany
Diglio A. Simoni, RTI International - Research Triangle Park, USA

INFOCOMP Special Area Chairs on Evaluation Context

Huong Ha, University of Newcastle, Australia (Singapore campus)
Philipp Kremer, German Aerospace Center (DLR), Institute of Robotics and Mechatronics, Oberpfaffenhofen, Germany

INFOCOMP Special Area Chairs on Biometry

Ulrich Norbisrath, Nazarbayev University, Kazakhstan / BIOMETRY.com, Switzerland

INFOCOMP 2016 Technical Program Committee

Wassim Abu Abed, Institute for Computational Modelling in Civil Engineering - Technische Universität Braunschweig, Germany
Ajith Abraham, Machine Intelligence Research Labs (MIR Labs), USA
Mehmet Akşit, University of Twente, Netherlands
Ali I. Al Mussa, King Abdulaziz City for Science and Technology (KACST), Saudi Arabia
Daniel Andresen, Kansas State University, USA
Bernadetta Kwintiana Ane, Institute of Computer-aided Product Development Systems, Universitaet Stuttgart, Germany
Douglas Archibald, University of Ottawa, Canada
John Ashley, NVIDIA Corporation, USA
Hazeline U. Asuncion, University of Washington, Bothell, USA
Simon Reay Atkinson, The University of Sydney, Australia
Mehmet Balman, VMware Inc. & Lawrence Berkeley National Laboratory, USA
Bernhard Bandow, Max Planck Institute for Solar System Research (MPS), Göttingen, Germany
Enobong Bassey, Auckland University of Technology, New Zealand
Khalid Belhajjame, Université Paris Dauphine, France
Belgacem Ben Youssef, King Saud University Riyadh, KSA / Simon Fraser University Vancouver, British Columbia, Canada
Martin Berzins, University of Utah, USA
Rupak Biswas, NASA Ames Research Center, USA
Rim Bouhouch, National Engineering School of Tunis, Tunisia
Elzbieta Lewańska, Poznan University of Economics, Poland
Hans-Joachim Bungartz, Technische Universität München (TUM) - Garching, Germany
Diletta Romana Cacciagrano, Computer Science Division, School of Science and Technology, University of Camerino, Italy
Xiao-Chuan Cai, University of Colorado Boulder, USA
Antonio Martí Campoy, Universitat Politècnica de València, Spain
Laura Carrington, University of California, San Diego/ San Diego Supercomputer Center, USA
Emre Celebi, Louisiana State University in Shreveport, USA
Hsi-Ya Chang, National Center for High-Performance Computing (NCHC), Taiwan

Jian Chang, Bournemouth University, UK
Chien-Hsing Chou, Tamkang University, Taiwan
Jerry Chi-Yuan Chou, National Tsing Hua University, Taiwan
Sung-Bae Cho, Yonsei University, Seoul, Korea
Noelia Correia, University of Algarve, Portugal
Matthew Leon Curry, Sandia National Laboratories, USA
Kei Davis, Los Alamos National Laboratory / Computer, Computational, and Statistical Sciences Division, USA
Sergio De Agostino, Sapienza University-Rome, Italy
Flávio de Oliveira Silva, Universidade Federal de Uberlândia, MG, Brasil
Vieri del Bianco, Università dell'Insubria, Italia
Šandor Dembitz, University of Zagreb, Faculty of Electrical Engineering and Computing, Croatia
Amine Dhraief, University of Kairouan, Tunisia
Beniamino Di Martino, Dipartimento di Ingegneria dell'Informazione, Seconda Università di Napoli, Italy
Zhong-Hui Duan, University of Akron, USA
Truong Vinh Truong Duy, JAIST / University of Tokyo, Japan
Vanessa End, Gesellschaft für wissenschaftliche Datenverarbeitung mbH Göttingen (GWDG), Germany
Jürgen Falkner, Fraunhofer-Institut für Arbeitswirtschaft und Organisation IAO, Stuttgart, Germany
Mohammed Farfour, Energy & Resources Eng. Dept., Chonnam National University, Gwangju, South Korea
Christophe Feltus, Luxembourg Institute of Science and Technology (LIST), Luxemborg
Lars Fischer, Research Group for IT Security, University of Siegen, Germany
Ian Flood, Rinker School, College of Design, Construction and Planning, University of Florida, USA
Dariusz Frejlichowski, West Pomeranian University of Technology, Poland
Huirong Fu, Oakland University - Rochester, USA
Munehiro Fukuda, Division of Computing and Software Systems, School of Science, Technology Engineering, and Math, University of Washington, Bothell, USA
Marta Gatius, Technical University of Catalonia, Spain
José Gracia, High Performance Computing Center Stuttgart (HLRS), University of Stuttgart, Germany
Alfred Geiger, T-Systems Solutions for Research GmbH, Germany
Andy Georgi, Dresden University of Technology, Germany
Birgit Frida Stefanie Gersbeck-Schierholz, Leibniz Universität Hannover/Certification Authority University of Hannover (UH-CA), Germany
Franca Giannini, Consiglio Nazionale delle Ricerche - Genova, Italy
Fabio Gomes de Andrade, Federal Institute of Science, Education and Technology of Paraíba, Brazil
Carina González, University of La Laguna, Spain
Conceicao Granja, Tromsø Telemedicine Laboratory - Norwegian Centre for Telemedicine, University Hospital of North Norway, Tromsø, Norway
Richard Gunstone, Bournemouth University, UK
Huong Ha, University of Newcastle, Australia (Singapore campus)
Björn Hagemeier, Juelich Supercomputing Centre, Forschungszentrum Juelich GmbH, Germany
Malgorzata Hanzl, Technical University of Lodz, Poland
Enrique Hernandez Orallo, Universitat Politecnica de Valencia, Spain
Abbas Hijazi, Lebanese University, Lebanon
Daniel Holmes, University of Edinburgh, UK
Wolfgang Hommel, Leibniz Supercomputing Centre - Munich, Germany
Tzyy-Leng Horng, Feng Chia University, Taiwan
Kuo-Chan Huang, National Taichung University of Education, Taiwan

Friedrich Hülsmann, Gottfried Wilhelm Leibniz Bibliothek - Hannover, Germany
Chih-Cheng Hung, Kennesaw State University, USA
Udo Inden, Cologne University of Applied Sciences, Research Centre for Applications of Intelligent Systems (CAIS), Germany
Lucjan Jacak, Wroclaw University of Technology - Institute of Physics, Poland
Oleg Jakushkin, Saint Petersburg State University, Russia
Mukesh Jha, Masdar Institute, Abu Dhabi, UAE
Jinyuan Jia, Tongji University, China
Kai Jiang, Shanghai Supercomputer Center, China
Seifedine Kadry, American University of the Middle East, Kuwait
David Kaeli, Northeastern University, USA
Tae-Wook Kang, KICT (Korea Institute of Construction Technology), Korea
Izabela Karsznia, University of Warsaw, Department of Cartography, Warsaw, Poland
Christos Kartsaklis, Oak Ridge National Laboratory (ORNL), USA
Stavros Kassinos, University of Cyprus, Cyprus
Takahiro Kawamura, Toshiba Corporation, Japan
Dae-Hyun Kim, Kyungpook National University, South Korea
Jinoh Kim, Texas A&M University-Commerce, USA
Marie Kim, Electronics and Telecommunications Research Institute (ETRI), Republic of Korea
Alexander Kipp, Robert Bosch GmbH., Germany
Christos Kloukinas, City University London, UK
Alexander Knapp, University of Augsburg, Germany
Manfred Krafczyk, Institute for Computational Modeling in Civil Engineering (iRMB), Braunschweig, Germany
Philipp Kremer, German Aerospace Center (DLR) / Institute of Robotics and Mechatronics - Oberpfaffenhofen, Germany
Herbert Kuchen, Westfälische Wilhelms-Universität Münster, Institut für Wirtschaftsinformatik, Praktische Informatik in der Wirtschaft, Münster, Germany
Michael Lang, Los Alamos National Lab, USA
Robert S. Laramee, Swansea University, UK
Scott Lathrop, University of Illinois at Urbana-Champaign, USA
Piotr Lech, West Pomeranian University of Technology, Poland
Sik Lee, Supercomputing Center / Korea Institute of Science and Technology Information (KISTI), Korea
Paulo Leitão, Polytechnic Institute of Braganca, Portugal
Edgar A. Leon, Lawrence Livermore National Laboratory, USA
Walter Lioen, SURFsara, Netherlands
Iryna Lishchuk, Institut für Rechtsinformatik - Leibniz Universität Hannover, Germany
Maciej Liśkiewicz, Universität zu Lübeck, Germany
Frank Loeffler, Louisiana State University, USA
Joan Lu, Informatics, University of Huddersfield, UK
Richard Lucas, University of Canberra and Charles Sturt University, Australia
Min Luo, Huawei Technologies Co., Ltd, USA
Tony Maciejewski, Colorado State University, USA
Tanu Malik, University of Chicago and Argonne National Lab., USA
Dirk Malzahn, Dirk Malzahn Ltd. / HfH University, Germany
Suresh Marru, Indiana University, USA
Antonio Martí Campoy, Universitat Politècnica de València (UPV), Spain
Nikolaos Matsatsinis, Technical University of Crete, Greece

Iris Weber, Institut für Planetologie, Westfälische Wilhelms-Universität Münster, Germany
Jacqueline Whalley, Auckland University of Technology, New Zealand
Wojciech Wiza, Poznan University of Economics, Poland
Michael Wrinn, Intel - Corporate Research division, USA
Dongrong Xu, Columbia University, USA
Ruini Xue, University of Electronic Science and Technology of China, China
Qimin Yang, Engineering Department, Harvey Mudd College, Claremont, CA, USA
Yi Yang, NEC Laboratories America, USA
Hongchuan Yu, Bournemouth University, UK
May Yuan, University of Texas at Dallas, USA
Peter Zaspel, University of Bonn, Germany
Yu-Xiang Zhao, National Quemoy University, Taiwan
Yunquan Zhang, Institute of Computing Technology - CAS, China
Sotirios Ziavras, New Jersey Institute of Technology, USA
Jason Zurawski, Lawrence Berkeley National Laboratory / Energy Sciences Network, USA

MODOPT 2016 Advisory Chairs

Ian Flood, University of Florida, USA
Claus-Peter Rückemann, Westfälische Wilhelms-Universität Münster / Leibniz Universität Hannover / North-German Supercomputing Alliance, Germany
Mauro Iacono, Seconda Universita' degli Studi di Napoli, Italy

Program Committee Members

Alnoor Allidina, IBI-MAAK Inc., Canada
Turgay Aytac, Prescience Technologies Inc., USA
Catherine Cleophas, RWTH Aachen University, Germany
Samuel da Costa Alves Basílio, Federal Center for Technological Education of Minas Gerais (CEFET-MG), Brazil
Madeline M. Diep, Fraunhofer Center for Experimental Software Engineering, USA
Ian Flood, University of Florida, USA
Rachel Harrison, Oxford Brookes University, UK
Hadi Hemmati, University of Manitoba, Canada
Frank Herrmann, OTH Regensburg - Technical University of Applied Sciences, Germany
Mauro Iacono, Seconda Universita' degli Studi di Napoli, Italy
Raymond R.R. Issa, Rinker School/University of Florida, USA
Marouane Kessentini, University of Michigan, USA
SangHyun Lee, Department of Civil and Environmental Engineering/University of Michigan, USA
Ulf Lotzmann, University of Koblenz-Landau, Germany
Roderick Melnik, Wilfrid Laurier University, Canada
Daniel Méndez Fernández, Technische Universität München, Germany
Akbar Siami Namin, Texas Tech University, USA
Claus-Peter Rückemann, Westfälische Wilhelms-Universität Münster / Leibniz Universität Hannover / North-German Supercomputing Alliance, Germany
Ravi S. Srinivasan, Rinker School/University of Florida, USA
Robert Wille, University of Linz & DFKI GmbH, Germany

Dietmar Winkler, Vienna University of Technology, Austria
Yimmin Zhu, Department of Construction Management/Louisiana State University, USA

Copyright Information

For your reference, this is the text governing the copyright release for material published by IARIA.

The copyright release is a transfer of publication rights, which allows IARIA and its partners to drive the dissemination of the published material. This allows IARIA to give articles increased visibility via distribution, inclusion in libraries, and arrangements for submission to indexes.

I, the undersigned, declare that the article is original, and that I represent the authors of this article in the copyright release matters. If this work has been done as work-for-hire, I have obtained all necessary clearances to execute a copyright release. I hereby irrevocably transfer exclusive copyright for this material to IARIA. I give IARIA permission or reproduce the work in any media format such as, but not limited to, print, digital, or electronic. I give IARIA permission to distribute the materials without restriction to any institutions or individuals. I give IARIA permission to submit the work for inclusion in article repositories as IARIA sees fit.

I, the undersigned, declare that to the best of my knowledge, the article is does not contain libelous or otherwise unlawful contents or invading the right of privacy or infringing on a proprietary right.

Following the copyright release, any circulated version of the article must bear the copyright notice and any header and footer information that IARIA applies to the published article.

IARIA grants royalty-free permission to the authors to disseminate the work, under the above provisions, for any academic, commercial, or industrial use. IARIA grants royalty-free permission to any individuals or institutions to make the article available electronically, online, or in print.

IARIA acknowledges that rights to any algorithm, process, procedure, apparatus, or articles of manufacture remain with the authors and their employers.

I, the undersigned, understand that IARIA will not be liable, in contract, tort (including, without limitation, negligence), pre-contract or other representations (other than fraudulent misrepresentations) or otherwise in connection with the publication of my work.

Exception to the above is made for work-for-hire performed while employed by the government. In that case, copyright to the material remains with the said government. The rightful owners (authors and government entity) grant unlimited and unrestricted permission to IARIA, IARIA's contractors, and IARIA's partners to further distribute the work.

Enterprise Architecture Quality Management Approach

Malgorzata Pankowska
Department of Informatics
University of Economics
Katowice, Poland
email: pank@ue.katowice.pl

Abstract—**Generally, the enterprise architecture (EA) is the discipline of designing enterprise guided with principles, frameworks, methodologies, requirements, tools, reference models, and standards. The EA is responsible for designing structures, engineering processes, developing working force, exploiting technology and creating opportunities for learning. The EA should be accessible for all the organization members to receive their acceptance as responsive to user needs. The EA modelling effectiveness and efficiency are determined by the EA elements quality. Therefore, the paper focuses on characterization of quality of enterprise architecture, consideration of key perspectives, measures and indicators.**

Keywords-enterprise architecture; quality; stakeholder; maturity model; ArchiMate.

I. INTRODUCTION

The term "enterprise" can be interpreted as an overall concept to identify a company, business organization or governmental institution. According to Robins, an enterprise is considered as a social entity, with a relatively identifiable boundaries [4]. The enterprise engineering is underpinned by two fundamental concepts, i.e., enterprise ontology and enterprise architecture.

The enterprise architecture (EA) is defined as a coherent and consistent set of principles and guidelines that guide system design [6]. Enterprise architecture is also defined as a strategic information asset base, which defines the business mission, the information and technology necessary to perform the mission, the transitional processes for implementing new technologies in response to the changing mission needs [2]. For the purpose of this paper, the enterprise architecture is a general plan or a direction of information communication technology (ICT) application in the enterprise to achieve strategic business goals. The enterprise architecture is a discipline that seeks to explain why organizations do what they do and how they can be changed to achieve a certain demanded purpose. The complete picture of the EA should include answers to the following questions: what will be done, i.e., what products, services and experiences, who will do the work, how well the work is done, who will be offered the results, why customers are expected to pay for what they receive, what technologies will be developed and applied. Firstly, the paper covers discussions on the EA quality issues included in the EA frameworks and some special approaches. Secondly, the role of stakeholders in the EA development and quality assurance is discussed. Thirdly, the proposed approach to quality of enterprise architecture (QoEA) evaluation is presented. In this approach, the stakeholder roles, EA principles and vision as well as the EA quality procedure are emphasized.

II. ENTERPRISE ARCHITECTURE AS PRODUCT AND PROCESS

ISO/IEC/IEEE 42010:2007 architecture standard is the fundamental organization, as well as the principles guiding its design and evolution. The EA can be considered as a process or as a product. The EA as a product serves to guide managers in designing business processes and system developers in building applications in a way that is in line with business objectives and policies. The EA as a process is to translate business vision and strategy into effective ICT components. It should be noticed that enterprise models are applied as a computational representation of the structure, activities, processes, information, people, goals, and constraints of a business. The EA is to ensure a holistic view of the business processes, systems, information, and technology of the enterprise [7]. The results of work of enterprise architect cover the derived IT strategies, the new and modified EA, the new and modified set of EA standards, and a roadmap describing the ICT projects for implementation of new architecture and achieving the target state, and a development plan [7].

Well architected systems can more quickly link with external business partners. The EA is to ensure the comprehensive understanding and evaluation of the current state or the desired state, as well as the interrelationships of processes, people and technology affected by ICT projects. The organization has bigger consistency of business processes and information across business units. The EA identifies opportunities for integration and reuse of ICT resources and prevents the development of inconsistent processes and low quality information. Especially important to users is the capability of integrating the information among applications and across data warehouses and data marts. The ISO/IEC/IEEE 42010: 2011 standard emphasizes the stakeholder object in the architecture description (Figure 1). Architecture description identifies stakeholders and system of interests, as well as expresses an architecture. The following stakeholders can be considered as having impact on the architecture description: system users, operators, acquirers, owners, suppliers, developers, and maintainers. The stakeholders are included in the EA quality evaluation process, because they are the EA work recipients, although they have different interests, risk awareness and impact on the system.

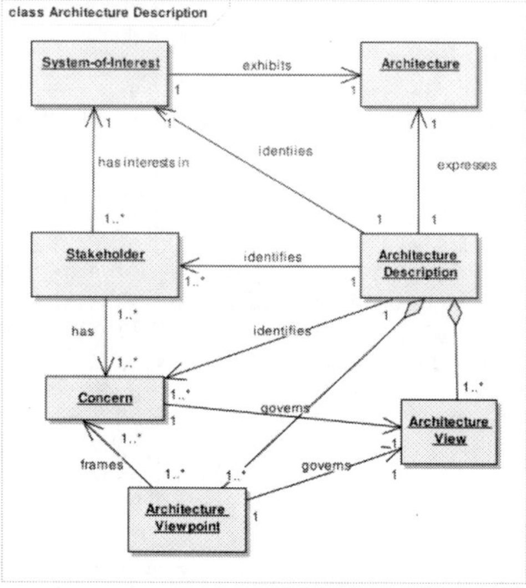

Figure 1. Enterprise Architecture in ISO/IEC/IEEE 42010:2011.

Architecture viewpoints establish the conventions for the construction, interpretation and use of architecture views to respect specific concerns. Architecture view expresses the architecture of the system from the perspectives of specific system concerns. Architecture views are the main categories that are evaluated in the aspect of quality of the EA. They are strongly dependent on EA stakeholders, whose qualifications for the EA process should also be evaluated. Architecture principles as general rules and guidelines are included in the EA views, and they guide how a chosen area of goal-oriented and efficient endeavor must be exploited and explored. Quality discussion should also concern the approval of the principles by users, and the principles development for better EA development.

III. RELATED WORKS ON EA QUALITY

A. *Enterprise Architecture evaluation problems*

The enterprise architecture as a process of translating business vision and strategy into effective enterprise can be viewed in many different aspects:

- business aspect - highlighting what business is conducted by the organization, what are its products and services,
- information aspect - providing the information engineering perspective of business solution architecture,
- work aspect - expressing in terms of work activities, associated resources, work locations and its optimal techniques, and needed information,
- application aspect - defining the automated business activities and business supporting software,
- technology aspect - focusing on the technology needed to facilitate other components of the architecture [8].

Evaluating refers to systematic activities undertaken to decide on a quality of particular phenomena and visualize them in a structural and formal way. The enterprise architecture evaluation is to decide on the value-in-use of EA objectives, activities, information resources, processes, actors, products, requirements and the relationships between these entities. The enterprise architecture evaluation can be used in different ways. Generally, it improves organization's work, allows the organizational members to review the enterprise and to design and implement business processes, to change the business structure and to increase the efficiency of the business reengineering and business strategy realization. Nowadays, the EA evaluation approaches do not offer mutually agreed languages, techniques and measures. The EA usually has many stakeholders, who establish their own techniques, schemas and measures. Although the EA is to provide a holistic approach to the enterprise information technology (IT) development, the quality of the EA requires different measurement methods depending on the stakeholder knowledge, competencies and activities. The EA frameworks' developers separate EA evaluation from EA implementation. They focus on analyzing the architecture models, languages, modeling techniques and propose methods for the evaluation of these artifacts. They notice in a pre-implementation analysis the necessity to ensure coherence among different models, they analyze the convergence of proposed models, their scalability, openness, agility, sustainability and ability to ensure security. The question on the EA quality is not popular in the EA engineering methodologies. However, in BIZBOK [1], beyond questions provided in Zachman Framework, there is a unique question on how well the EA is developed, and what metrics and measures are to be applied.

B. *Stakeholders and Quality issues in EA Frameworks*

Nowadays, the EA is considered as the discipline of describing enterprises guided with principles, frameworks, methodologies, requirements, tools, reference models and standards. There are many frameworks that support the EA modeling and development, e.g., Zachman Framework (ZF), the Open Groups Architecture Framework (TOGAF), the Generic Enterprise Reference Architecture and Methodology (GERAM), the Purdue Enterprise Reference Architecture (PERA), Computer Integrated Manufacturing Open System Architecture (CIMOSA), the Lightweight Enterprise Architecture (LEA), Nolan Norton Framework (NNF), the Extended Enterprise Architecture Framework (E2AF), Enterprise Architecture Planning (EAP), the Federal Enterprise Architecture Framework (FEAF), Treasury Enterprise Architecture Framework (TEAF) [6], [7], [11]. However, the frameworks mentioned above are product oriented and the quality issues are not well discussed in their general descriptions. Only some of them, i.e., ZF, TOGAF,

FEAF, CIMOSA and MODAF emphasize the role of stakeholders in the EA development process.

The ZF provides a basic structure for organizing a business architecture through dimensions, such as data, function, network, people, time and motivation [13]. Zachman describes the ontology for the creation of EA through negotiations among several actors. The ZF presents various views and aspects of the enterprise architecture in a highly structured and clear form. Zachman differentiates between the levels: Scope (contextual, planner view), Enterprise Model (conceptual, owner view), System Model (logical, designer view), Technology Model (physical, builder model), Detailed Representation (out-of-context, subcontractor), and Functioning Enterprise (user view). Each of these views is presented as a row in the matrix. The lower the row, the greater the degree of detail of the level represented. The model works with six aspects of the enterprise architecture: Data (what?), Function (how?), Network (where?), People (who?), Time (when?), and Motivation (why?). Each view (i.e., column) interrogates the architecture from a particular perspective. Taken together, all the views create a complete picture of the enterprise. In this enterprise ontology there is no place for quality considerations.

Since 1999, the FEAF components of an enterprise architecture cover architecture drivers, strategic direction, current architecture, target architectures, transitional processes, architectural components, architectural models, and standards. The architect has a responsibility for ensuring the completeness of the architecture, in terms of adequately addressing all the concerns of all the various views, satisfactorily reconciling the conflicts among different stakeholders. The framework emphasizes the role of planner, owner, designer, builder and subcontractor in the EA development process. The FEAF is derived from the Zachman Framework, however, the user of the realized architecture is not included in the development team. In FEAF, the Performance Reference Model (PRM) is a standardized framework to measure the performance of major IT investments and their contribution to program performance. Within that model the customer service quality, process and activity quality, and technology quality are measured [7].

The Ministry of Defense Architectural Framework (MODAF) is the UK Government specification for architectural frameworks for the defense industry [9]. The MODAF covers 7 viewpoints, i.e., All View, Acquisition, Strategic, Operational, System, Service, and Technical. The All View viewpoint is created to define the generic, high-level information that applies to all the other viewpoints. In this approach, the architect role is hidden in the particular viewpoints. The Acquisition viewpoint is used to identify programmes and projects that are relevant to the framework and that will be executed to deliver the capabilities that have been identified in the strategy views. The Strategic viewpoint defines views that support the analysis and the optimization of a domain capability. The intention is to capture long-term missions, goals and visions, and to define what capabilities are required to realize them. The Operational viewpoint contains views that describe the operational elements required to meet the capabilities defined in the strategic views. This is achieved by considering a number of high-level scenarios, and then defining the element sorts existing in the scenarios. The operational views are solution-independent and do not describe an actual solution. These views are available to suppliers and form the basis of evaluating the System views that are provided as the supplier's proposed solution. The Service viewpoint concerns views that allow the solution to be described in terms of its services. This allows a solution to be specified as a complete service-oriented architecture. The Technical viewpoint contains two views that allow all the relevant standards to be defined. This is split into two categories: current standards and predicted future standard [9].

The CIMOSA framework is based on four abstract views (function, information, resource and organization views) and three modeling levels (i.e., requirements definition, design specification, and implementation description) [10]. The four modeling views are provided to manage the integrated enterprise model (covering the design, manipulation and access). For the management of views, CIMOSA assumes a hierarchy of business units that are grouped into divisions and plants. The TOGAF standard takes a holistic approach to the enterprise architecture. TOGAF divides the EA into four categories of architecture, i.e., business, application, data and technology. Similarly to the ISO/IEC/IEEE 42010:2007 standard, in TOGAF the minimum set of stakeholders for a system covers users, system and software engineers, operators, administrators, managers and acquirers. Beyond that there are other stakeholders:

- the executive management, who defines strategic goals,
- the client, who is responsible for the allocated budget, with regard to the expected goals,
- the provider, who delivers the component elements of the architecture,
- the sponsors, who drive and guide the work,
- the enterprise architects, who turn business goals into reality within the structure of its system.

In TOGAF, the holistic approach to the EA quality management is possible through the application of the Architecture Maturity Model (AMM), which is based upon capability maturity models as formal ways to gain control over and improve architecture processes as well as to assess the organization's development competence. Van Den Berg and Van Steenbergen consider eighteen key areas of architecture maturity, which can be included in the EA evaluation process [12]. They are as follows: architecture development, use of architecture, alignment with business, alignment with the development process, alignment with operations, suitability of the architecture, roles and responsibilities, coordination of development, monitoring, quality management, architectural process maintenance, maintenance of architectural deliverables, commitment and motivation, architectural roles and training, use of architectural roles and training, use of an architectural method, consultation, architectural tools, budgeting and planning. The development of architecture should be budgeted and planned, however, in such a wide spectrum of variables included in the evaluation process, there is a question of who is the beneficiary of the multicriteria evaluation and what priorities have been established for these criteria. In TOGAF 9.1, the enterprise architecture process maturity levels are as follows:

- Level 0: No enterprise architecture program,
- Level 1: Informal enterprise architecture process underway,
- Level 2: Enterprise architecture process under development,
- Level 3: Defined enterprise architecture including detailed written procedures, Technical Reference Model (TRM) and Standards Profile framework,
- Level 4: Managed and measured enterprise architecture process,
- Level 5: Continuous improvement of enterprise architecture process.

That model is a result of the Enterprise Architecture Capability Maturity Model delivered by DoC (US Department of Commerce) [3].

IV. Stakeholders and Visions as Fundamental of EA Quality Management

Stakeholders are the individuals who have a stake in the success or failure of a business. They are people, for whom the value is created, who are beneficiaries of the EA development decision. Among others, a particularly important role belongs to enterprise architect, whose competencies should be planned and addressed at two levels: the enterprise and the personal level. An enterprise competence is an integrated complex of enterprise skills, knowledge and technology. To a considerable extent, enterprises competencies rest on the competencies of employees, i.e., the competencies at the personal level. Competencies are defined in measurable behavior characteristics that determine the ability to function successfully - knowledge, skills, craftsmanship, attitudes, social skills, and personal traits. The competencies cover the abilities to cooperate, to take initiative, or show user-orientation and decision making skills [4]. The important for the enterprise architect knowledge aspects cover system thinking, business and organization, information, information technology, enterprise development, and its change. The enterprise architects should be able to translate the strategic initiatives and areas of concerns into a particular enterprise design. Usually, the enterprise architects are responsible for documenting, analyzing, and designing the business processes, business functions, business objects, and the interactions among them. By the analysis of the entire organization model, the architects are able to uncover the points where there is a need for action and the potential of optimization. There is a necessity to ensure the cohesion among roles: application managers, project managers, process architects, business analysts, organization consultants, infrastructure acquirers, project portfolio components' controllers, ICT strategists, IT managers, security representatives, risk managers and quality managers.

The enterprise architect is placed in a network of stakeholders. As actors in network, they achieve their significance by being in relations with other actors. The position of the architect in the enterprise determines the associated controls of the EA development activities. Techniques used frequently to clarify responsibilities are RACI and RAEW [12]. RACI model includes the following characteristics: Responsible (i.e., the individual delivering the end result), Accountable (i.e., the person bearing the ultimate responsibility for the result), Consulting (i.e., the person providing input to reach the result), Informed (i.e., the individuals informed about the result) (see Table I). In RAEW model, the enterprise architect should be the person of Responsibility, Authority, Expertise and Work. Assuming that EA quality depends on the stakeholders' qualifications, the stakeholder network quality problem could be analyzed through the detail specification and evaluation of stakeholders' competencies.

For the illustration of EA quality considerations, the e-healthcare system architecture is presented in Figure 2. The project was supported by the National Centre of Science, grant number 4100/B/H03/2011/40. Stakeholders of the e-healthcare system contribute to the three kinds of architecture (i.e., Business, Application and Technology Infrastructure) in a consistent way. Architects in each of the architectural areas influence each other's decisions. Software architects designing for software reliability need the design support of system architects as well as knowledge brokers and end users.

For e-healthcare architecture modeling, the ArchiMate language is applied to emphasize the stakeholders in a suitable manner to support business agility. In Figure 2, a system architecture model in ArchiMate presents the whole complexity of EA e-healthcare and as such should be considered, although it is organized into some basic layers:

- BUSINESS containing the following elements: actor (i.e., Patient), role (i.e., e-Healthcare Service Recipient, Knowledge Broker), process (i.e., e-Healthcare Consultation Process covering 7 subprocesses), service (i.e., e-Healthcare Service Information Browsing, e-Healthcare Service Conceptualization, e-Healthcare Service Knowledge Component Registration, e-Healthcare Service Knowledge Components' Catalogue, e-Healthcare Service Knowledge Components' Management). In this paper, the e-healthcare knowledge management is component-oriented. Therefore, each service consists of some knowledge components, which are designed, constructed and selected to provide optimal advice to patients and their guardians. The knowledge components can be further designed as learning objects for education of end users and for their community considered as organization of learning good medical practices.
- APPLICATION covering elements, such as Financial Application, Knowledge Component Management System, Portal to External Sources of Knowledge (e.g., libraries, journals, document repositories), Service Management System, Knowledge Broker- Patient

Relation System, e-Healthcare Service Politics and Regulations, Risk Evaluation, IT Support.

- TECHNOLOGY including elements, such as Data Server, Application Server.
- MOTIVATION containing the following elements: drivers (i.e., e-Healthcare Consultation Needs), principles (i.e., e-Healthcare Knowledge Development Principles), assessment (i.e., e-Healthcare Consultation Evaluation), goals (i.e., Patient Satisfaction, Efficient and Effective Response for Patient), requirements (i.e., Patient e-Healthcare Requests), stakeholders (e.g., Patients and their Guardians).

In Table I, proposed e-Healthcare organizational structure covers the most important stakeholders, i.e., Patients and their Guardians (PG), Medical Staff (MS), Institutional Investors (II), Knowledge Brokers (KB), Information System Developers (ISD), Information Technology Architects (ITA), Public Healthcare Managers (PHM).

TABLE I. RACI CHART FOR E-HEALTHCARE

Key Management Practices	PG	MS	II	KB	ISD	ITA	PHM
e-Healthcare Strategic Planning	I	C	R	C	R	R	C
e-Healthcare Knowledge Brokering	C	C	R	A	R	R	C
e-Healthcare Vision Development	R	C	C	R	I	I	C
Cultural Environment Capabilities & Performance	A	R	R	R	R	A	C
IT Capabilities Development	C	C	R	C	A	A	C
The ICT Investment Development & Project Planning	R	R	A	R	R	C	C

Their activities are further precisely specified and verified in particular projects. However, at the pre-implementation stage each person can be evaluated according to the following criteria:

- Reliability: capability to maintain a level of performance under stated conditions for a stated period of time,
- Efficiency: ability to work properly to the amount of resources used under stated conditions,
- Suitability: ability to meet stated and implied needs,
- Agility: capability to receive required effects in stated time,
- Compliance: complying with laws, regulations and contractual agreements.

At the EA development, quality can be evaluated as the conformance to the requirements. Every EA product or service has a requirement, i.e., a description of what the service recipient needs. When a particular product meets that requirement, it has achieved quality. The requirements are formulated for information, applications, and services. TECHNOLOGY layer components are strongly standardized and their quality can be evaluated through IT benchmarking.

The EA quality evaluation focuses on the evaluation of certain vision provided by a stakeholder as it is in Figure 2. Usually, the vision is supported by the set of principles, which support the EA analysis, development and implementation. The exemplar principles of EA are as follows:

- data quality is a major factor in enhancing value of e-healthcare,
- reusing existing services and knowledge components reduces the work required to implement new ones,
- real-time e-healthcare system monitoring allows immediate action to resolve failures and incidents,
- standardization of EA components help achieve economies of scale and improves flexibility,
- processes must be designed from the patient perspective,
- decision-making must take place at the lowest possible organizational level,
- patient interaction processes must have error correction capabilities,
- all knowledge must have authorizing source,
- information structure must be based on ArchiMate standards,
- patient data must be accessible to the patient.

The EA vision and principles are evaluated in the following way:

- identification of the intended stakeholders of the quality measurement results,
- determination of the post-evaluation decision-making responsibilities, decisions will be some procedures with respect to the architecture vision,
- defining the measures, e.g., :
  - accuracy : data in the EA vision correctly define the event or object which they describe,
  - completeness: all the necessary data are present,
  - validity: the data fall between acceptable ranges defined by the system architect,
  - consistency: data elements are consistently defined and understood,
  - relevance: the EA vision components support a decision that needs to be made or a task that needs to be performed,
  - presentation: the EA vision is presented in a form that makes it easily understandable
- for each measure, specification of feasible quantifiers, and if it is not possible using the "check-mark" technique for the acceptance of requirement level achievement.
- on the basis of the assessments in the step above, re-improvement of the EA vision and principles specification. The results of such evaluations of measurements will address questions related to the occurrence of the undesirable conditions, outcomes or principles. The process is also developed to reveal omissions, redundancies and any other weaknesses.

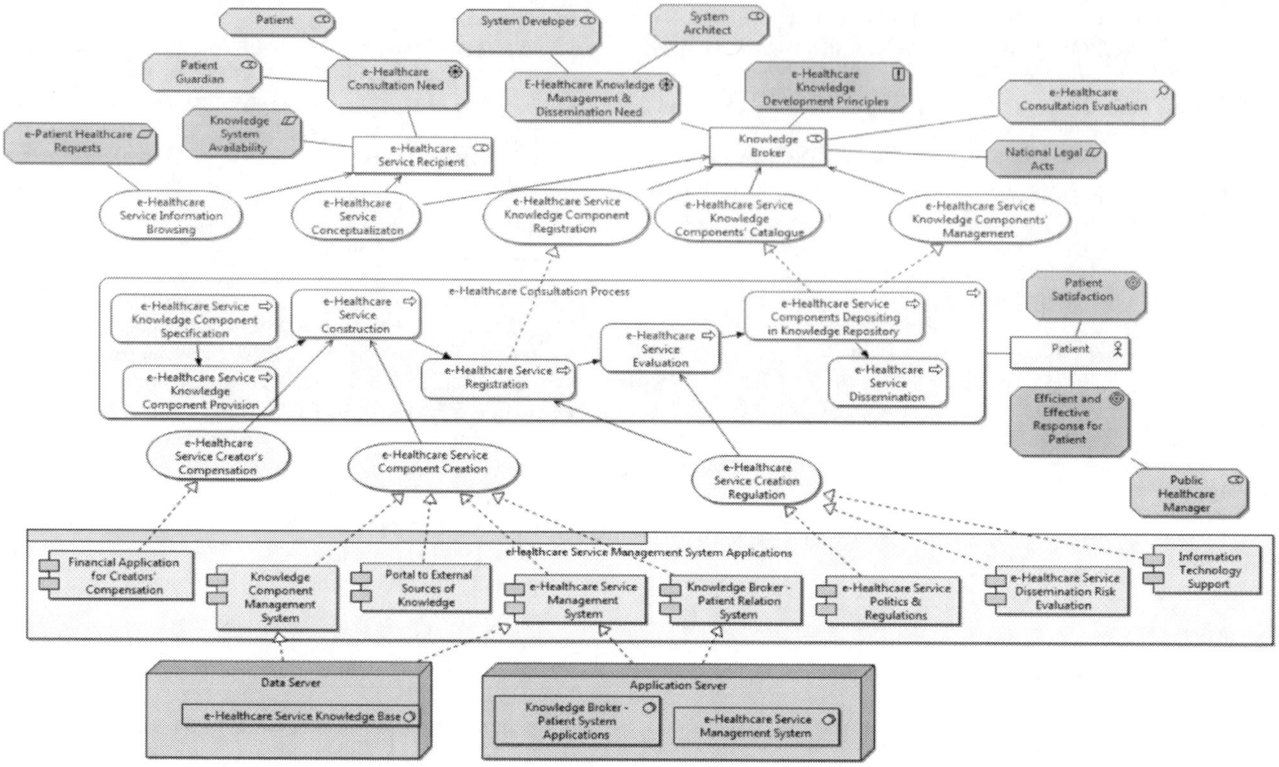

Figure 2. e-Healthcare Architecture Model.

V. Conclusion

Although holistic approach to the EA quality evaluation was provided in TOGAF as the Architecture Maturity Modeling, in this paper, the EA quality evaluation is a complex process. Taking into account the ISO/IE/IEEE 42010 definition, quality of each of the EA elements should be evaluated separately. Although the TOGAF framework focuses on EA process quality, this paper is to emphasize that EA stakeholders and vision are the most important in the quality evaluation process. The stakeholders as EA development beneficiaries should be the EA quality evaluators. The exemplar specification of quality measures were proposed for that EA objects.

References

[1] BIZBOK™ guide version 4.0. [Online] Available from http://c.ymcdn.com/sites/www.businessarchitectureguild.org/resource/resmgr/BIZBOKV4IntroductiIn.pdf. 2014.10.12

[2] CIO Council, Updating the Clinger-Cohen Competencies for Enterprise Architecture, 2003, [Online] Available from http://www.cio.gov/documents/FINAL_White_Paper_on_EA_v62.doc, 2016.01.11

[3] P. Desfray and G. Raymond, "Modeling Enterprise Architecture with TOGAF A Practical Guide Using UML and BPMN," Amsterdam, Elsevier, 2014

[4] J.A.P. Hoogervorst, "Enterprise Governance and Enterprise Engineering," Berlin, Springer, 2009.

[5] ISO/IEC 42010, System and software engineering - Architecture description. International Standard, Geneva, 2011.

[6] M. Lankhorst, "Enterprise Architecture at Work," Berlin, Springer, 2005.

[7] D. Minoli, "Enterprise Architecture A to Z, Frameworks, Business Process Modeling, SOA, and Infrastructure Technology," London, CRC Press, 2008.

[8] M. Op't Land, E. Proper, M. Waage, J. Cloo, and C. Steghuis, "Enterprise Architecture, creating value by Informed Governance," Berlin, Springer, 2009.

[9] C. Perks and T. Beveridge, T., "Guide to Enterprise IT Architecture," New York, Springer, 2003.

[10] M. Spadoni and A. Abdmouleh, "Information Systems Architecture for Business Process Modelling" in Handbook of Enterprise Systems Architecture in Practice, P.Saha, Ed. Hershey, Information Science Reference, 2007, pp. 366-382,.

[11] F. Theuerkorn, "Lightweight Enterprise Architectures," London, Auerbach Applications, 2005.

[12] M. Van Den Berg and M. Van Steenbergen, "Building an Enterprise Architecture Practice, Tools, Tips, Best Practices, Ready-to-Use Insights," Sogeti, Springer, 2006.

[13] J.A. Zachman, "Frameworks Standards: What's It All About?" In The SIM Guide to Enterprise Architecture, L.A. Kappelman L.A. Eds. Boca Raton, CRC Press, 2010, pp.66-70.

Automatic Image Marking Process

Aeman I.G. Masbah
School of Computing and Engineering
University of Huddersfield
Huddersfield, UK
E-mail: Aeman.Masbah@hud.ac.uk

Joan Lu
School of Computing and Engineering
University of Huddersfield
Huddersfield, UK
E-mail: J.lu@hud.ac.uk

***Abstract*-Efficient evaluation of student programs and timely processing of feedback is a critical challenge for faculty. Despite persistent efforts and significant advances in this field, there is still room for improvement. Therefore, the present study aims to analyse the system of automatic assessment and marking of computer science programming students' assignments in order to save teachers or lecturers time and effort. This is because the answers are marked automatically and the results returned within a very short period of time. The study develops a statistical framework to relate image keywords to image characteristics based on optical character recognition (OCR) and then provides analysis by comparing the students' submitted answers with the optimal results. This method is based on Latent Semantic Analysis (LSA), and the experimental results achieve high efficiency and more accuracy by using such a simple yet effective technique in automatic marking.**

Keywords-Automatic Image Marking Process; Optical Character Recognition; Test and Evaluation; Operational Test and Evaluation.

I. Introduction

Computer-based Assessment Systems (CAS) has grown exponentially in the last few years because of the growing number of university students and increasing contributions of e-learning approaches to asynchronous and ubiquitous education.

The marking of student assignments can be classified as manual and automatic. Unfortunately, instructors and teaching assistants are already overburdened with work teaching computer science courses; they have little time to devote to additional assessment activities. As a result, an automated tool for grading student assignments must be devised.

Many educators have used automated systems to assess and provide quick feedback on large volumes of student programming assignments [1][2]. Such systems typically focus on the compilation and execution of student programs against some form of instructor-provided test data. However, this approach ignores any testing that the student has undertaken, and fails to provide both the assessment and feedback necessary for facilitating Test-Driven Development (TDD) [3].

Marking the programming assignments of many students is not often an easy job for instructors. Thus, making the marking easier benefits the automated marking program. Such innovation in marking programming class assignments electronically is, arguably, as important as the learning curriculum for programming classes [4]. Automated marking applications are more accurate in detecting errors and providing feedback.

This paper presents a novel automatic image marking process technique. Section 2 discusses the related work, and section 3 describes the design of the proposed technique. Section 4 presents the experimental results, and section 5 concludes the study.

II. Related Work

The problem of marking automation has attracted much research attention. Early studies on computerisation considered the practicality of the general approach to different programming dialects by exploring diverse evaluation systems. The early Ceilidh framework checked understudy assignments in dialects that included Standard ML [5] in a similar way as that presented in this work, but without high-level, consistent joining using a cutting-edge Learning Management System (LMS) [6].

Recent studies have focused on the specifics of Java assessment and interactive learning. Truong et al. [7] attempted to assess semi-automatically Java programs via static analysis without compiling and executing programs. Tremblay et al. [8] assessed Java programs using a command-line tool available to students who use a Unix-based system and noted the possibility of a future Web-based application. Blumenstein et al. [9] developed a generic GAME system that can be used as a framework for the automated grading of assignments in programming languages, including Java.

Web-CAT is a web-based application that is implemented using the WebObjects framework of Apple [10]. This application is designed to be language independent, but focuses on grading object-oriented programs that are written in Java. For Java programs, students write JUnit-compatible test cases and submit them along with the assignments in their other classes. The reports produced by these tools are merged into one seamless source code mark-up, which can be viewed on the Web by students.

Redish et al. [11] developed a tool called AUTOMARK to evaluate student style based Pascal programs. Berry et al. [12] [13] developed another tool to assess student programs written in C language depending on style. Jones used the concept of testing to automate the evaluation of student programs [14].

Furthermore, Jackson and Usher developed a tool called ASSYST to automate student programs depending on their correctness, efficiency, complexity and style [1]. Jumaa developed a tool to evaluate structural languages such as Pascal, FORTRAN, C and Basic based on Halstead, McCabe, Style and Lipow and Thayler models [15]. The instructor evaluated student programs against it. The tool proved to be suitable for intermediate courses. As for advanced courses with big projects, it was impractical for the instructor to write a model program for each assignment. Also, in the industry it is difficult to write a model program in order to assess an industrial program.

One of the very early applications in the course of automated program marking, Hollingworth's grader, was specifically developed to test punched card programs [16]. Many other applications with similar functions have been introduced, for instance, the Online Judge [17], and, more recently, Sakai, which was developed with much more sophisticated ware introduced by Suleman [18]. Although the varieties of Automated Marker available can differ in name or other peripheries, their principal functionality is to evaluate programs written by students indirectly through the output. This process of indirect test is not without some deficiency. According to experts, the deficiency of the indirect approach of testing programs includes, but is not limited to, "limited quality of feedback", "heavy hindrances on evaluation" and "over sensitivity to minor errors". Another noticeable pitfall of the available series of automatic program markers is the inability to mark non-textual programs, interactive programs and tasks with specific algorithms; some examples are animation or drawing programs that students are sometimes required to write. Pragmatically, it is important to explore ways of upgrading the functionalities of the already existing automated markers and suggest solutions to the currently noticeable pitfalls. Other common approaches, amongst the available automated program makers in the literature, are those that apply the file-system-based organisational strategy. For instance, the Isong [19] automated program marker was developed to focus on compiling student programs automatically. This is done by comparing the instructor-provided data against the student program output. Isong's marker was written with the help of Unix-shell scripts. Reek developed a similar grader long before Isong's marker [2]. Like Isong's marker Reek's grader is also a Unix-based system that was developed for inductor programing courses. This grader also adopted the file-system organisational strategy for evaluating assignments and student submission. The submissions are graded against instructor-provided data. Hence, instructors control the grader's feedback and evaluation process.

BOSS is also an automated program marker developed with a battery of Unix-based programs, which adopts file-system-based organisational strategy for submission of test cases tested against instructor-provided test criteria [20]. Through these studies, the proposed system will differ from other systems by depending on accuracy and efficiency in the operations of automatic marking. It will use a new technology based on Images and OCR.

III. RESEARCH APPROACH

A systematic investigative process was employed to increase or revise current knowledge of automatic marking. This section discusses the research approach, which consists of two sub-phases: (A) designing an improved automatic image marking process system and (B) testing and evaluating the developed system.

A. Automatic Image Marking Process System Design

The entry point of the proposed system will be the submission of the programming assignments in image format. Optional Character Recognition (OCR) will then be used to extract the text from the submitted assignments and to save the text file. The proposed system is a combination of OCR, web technology and database. Web technology is used to develop a Web interface that enables students to submit their assignments, and teachers to mark the submitted answers and manage students' marks. Furthermore, this process will be explained with more detail in phases: (1) submission process and (2) marking process. The database is used to save the students' marks, and the saved data are used later by the teachers to generate their reports. This section consists of two sub-sections: (1) submission process and (2) marking process. Figure 1 shows the architecture of the proposed system.

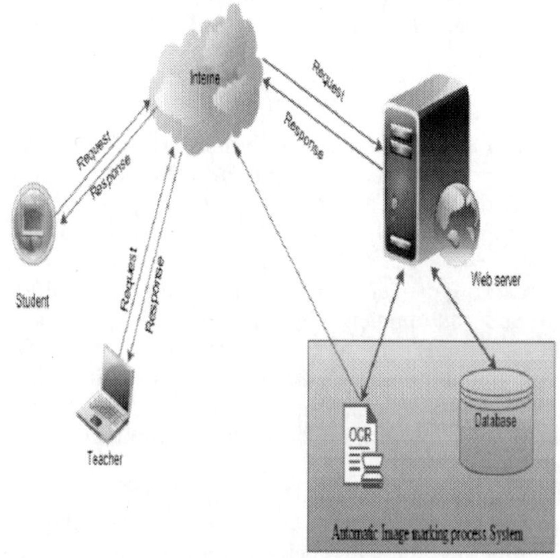

Figure 1. Architecture of the proposed system.

1. Submission Process

The computer science programming assignments undergo the stages of (1) compilation, (2) execution and (3) testing. The submission process, which begins after the execution stage, is described as follows:

- The student executes his/her programming assignment using programming IDE.
- The student converts the result of the execution into an image (e.g., a snapshot of the result).
- The student logs into the system using his/her metric number. In order to enforce proper security, each user must first register onto the system before he/she can use any of the other functionalities. Registration ensures that a proper ID and password are created for each new user.
- The student uploads the image that contains his/her answer.
- The system creates a folder named after the metric number of the student and then saves the uploaded image inside the folder.

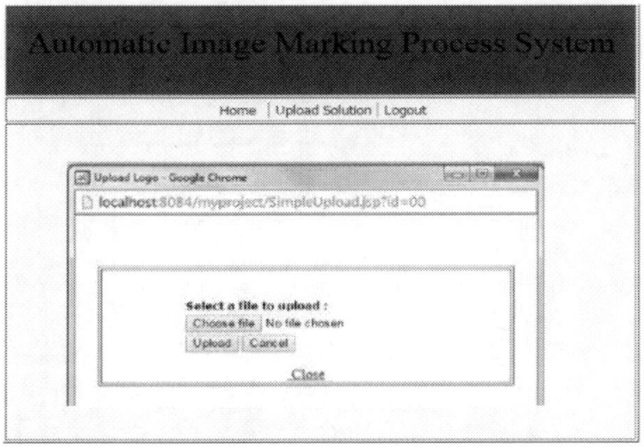

Figure 2. Web interface for uploading assignment answers.

The proposed system provides a web interface for students to upload their assignment answers. Figure 2 shows the web interface.

2. Marking Process
   The proposed system provides an automatic marking process for the submitted answers. The marking process is described as follows:
   - The teacher logs onto the system using his/her teacher ID.
   - The teacher selects one of the submitted answers.

The system allows the teacher to upload the optimal Answer and to enter the assignment mark. Figure3 shows the upload of the optimal answer.

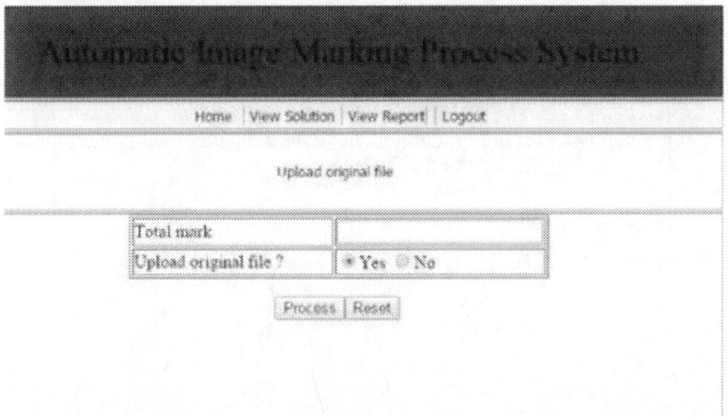

Figure 3. The upload of the optimal answer and the assignment mark box.

- The system uses the OCR web service to extract the text from the answer of the student and the optimal answer of the teacher.
- The system compares both texts (i.e., the submitted and optimal answer) and computes the similarity percentage.

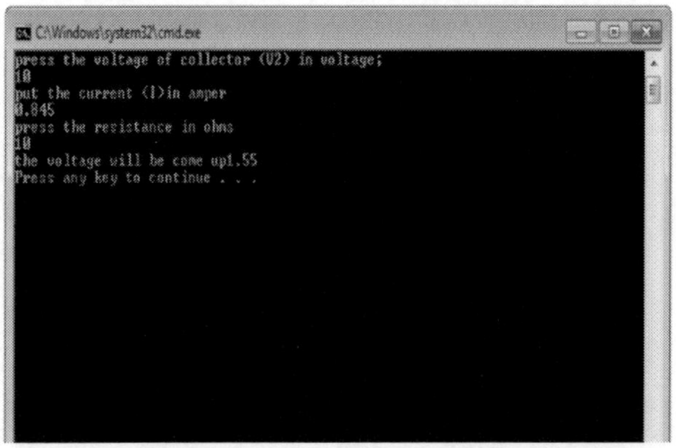

Figure 4. Submitted image that represents the student's answer.

The accuracy of the text extraction is positively affected by a high image quality. Figure 4 shows the submitted image for the student's answer.

Figure 5 shows the text extracted from the image using the OCR web service.

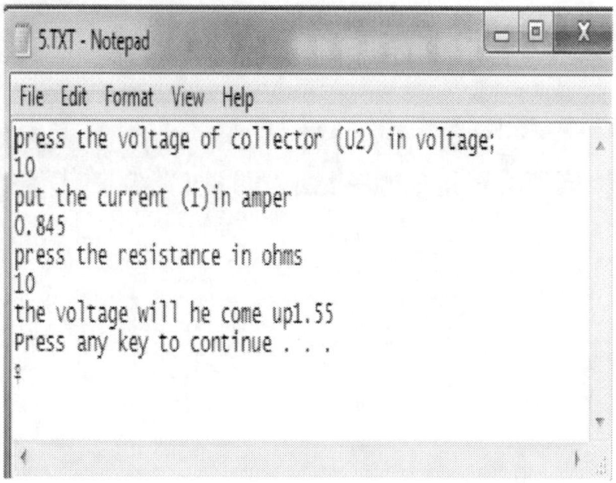

Figure 5. Text extracted from the image using the OCR web service.

B. Testing and Evaluation

Test and Evaluation (T&E) is the process by which a system or its components are compared against the requirements and specifications through testing. The results are evaluated to assess the progress of design, performance, supportability and more. Developmental Testing and Evaluation (DT&E) is an engineering tool used to reduce risk throughout the acquisition cycle. Operational Test and Evaluation (OT&E) is the actual or simulated employment, by typical users, of a system under realistic operational conditions [21]. In this phase, the proposed system is tested against the student answer samples to check the matching percentage of the proposed system.

IV. Experimental Result

The proposed system is tested on a sample of 65 student answers. The targeted samples are divided into five groups as follows: (1) Group A, (2) Group B, (3) Group C, (4) Group D and (5) Group E.

Group A consists of students' answers with zero matching optimal answers, while Groups B ,C and D consist of students' answers with partial matching of optimal answers. Group E consists of students' answers with identical matching of optimal answers.

The students upload different answers to computer science programming questions. The teacher selects a specific answer, uploads the optimal answer, and gives the total mark for a particular question. The system calculates the matching percentage using (1). Figure 6 shows the matching percentage for each group.

$$\text{Percentage of matching} = \frac{\textit{Number of matched lines}}{\textit{Total number of the optipal answer line}} \ldots \text{“(1)”}$$

Mathematically, this can be explained as the simultaneous representation of all optimal answers uploaded in the assignments corpus as points in semantic space, with the initial dimensionality of the sequences of answers in the developing system. To classify the correct representation of optimal answers, we represent it as a vector, and determine which answer is nearest to the optimal answer, where the distance measure between two vectors x_n and y_n is defined as:

$$d\left((x_n - y_n)^n = log \sum_{k=0}^{n} (x_n - y_n)x^k\right)$$

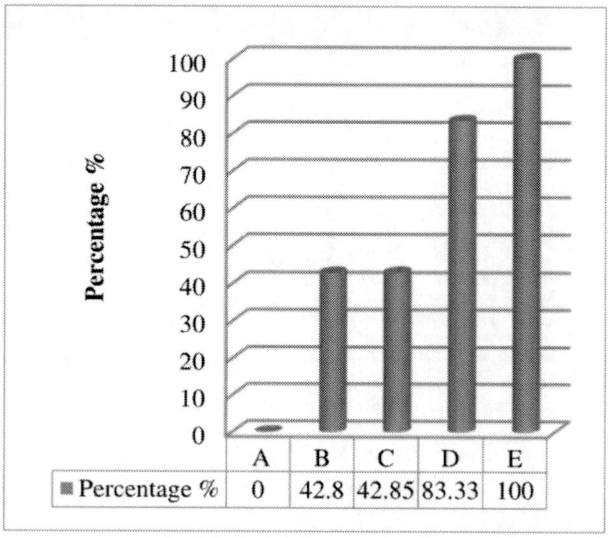

Figure 6. The matching percentage for each group.

The entire sample is submitted and evaluated. A zero matching percentage is obtained if these answers do not match each other as shown in Group A. B 42.8%, C 42.85% and D 83.33% decreased matching percentage is obtained if these answers partially match each other as shown in Group B, C and D. E 100% matching percentage is achieved in group E when the submitted and optimal answers exactly match each other.

The matching accuracy depends on the adoption of OCR and the advanced analysis that is applied to the submitted answers. However, such accuracy is negatively affected by the quality of the uploaded image that represents the student answer. Image quality is one of the most important factors for improving the quality of recognition. A resolution of 200 DPI to 400 DPI is recommended for a better recognition. An example of a system output is shown in Figure 7.

The content of the submitted image is extracted, and each line of the extracted content compared with the corresponding line in the optimal answer to check whether they match each other.

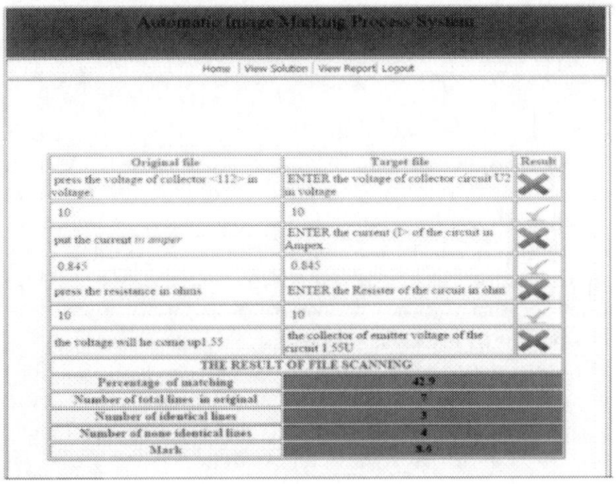

Figure 7. Example of output.

V. Conclusion And Future Work

An approach to automatically evaluating computer students' assignments has been described. The framework is based on Optical Character Recognition (OCR). Automatic Assignment Scoring (AAS) aims to extend the system's capabilities to provide more efficient and accurate results, as well as to save teachers or lecturers time and effort. This paper has illustrated the students' group matching with optimal answers. The 100% matching percentage is achieved in group A. The experimental results validate the efficiency of the proposed system in the automatic marking process.

In future, the proposed system will be integrated with the interface of Huddersfield University website. Furthermore, the prototype will be evaluated through task-based trials and comparative qualitative evaluation and testing with other systems.

References

[1] D. Jackson and M. Usher, "Grading student programs using ASSYST," in ACM SIGCSE Bulletin, 1997, pp. 335-339.

[2] K. A. Reek, "A software infrastructure to support introductory computer science courses," in ACM SIGCSE Bulletin, 1996, pp. 125-129.

[3] K. Beck, Test-driven development: by example: Addison-Wesley Professional, 2003.

[4] J. Al-Jáafer and K. E. Sabri, "Automark++: A case tool to automatically mark student Java programs," Int. Arab J. Inf. Technol., vol. 2, pp. 87-96, 2005.

[5] S. P. Foubister, G. Michaelson, and N. Tomes, "Automatic assessment of elementary Standard ML programs using Ceilidh," Journal of Computer Assisted Learning, vol. 13, pp. 99-108, 1997.

[6] Q. Wang, H. L. Woo, C. L. Quek, Y. Yang, and M. Liu, "Using the Facebook group as a learning management system: An exploratory study," British Journal of Educational Technology, vol. 43, pp. 428-438, 2012.

[7] R. Saikkonen, L. Malmi, and A. Korhonen, "Fully automatic assessment of programming exercises," in ACM Sigcse Bulletin, 2001, pp. 133-136.

[8] G. Tremblay, F. Guérin, A. Pons, and A. Salah, "Oto, a generic and extensible tool for marking programming assignments," Software: Practice and Experience, vol. 38, pp. 307-333, 2008.

[9] M. Blumenstein, S. Green, A. Nguyen, and V. Muthukkumarasamy, "Game: A generic automated marking environment for programming assessment," in Information Technology: Coding and Computing, 2004. Proceedings. ITCC 2004. International Conference, 2004, pp. 212-216.

[10] S. H. Edwards and M. A. Perez-Quinones, "Web-CAT: automatically grading programming assignments," in ACM SIGCSE Bulletin, 2008, pp. 328-328.

[11] K. Redish and W. Smyth, "Program style analysis: A natural by-product of program compilation," Communications of the ACM, vol. 29, pp. 126-133, 1986.

[12] R. E. Berry and B. A. Meekings, "A style analysis of C programs," Communications of the ACM, vol. 28, pp. 80-88, 1985.

[13] W. Harrison and C. R. Cook, "A note on the Berry-Meekings style metric," Communications of the ACM, vol. 29, pp. 123-125, 1986.

[14] E. L. Jones, "Grading student programs-a software testing approach," Journal of Computing Sciences in Colleges, vol. 16, pp. 185-192, 2001.

[15] Jumaa, "A Computer Model for Evaluation of Programs," University of Engineering and Science, 1992.

[16] J. Hollingsworth, "Automatic graders for programming classes," Communications of the ACM, vol. 3, pp. 528-529, 1960.

[17] B. Cheang, A. Kurnia, A. Lim, and W.-C. Oon, "On automated grading of programming assignments in an academic institution," Computers & Education, vol. 41, pp. 121-131, 2003.

[18] H. Suleman, "Automatic marking with Sakai," in Proceedings of the 2008 Annual Research Conference of the South African Institute of Computer Scientists and Information Technologists on IT Research in Developing Countries: Riding the Wave of Technology, 2008, pp. 229-236.

[19] J. Isong, "Developing an automated program checker," Journal of Computing Sciences in Colleges, 2001, pp. 218-224.

[20] M. Luck and M. Joy, "A secure on-line submission system," Software-Practice and Experience, vol. 29, pp. 721-40, 1999.

[21] K. T. Weber and J. S. Janicki, "Cardiopulmonary exercise testing for evaluation of chronic cardiac failure," The American Journal of Cardiology, vol. 55, pp. A22-A31, 1985.

A Novel MILP Model to Solve Killer Samurai Sudoku Puzzles

José B. Fonseca
Department of Electrical Engineering and Computer Science
Faculty of Sciences and Technology, New University of Lisbon
Monte de Caparica, Portugal
e-mail: jbfo@fct.unl.pt

***Abstract*— A Killer Samurai Sudoku puzzle is a NP-Hard problem and very nonlinear since it implies the comparison of areas or cages sums with their desired values, and humans have a lot of difficulty to solve these puzzles. On the contrary, our mixed integer linear programming (MILP) model, using the Cplex solver, solves easy puzzles in few seconds and hard puzzles in few minutes. We begin to explain why humans have such a great difficulty to solve Killer Samurai Sudoku puzzles, even for low level of difficulty ones, taking into account the cognitive limitations as the very small working memory of 7-8 symbols. Then, we briefly review our previous work where we describe linearization techniques that allow solving any nonlinear problem with a linear MILP model. Next we describe the sets of constraints that define a Killer Sudoku puzzle and the definition of the objective variable and the implementation of the solution of a Killer Samurai Sudoku puzzle as a minimization problem formulated as a MILP model and implemented with the GAMS software. Finally, we present the solutions of a hard Killer Samurai Sudoku puzzles with our MILP model using the Cplex solver.**

Keywords-intelligence; MILP; puzzles

I. INTRODUCTION

The first problems solved by Artificial Intelligence (AI) and Operations Research (OR) were toy problems, games and more recently puzzles. In the eighties, there were annual tournaments of chess computer programs and Kasparov was even defeated by one of these chess programs. More recently Sudoku appeared in Japan and then Kakuro and Killer Sudoku puzzles that were rapidly disseminated through the rest of the world. More recently arose the Killer Samurai Sudoku puzzles that consist of five Killer Sudoku puzzles with the fifth puzzle overlapping over the remaining four puzzles. As an alternative approach to AI, in this work we formulate the Killer Samurai Sudoku puzzle problem solution as an optimization problem with constraints in the framework of a Mixed Integer Linear Program (MILP) model and then solve it using the Cplex solver with the GAMS software and using the linearization techniques developed in our previous work [1]. A Killer Sudoku puzzle consists of a matrix of dimension 9x9 where each line and column must be a permutation of integers between 1 and 9, each sub-matrix 3x3 must be a permutation of these numbers and there are a set of colour areas or cages that must have a predefined sum. The runtimes of the solution of a black belt Killer Samurai Sudoku puzzle from [2] using our MILP model were very small, just some few seconds. To our knowledge this is the first proposal to solve a Killer Samurai Sudoku puzzle with a MILP model. Although exists a site to solve Killer Samurai Sudoku puzzles online, we believe that our solution is faster and can be understood by non specialists of computer science. Nevertheless in a previous work [3] we solved Kakuro puzzles with a MILP model and the runtimes showed to be much lower than then the runtimes of previous proposals [4-5].

Next we describe the structure of our paper. In Section 2, we give a brief overview of what mathematical programming is, the MILP models and their implementation with the GAMS software and solution with the Cplex solver. In Section 3, we describe our MILP model giving a detailed presentation of the main sets of constraints and their implementation with the GAMS software. In Section 4, we present the main conclusions and possible evolution of our work.

II. WHAT IS MATHEMATICAL PROGRAMMING? WHAT IS A MILP MODEL?

A mathematical program is a set of inequalities and equalities defined in terms of the model variables, one of them defining the objective variable that must be maximized or minimized. In a linear model all constraints are linear and it cannot be applied any nonlinear operation over a model variable neither exists the product between two model variables. A mixed integer linear program (MILP) is a linear model with integer, binary and continuous variables. In this work we used the GAMS modeling language to formulate the puzzle as an optimization problem and solve it with an algorithm, the Cplex solver. For example the simplified code that implements a MILP model to obtain the maximum and minimum of a given array would be:

```
sets i /1*20/;
parameter a_p(i);
a_p(i)=ord(i)-10;
variable a(i), minimum, maximum, obj;

**CONSTRAINTS**
**set the array elements:
set_a(i).. a(i)=e=a_p(i);
**the minimum is less or equal to all
elements of a(i):
calc_min(i).. minimum =l= a(i);
```

```
**the maximum is greater or equal to all
elements of a(i):
calc_max(i).. maximum =g= a(i);
**to prevent trivial solutions we must
maximize the minimum and minimize the
maximum:
calc_obj.. obj=e= minimum - maximum;
Model MaxMin /all/;
Solve MaxMin using MIP maximizing obj;
display a.l, obj.l, maximum.l,
minimum.l;
```

The constraint *calc_max(i)* implements the set of inequalities (1).

$$\forall i, maximum \geq a(i) \qquad (1)$$

The output of this small MILP model using the Cplex solver looks like the following:

```
GAMS Rev 229  WIN-VIS 22.9.2 x86/MS Windows
03/09/16 17:01:32 Page 6
General Algebraic Modeling System
Execution

----    26 VARIABLE a.L

1 -9.000,   2 -8.000,   3 -7.000,   4 -6.000,   5 -5.000,
6 -4.000 7 -3.000,   8 -2.000,   9 -1.000,   11  1.000,
12  2.000,   13  3.000 14 4.000,   15  5.000,   16  6.000,
17  7.000,   18  8.000,   19  9.000 20 10.000

----    26 VARIABLE obj.L          =    -19.000
          VARIABLE maximum.L      =     10.000
          VARIABLE minimum.L      =     -9.000
```

III. Description of our MILP Model to Solve Killer Samurai Sudoku Puzzles

The main element of our Killer Samurai Sudoku MILP model is an indexed binary variable with three indexes that defines the 9x9 matrix which must be filled with integer numbers between 1..9. The first and second indexes represent the line and column of the matrix element, respectively, and the third index represents the value of the matrix element, i.e., there is only one value of the third index for which the binary variable is one and all the remaining are zero for a given line and column. This way the order of the last index of this indexed binary variable is translated into the value of the Killer Samurai Sudoku matrix element. The use of this indexed binary variable is the main idea to linearize this so nonlinear problem. With this approach the constraints, like the *all different* constraints, are very elegant and simple and the runtimes are very small.

First we must impose that each matrix element has only one value, which seems obvious but must be declared since the value of the matrix element is expressed by the order of the third index of the indexed binary variable *a_bin(l,c,v)*, *l* and *c*, being the line and column of the matrix element and the order of index *v* its value. This condition is expressed by (2).

$$\forall l, c, \textstyle\sum_v a\_bin(l,c,v) = 1 \qquad (2)$$

The set of constraints (2) can be implemented with GAMS syntax as:

only_one(*l,c*).. **sum**(*v, a_bin(l,c,v)*)**=1=**1;

Next, we must impose that there are no repetitions in each line *l*, the *all different constraint*, i.e., for each pair of values (*l,v*) summing the binary indexed variable *a_bin(l,c,v)* over all columns *c*, this sum must be equal to 1, since in a Killer Samurai Sudoku puzzle each line is a permutation of integer numbers between 1 and 9. This set of logical conditions or constraints is expressed by (3).

$$\forall l, v, \textstyle\sum_c a\_bin(l,c,v) = 1 \qquad (3)$$

The set of constraints (3) can be implemented with GAMS syntax as:

all_different_line(*l,v*).. **sum**(*c, a_bin(l,c,v)*)**=e=**1;

In other words (3) ensures that each line is a permutation of integers between 1 and 9. And there must not exist repetitions in each column, which is expressed by the similar set of logical conditions or constraints (4), the *all different* constraint for each column *c*.

$$\forall c, v, \textstyle\sum_l a\_bin(l,c,v) = 1 \qquad (4)$$

The set of constraints (4) can be implemented with GAMS syntax as:

all_different_column(*c,v*)..
sum(*l, a_bin(l, a_bin(l,c,v)*)**=e=**1;

Next we impose that each sub-matrix 3x3 must be a permutation of integers between 1 and 9. To express this set of logical conditions we created an auxiliary indexed parameter, *square*(l_1,c_1,*l,c*) which is initialized by (5).

$$\forall l_1, c_1, l, c, square(l_1, c_1, l, c,) = \Big(l \geq \big((l_1 - 1)Order + 1\big)\Big)\big(l \leq \big((l_1 - 1)Order\big) + Order\big)\,(c \geq (c_1 - 1)Order + Order)) \qquad (5)$$

In (5) the multiplication of inequalities must be interpreted as the logical AND of the logical values of the inequalities. The scalar *Order* defines the dimension of the Killer Sudoku puzzle sub-matrix and for the classical Killer Sudoku puzzles *Order*=3. Then the set of logical conditions or constraints that impose that each sub-matrix *Order* x *Order* must have no repetitions is expressed by (6).

$$\forall l_1, c_1, v_1, \sum_{(l,c):square(l_1,c_1,l,c)=1} a\_bin(l,c,v_1) = 1 \quad (6)$$

The set of equations (6) can be written using GAMS syntax as:

all_different_square(*l*1,*c*1,*v*1)..
sum((*l*,*c*)**$**(square(*l*1,*c*1,*l*,*c*)), *a_bin*(*l*,*c*,*v*1))**=e=**1;

The dollar operator has the meaning of restriction to the values for which the expression next to **$** is true. Then we impose that each colour segment must has a predefined sum saved in an auxiliary indexed parameter *sum_colour*(*col*). Each colour segment is defined by a logical auxiliary indexed parameter *colour_bin*(*col*,*l*,*c*) which has the value 1 when the Killer Sudoku element (*l*,*c*) belongs to the colour segment of order *col*. This set of conditions or constraints is expressed by (7).

$$\forall col, \sum_{v,(l,c):colour\_bin(col,l,c)=1} v\, a\_bin(l,c,v) = sum\_colour(col) \quad (7)$$

The set of equatons (7) can be written using GAMS syntax as:

sum_colour_segment(*col*)..
sum((*l*,*c*,*v*1)**$**(*colour_bin*(*col*,*l*,*c*)),**ord**(*v*)**a_bin*(*l*,*c*,*v*1))**=e=** *sum_colour*(*col*);

Finally to prevent trivial solutions with all values of *a_bin*(*i*,*j*,*v*)=1 we must minimize the objective variable defined as the number of matrix elements, which is expressed by (8).

$$obj = \sum_{i,j,v} a\_bin(i,j,v) \quad (8)$$

Equation (8) can be implemented in GAMS code as:

calc_obj.. *obj*=**e=sum**((*i*,*j*,*v*), *a_bin*(*i*,*j*,*v*));

In Figure 1, we show a hard Killer Samurai Sudoku puzzle taken from [2] that we solved with our MILP model showed in appendix A in just few seconds in a PC with 2GHz clock and in appendix B we show the output of the GAMS software code that corresponds to the solution of the puzzle. Note that in this hard Killer Samurai Sudoku puzzle, each different area of matrix elements whose sum must be equal to the number printed in the region. Moreover this puzzle has two regions with four elements which contribute to the combinatorial explosion in the ways the matrix elements may be filled.

IV. Conclusions and Future Work

We showed that our MILP model to solve Killer Samurai Sudoku puzzles is very efficient and elegant. In a near future, we plan to expand our MILP model to solve variants of Killer Sudoku like Killer Sudoku Greater Than and then adapt them to develop a MILP model to make production planning based on a MILP model and the Cplex solver.

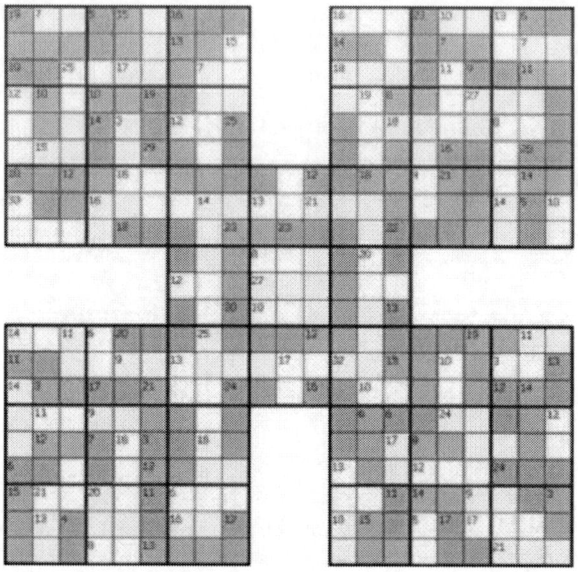

Figure 1. Killer Sudoku puzzle solved by our MILP model.

References

[1] J. Barahona da Fonseca, "Solving any nonlinear problem with a MILP model," Proceedings of Escape-19 Conference, pp.647–652, 2009.

[2] D. J.. Ape, .Killer Sudoku and other puzzle variants, Createspace, 2010.

[3] J. Barahona da Fonseca, "A novel linear MILP model to solve Kakuro puzzles," Proceedings of Controlo 2012 Conference, pp. 185-190, 2012.

[4] R. P. Davies, An investigation into the solution to, and evaluation of, Kakuro puzzles, MSc thesis, 2009.

[5] H. Simonis,, "Kakuro as a constraint problem," Proceedings of Modref Conference, pp. 201-216, 2008.

Appendix A

In the following GAMS code the names of constraints always finish with "..".

```
sets l /1*21/;

alias(c,  l);

set v1 /1*9/;
alias(v, v1);

set c1 /1*3/;
```

```
alias(l1, c1);

set col /1*129/;
*121-

*positive variable a(l,c);

binary variable a_bin(l,c, v1);



scalar Order /3/;

Parameter square(l1,c1,l,c), square2(l1,c1,l,c),
square3(l1,c1,l,c), square4(l1,c1,l,c),
square5(l1,c1,l,c), cor_bin(col, l, c),
soma_cor(col);


square(l1,c1,l,c)=(ord(l) ge ((ord(l1)-1)*Order+1)
)*(ord(l) le ((ord(l1)-1)*Order+Order))
*(ord(c) ge ((ord(c1)-1)*Order+1))*(ord(c) le
((ord(c1)-1)*Order+Order));

square2(l1,c1,l,c)=(ord(l) ge ((ord(l1)-
1)*Order+1) )*(ord(l) le ((ord(l1)-
1)*Order+Order))
*(ord(c) ge (12+(ord(c1)-1)*Order+1))*(ord(c) le
(12+(ord(c1)-1)*Order+Order));

square3(l1,c1,l,c)=(ord(l) ge (12+(ord(l1)-
1)*Order+1) )*(ord(l) le (12+(ord(l1)-1)
*Order+Order))
*(ord(c) ge ((ord(c1)-1)*Order+1))*(ord(c) le
((ord(c1)-1)*Order+Order));

square4(l1,c1,l,c)=(ord(l) ge (12+(ord(l1)-
1)*Order+1) )*(ord(l) le (12+(ord(l1)-1)*
Order+Order))
*(ord(c) ge (12+(ord(c1)-1)*Order+1))*(ord(c) le
(12+(ord(c1)-1)*Order+Order));

square5(l1,c1,l,c)=(ord(l) ge (6+(ord(l1)-
1)*Order+1) )*(ord(l) le (6+(ord(l1)-1)
*Order+Order))
*(ord(c) ge (6+(ord(c1)-1)*Order+1))*(ord(c) le
(6+(ord(c1)-1)*Order+Order));

*Next we define the cages of the first puzzle
cor_bin(col, l, c)=0;
soma_cor(col)=0;

cor_bin('1', '1', '1')=1;
cor_bin('1', '2', '1')=1;


soma_cor('1')=6;

************************************

cor_bin('2', '1', '2')=1;
cor_bin('2', '2', '2')=1;
cor_bin('2', '3', '2')=1;
cor_bin('2', '3', '1')=1;

soma_cor('2')=23;

************************************

cor_bin('3', '1', '3')=1;
cor_bin('3', '1', '4')=1;

soma_cor('3')=13;

************************************

cor_bin('4', '1', '5')=1;
cor_bin('4', '1', '6')=1;


soma_cor('4')= 17;

************************************

cor_bin('5', '1', '7')=1;
cor_bin('5', '1', '8')=1;
cor_bin('5', '1', '9')=1;

soma_cor('5')=8;

************************************

cor_bin('6', '2', '3')=1;
cor_bin('6', '2', '4')=1;
cor_bin('6', '2', '5')=1;
cor_bin('6', '2', '6')=1;

soma_cor('6')=15;
* snip! some instructions omitted

variable obj;

* CONSTRAINTS:
*only_one(l,c).. sum(v1, a_bin(l,c,v1))=e=1;

only_one(l,c)$( (ord(l) ge 1) * (ord(l) le 9) *
(ord(c) le 9) * (ord(c) ge 1) )..
 sum(v1, a_bin(l,c,v1))=e=1;
only_one2(l,c)$( (ord(l) ge 1) * (ord(l) le 9) *
(ord(c) le 21) * (ord(c) ge 13) ) ..
 sum(v1, a_bin(l,c,v1))=e=1;

only_one3(l,c)$( (ord(l) ge 7) * (ord(l) le 15) *
(ord(c) le 15) * (ord(c) ge 7) )..
 sum(v1, a_bin(l,c,v1))=e=1;

only_one4(l,c)$( (ord(l) ge 13) * (ord(l) le 21) *
(ord(c) le 9) * (ord(c) ge 1) )..
 sum(v1, a_bin(l,c,v1))=e=1;

only_one5(l,c)$( (ord(l) ge 13) * (ord(l) le 21) *
(ord(c) le 21) * (ord(c) ge 13) )..
 sum(v1, a_bin(l,c,v1))=e=1;


all_different_line(l,v1)$( ord(l) le 9)..
sum(c$(ord(c) le 9), a_bin(l,c,v1))=e=1;
all_different_line2(l,v1)$( ord(l) le 9)..
 sum(c$( (ord(c) le 21) * (ord(c) ge 13) ),
a_bin(l,c,v1))=e=1;

all_different_line3(l,v1)$( (ord(l) le 15) *
(ord(l) ge 7) )..
 sum(c$( (ord(c) le 15) * (ord(c) ge 7) ),
a_bin(l,c,v1))=e=1;

all_different_line4(l,v1)$( (ord(l) le 21) *
(ord(l) ge 13) )..
 sum(c$( (ord(c) le 9) * (ord(c) ge 1) ),
a_bin(l,c,v1))=e=1;
```

```
all_different_line5(l,v1)$( (ord(l) le 21) *
(ord(l) ge 13) )..
 sum(c$( (ord(c) le 21) * (ord(c) ge 13) ),
a_bin(l,c,v1))=e=1;

all_different_column(c,v1)$(ord(c) le 9)..
sum((l)$(ord(l) le 9), a_bin(l,c,v1))=e=1;
all_different_column2(c,v1)$( (ord(c) le 21) *
(ord(c) ge 13) )..
 sum((l)$( ord(l) le 9 ), a_bin(l,c,v1))=e=1;

all_different_column3(c,v1)$( (ord(c) le 15) *
(ord(c) ge 7)  )..
 sum((l)$( (ord(l) le 15) * (ord(l) ge 7) ),
a_bin(l,c,v1))=e=1;

all_different_column4(c,v1)$( (ord(c) le 9) *
(ord(c) ge 1) )..
 sum((l)$( (ord(l) le 21) * (ord(l) ge 13) ),
a_bin(l,c,v1))=e=1;

all_different_column5(c,v1)$( (ord(c) le 21) *
(ord(c) ge 13) )..
 sum((l)$( (ord(l) le 21) * (ord(l) ge 13) ),
a_bin(l,c,v1))=e=1;

zero_elements(l,c,v)$( (ord(l) le 6)* (ord(l) ge
1) * (ord(c) ge 10) * (ord(c) le 12) +
(ord(l) ge 16) * (ord(l) le 21) * (ord(c) ge 10)
*(ord(c) le 12) + (ord(l) ge 10) *
 (ord(l) le 12) * (ord(c) le 6)+
(ord(l) ge 10) * (ord(l) le 12) * (ord(c) ge 16) *
(ord(c) le 21) ).. a_bin(l,c,v)=e=0;

all_different_square(l1,c1,v1)..
 sum((l,c)$(
 square(l1,c1,l,c) *(ord(l) ge 1) * (ord(l) le
9)*(ord(c) le 9)*(ord(c) ge 1) ),
  a_bin(l,c,v1)) =e= 1;

 all_different_square2(l1,c1,v1)..
 sum((l,c)$(
 square2(l1,c1,l,c) *(ord(l) ge 1) * (ord(l) le
9)*(ord(c) le 21)*(ord(c) ge 13) ),
 a_bin(l,c,v1)) =e= 1;

all_different_square3(l1,c1,v1)..
 sum((l,c)$(
 square3(l1,c1,l,c) *(ord(l) ge 13) * (ord(l) le
21)*(ord(c) le 9)*(ord(c) ge 1) ),
 a_bin(l,c,v1)) =e= 1;

all_different_square4(l1,c1,v1)..
 sum((l,c)$(
 square4(l1,c1,l,c) *(ord(l) ge 13) * (ord(l) le
21)*(ord(c) le 21)*(ord(c) ge 13) ),
 a_bin(l,c,v1)) =e= 1;

all_different_square5(l1,c1,v1)..
 sum((l,c)$(
 square5(l1,c1,l,c) *(ord(l) ge 7) * (ord(l) le
15)*(ord(c) le 15)*(ord(c) ge 7) ),
 a_bin(l,c,v1)) =e= 1;

sum_color_segment(col)..
 sum((l,c,v1)$(cor_bin(col,l,c)=1),
ord(v1)*a_bin(l,c,v1)) =e=soma_cor(col);

calc_obj.. obj=e=sum((l,c,v1), a_bin(l,c,v1));

model KillerSamuraiSudoku /all/;
```

```
option IterLim=1000000000;
option ResLim=1000000000;

option optcr=0;
option optca=0;

solve KillerSamuraiSudoku using MIP minimizing
obj;

display  a_bin.l, obj.l;
```

APPENDIX B

Next we show the output of the Cplex solver that results from a run of the GAMS model that corresponds to the solution of the puzzle presented in figure 1.

---- 910 VARIABLE a_bin.L

	1	2	3	4	5	6
1 .1		1.000				
1 .2					1.000	
1 .3						1.000
1 .7			1.000			
1 .8	1.000					
1 .9				1.000		
1 .13		1.000				
1 .14			1.000			
1 .15					1.000	
1 .16						1.000
1 .18				1.000		
1 .21	1.000					
2 .1				1.000		
2 .4			1.000			
2 .5	1.000					
2 .6		1.000				
2 .7						1.000
2 .9					1.000	
2 .14				1.000		
2 .16		1.000				
2 .17	1.000					
2 .19			1.000			
2 .20					1.000	
2 .21						1.000
3 .1			1.000			
3 .3	1.000					
3 .4				1.000		
3 .5					1.000	
3 .6						1.000
3 .9		1.000				
3 .14						1.000
3 .15	1.000					
3 .16			1.000			
3 .17					1.000	
3 .19		1.000				
3 .20				1.000		
4 .2				1.000		
4 .3					1.000	
4 .5						1.000
4 .7	1.000					
4 .8		1.000				
4 .9			1.000			
4 .13					1.000	
4 .14		1.000				
4 .15			1.000			
4 .18	1.000					
4 .19				1.000		
4 .20						1.000
5 .1						1.000
5 .3			1.000			
5 .4	1.000					
5 .5		1.000				
5 .7					1.000	
5 .8				1.000		
5 .13						1.000
5 .15				1.000		
5 .16					1.000	
5 .18		1.000				
5 .19	1.000					
5 .21			1.000			
6 .1	1.000					
6 .2		1.000				
6 .4					1.000	
6 .5			1.000			
6 .6				1.000		
6 .8						1.000
6 .13	1.000					
6 .16				1.000		
6 .17						1.000
6 .18			1.000			
6 .20		1.000				
6 .21					1.000	
7 .2						1.000
7 .3				1.000		
7 .6					1.000	
7 .7		1.000				

7 .8			1.000			
7 .9	1.000					
7 .10					1.000	
7 .11				1.000		
7 .12						1.000
7 .16	1.000					
7 .17		1.000				
7 .18					1.000	
7 .19						1.000
7 .20			1.000			
7 .21				1.000		
8 .2			1.000			
8 .4		1.000				
8 .6	1.000					
8 .7				1.000		
8 .8					1.000	
8 .9						1.000
8 .13			1.000			
8 .14	1.000					
8 .15		1.000				
8 .17				1.000		
8 .18						1.000
8 .19					1.000	
9 .1					1.000	
9 .2	1.000					
9 .3		1.000				
9 .4						1.000
9 .5				1.000		
9 .6			1.000			
9 .10			1.000			
9 .11		1.000				
9 .12	1.000					
9 .13				1.000		
9 .14					1.000	
9 .15						1.000
9 .17			1.000			
9 .20	1.000					
9 .21		1.000				
10.7						1.000
10.8				1.000		
10.9			1.000			
10.12					1.000	
10.13		1.000				
10.15	1.000					
11.6	1.000					
11.10				1.000		
11.11						1.000
11.12		1.000				
11.13					1.000	
11.14			1.00			

**snip! some lines omitted

Licensing Implications of the Use of Open Source Software in Research Projects

Iryna Lishchuk
Institut für Rechtsinformatik
Leibniz Universität Hannover
Hannover, Germany
e-mail: lishchuk@iri.uni-hannover.de

***Abstract*—As more and more areas of science make use of the open source software (OSS), legal research in the field seeks to reconcile various open source licenses (which may be used in a single research project) and explores solutions to allow exploitation of project components in a license compliant way. Innovative software solutions contribute to the field of computer science from the technical side, while exploration of the legal implications of open source licensing enriches the topic from the legal perspective. In this paper, we consider what uses of what OSS may have licensing implications and suggest some solutions on how software developments may be used and distributed in a license compliant way.**

Keywords-open source software; free software; open source licensing; copyleft.

I. INTRODUCTION

Some key areas of computing, such as Linux/GNU, Google/Android, rely on open source software. Many research projects use the potential of OSS and contribute to the open source movement as well. One example is the EU FP7 CHIC project in the health informatics (full title "Computational Horizons In Cancer (CHIC): Developing Meta- and Hyper-Multiscale Models and Repositories for In Silico Oncology" [1]). CHIC is engaged in "*the development of clinical trial driven tools, services and infrastructures that will support the creation of multiscale cancer hypermodels (integrative models)*" [1]. In the course of this, it makes use of OSS and explores the possibility of open sourcing the project outcomes itself. For example, the hypermodelling framework VPH-HF relies on an open source domain-independent workflow management system Taverna [2], while an open source finite element solver, FEBio, is used in biomechanical and diffusion modeling [3].

This is part of a wider trend, in which OSS is becoming increasingly popular in all areas of scientific research. However, while the use of OSS may benefit the conduct of the project and promote its outcomes, it may later also have the effect of limiting the project exploitation options.

In this paper, we look into the licensing implications associated with the use of OSS and open sourcing the project outcomes. Also, we seek to suggest solutions on how licensing implications (and incompatibility risks) may best be managed. The rest of this paper is organized as follows. Section II describes the notion of free and open source software (FOSS) and elaborates on the license requirements for software distribution. Section III addresses peculiarities of the set of General Public Licenses (GPL) and points up some specific aspects stemming from the use of GPL software. In Section IV, the article concludes by way of a case study showing how the use of OSS may impact on future licensing of a project component.

II. FREE AND OPEN SOURCE SOFTWARE

Open source software is not simply a popular term, but it has its own definition and criteria, which we describe below.

A. Open Source Software

According to the Open Source Initiative (OSI), "*Open source doesn't just mean access to the source code. The distribution terms of open-source software must comply with the following criteria...*" [4]. These requirements normally determine how the program may be distributed either in its source code (a script in a human readable form, usually written in one or another programming language, such as C^{++}, Java, Python, etc.) or as a compiled executable, i.e., object code ("*a binary code, simply a concatenation of "0"'s and "1"'s.*" [5]).

The basic requirements of open source are as follows:

1. *Free Redistribution.* The license may not restrict distributing a program as part of an aggregate software distribution and/or may not require license fees.
2. *Source Code.* The license must allow distribution of the program both in source code and in compiled form. By distribution in object code, the source code should also be accessible at a charge not higher than the cost of copying (download from Internet at no charge).
3. *Derived Works.* The license must allow modifications and creation of derivative works and distribution of such works under the same license terms.
4. *Integrity of The Author's Source Code.* The license may require derivative works to be identified from original, such as by a version number or by name.
5. *No Discrimination Against Persons or Groups.*
6. *No Discrimination Against Fields of Endeavor.*
7. *Distribution of License.* The license terms apply to all users without the need of concluding a separate license agreement with every user.
8. *License Must Not Be Specific to a Product.* The license may not be dependent on any software distribution.

9. License Must Not Restrict Other Software. The license must not place restrictions on software distributed with the program (e.g., on the same medium).

10. License Must Be Technology-Neutral. The license may not be pre-defined for a specific technology [4].

There are currently more than 70 open source licenses, which can be categorized according to the license terms.

B. Free Software

One category is free software, which also has its own criteria. As defined by the Free Software Foundation (FSF), a program is free software, if the user (referred to as "you") has the four essential freedoms:

1. "The freedom to run the program as you wish, for any purpose (freedom 0).

2. The freedom to study how the program works, and change it so it does your computing as you wish (freedom 1). Access to the source code is a precondition for this.

3. The freedom to redistribute copies so you can help your neighbor (freedom 2).

4. The freedom to distribute copies of your modified versions to others (freedom 3). By doing this you can give the whole community a chance to benefit from your changes. Access to the source code is a precondition for this." [6].

The GPL, in its different versions, is a true carrier of these freedoms and GPL software (when distributed in a GPL compliant way) is normally free. The licenses, which qualify as free software licenses are defined by the FSF [7].

C. Free Software and Copyleft

The mission of free software (providing the users with these essential freedoms) is achieved in a way that not only the original author, who licenses his program under a free license, but also the subsequent developers, who make modifications to such free program, release their modified versions in the same "free" way.

Maintaining and passing these freedoms for subsequent software distributions is usually achieved by the so called copyleft principle. "*Copyleft is a general method for making a program (or other work) free, and requiring all modified and extended versions of the program to be free as well.*" [8]. A copyleft license usually requires that modified versions be distributed under the same terms. This distinguishes copyleft from non-copyleft licenses: copyleft licenses pass identical license terms on to derivative works, while non-copyleft licenses govern the original code only.

However, a free license does not necessarily involve copyleft and a copyleft license is not always free. On the other hand, a license that "*requires modified versions to be nonfree does not qualify as a free license*" [6].

D. Licensing Implications on Software Distribution

From the whole spectrum of FOSS licenses, mostly the free licenses with copyleft produce licensing implications on software exploitation. Some other free licenses without copyleft are, in contrast, rather flexible, provide for a wider variety of exploitation options, subject to rather simple terms: acknowledgement of the original developer and replication of a license notice and disclaimer of warranties.

Such more relaxed non-copyleft licenses usually allow the code to be run, modified, distributed as standalone and/or as part of another software, either in source form and/or as a binary executable, provided the license terms for the original code are met. Among the popular non-copyleft licenses are: the Apache License [9], the MIT License [10], the BSD 3-Clause License [11], to name a few. "*Code, created under these licenses, or derived from such code, may "go "closed" and developments can be made under that proprietary license, which are lost to the open source community.*" [12].

As a condition for distributing the MIT or BSD licensed code (or its modified versions), these licenses require that the use of the original code should be acknowledged. For this, the developers of the original program and the program license with disclaimer should be replicated (maintained) throughout the whole re-distribution chain. For instance, the MIT license requires that "*copyright notice and this permission notice shall be included in all copies or substantial portions of the Software*" [10]. Failure to do so may, at one hand, compromise the ability of the developer to enforce his own copyright in parts of the code, which he wrote himself, and, on the other hand, put him at risk of being found liable for copyright infringement, because distribution of the program in breach of the license terms may be a ground for claiming copyright violation [12]. Once these requirements of notice preservation are met, a developer may exploit the software as he deems fit.

E. Copyleft Licenses

In contrast, the free licenses with copyleft by promoting the four essential freedoms to the users may at the same time take away the developer´s freedom to decide on licensing of his own software, pre-determining a license choice for him. While supporters of free software speak about copyleft as protecting the rights, some developers, affected by the copyleft against their will, tend to refer "*to the risk of "viral" license terms that reach out to infect their own, separately developed software and of improper market leverage and misuse of copyright to control the works of other people.*" [13].

The GPL Version 2 (GPL v2) [14] and Version 3 (GPL v3) [15] are examples of free licenses with copyleft. GPL copyleft looks as follows. GPL v2, in Section 1, allows "*to copy and distribute verbatim copies of the Program's source code… in any medium*" under the terms of GPL, requiring replication of the copyright and license notice with disclaimer and supply of the license text. In Section 2, the GPL license allows modifying the program, "*thus forming a work based on the Program, and copy and distribute such modifications or work under the terms of Section 1 above*", i.e., under GPL itself. In doing so, it implies that a developer may distribute his own developments, only if he licenses under GPL. In some cases, it may put a developer up to a dilemma: either to license under GPL or not to license at all.

A more positive aspect of GPL is that at times it may be rather flexible. In particular, not all modes of using a GPL program create a modified version and not all models of software distribution are necessarily affected by GPL.

III. GPL AND GPL COPYLEFT

Among the decisive factors whether software is affected by GPL copyleft are: the mode, in which software uses a GPL program, the version and wording of the applicable GPL license, and the method of how software will be distributed.

A. *Mode of Use*

The mode of use essentially determines whether a development qualifies as "*a work based on a GPL program*" or not. If because of using a GPL program, software qualifies as a *"work based on the Program"*, then according to the terms of GPL it shall go under GPL [14]. Otherwise, if a program is not a modified version of GPL, then there is no binding reason for it to go under GPL.

In this regard, not all uses of a GPL program will automatically produce a derivative work. For example, developing a software using the Linux operating system, or creating a piece of software designed to run on Java or Linux (licensed under GPL v2 [16]) does not affect licensing of this software (unless it is intended to be included into the Linux distribution as a Linux kernel module). Also, calculating algorithms by means of a GPL licensed R (a free software environment for statistical computing and graphics [17]) in the course of developing a software model does not affect licensing of a model, because the model is not running against the GPL code.

Another distinctive feature of GPL is that, in contrast to the majority of other open source licenses, which do not regard linking as creating a modified version (e.g., Mozilla Public License [18], Apache License [9]), the GPL license considers linking, both static and dynamic, as making a derivative work. Following the FSF interpretation criteria, "*Linking a GPL covered work statically or dynamically with other modules is making a combined work based on the GPL covered work. Thus, the terms and conditions of the GNU General Public License cover the whole combination*" [19]. This position may be tested against the technical and legal background involved [20].

The controversy Android v Linux [21] illustrates how Google avoided licensing of Android under GPL because the mode how it used Linux was beyond the scope of applicability of Linux GPL license. This case concerned the Android operating system, which relies on the GPL licensed Linux kernel and which was ultimately licensed under the Apache License. Android is an operating system, primarily used by mobile phones. It was developed by Google and consists of Linux kernel, some non-free libraries, a Java platform and some applications. Despite the fact that Android uses Linux kernel, licensed under GPL v2 [16], Android itself was licensed under Apache 2.0 License. "*To combine Linux with code under the Apache 2.0 license would be copyright infringement, since GPL version 2 and Apache 2.0 are incompatible*" [21]. However, the fact that the Linux kernel remains a separate program within Android, with its source code under GPL v2, and the Android programs communicate with the kernel via system calls clarified the licensing issue. Software communicating with Linux via system calls is expressly removed from the scope of derivative works, affected by GPL copyleft. A note, added to the GPL license terms of Linux by Linus Torvalds, makes this explicit:

*"NOTE! This copyright does *not* cover user programs that use kernel services by normal system calls - this is merely considered normal use of the kernel, and does *not* fall under the heading of "derived work". Also note that the GPL below is copyrighted by the Free Software Foundation, but the instance of code that it refers to (the linux kernel) is copyrighted by me and others who actually wrote it."* [16].

Examples of normal system calls are: *fork(), exec(), wait(), open(), socket()*, etc. [21]. Such system calls operate within the kernel space and interact with the user programs in the user space [22]. Taking into consideration these technical details, "*Google has complied with the requirements of the GNU General Public License for Linux, but the Apache license on the rest of Android does not require source release.*" [21]. In fact, the source code for Android was ultimately released, however, in the view of the FSF, even the use of Linux kernel and release of the source code do not make Android free software. As explained by Richard Stallman [21], the aspects that Android comes up with some non-free libraries, proprietary Google applications, proprietary firmware and drivers, prevents the users from installing and running their own modified software, accepting versions approved by some company, and – what is most interesting – that the Android code is insufficient to run the device undermine the philosophy of free software [21].

B. *GPL Weak Copyleft and Linking Exceptions*

Another factor that matters whether a development is subject to GPL copyleft is the GPL license used.

Some GPL licenses have so-called weak copyleft. Examples are the GNU Library or "Lesser" General Public License, Version 2.1 (LGPL-2.1) [23] and Version 3.0 (LGPL-3.0) [24]. In these cases, a program, which merely links to a LGPL program or library (without modifying it), does not have to be licensed under LGPL. As LGPL-2.1 explains, "*A program that contains no derivative of any portion of the Library, but is designed to work with the Library by being compiled or linked with it, is called a "work that uses the Library". Such a work, in isolation, is not a derivative work of the Library, and therefore falls outside the scope of this License.*" [23]. LGPL allows combining external programs with a LGPL library and distributing combined works under the terms at the choice of the developer, provided: (a) the library stays under

LGPL; and (b) license of the combined work allows *"modification of the work for the customer's own use and reverse engineering for debugging such modifications"* [23].

Some practical consequences of how a switch from LGPL to GPL in one software product may affect exploitation and usability of another software product are demonstrated by the controversy: MySQL v PHP [20].

PHP is a popular general-purpose scripting language that is especially suited to web development [25]. PHP was developed by the Zend company and licensed under the PHP license, which is not compatible with GPL [26]. PHP is widely used and distributed with MySQL in web applications, such as in the LAMP system (standing for: Linux, Apache, MySQL and PHP), which is used for building dynamic web sites and web applications [27]. MySQL is the world's most popular open source database, originally developed by MySQL AB, then acquired by Sun Microsystems in 2008, and finally by Oracle in 2010 [28]. In 2004, MySQL AB decided to switch the MySQL libraries from LGPL to GPL v2. That is when the controversy arose. The PHP developers responded with disabling an extension in PHP 5 to MySQL. If PHP was thus not able to operate with MySQL, the result would be negative for the open source community [20], which widely relied on PHP for building web applications with MySQL. To resolve the conflict, MySQL AB came up with a FOSS license exception. The FOSS license exception (initially called the FLOSS License Exception) allowed developers of FOSS applications to include MySQL Client Libraries (also referred to as "MySQL Drivers" or "MySQL Connectors") within their FOSS applications and distribute such applications together with GPL licensed MySQL Drivers under the terms of a FOSS license, even if such other FOSS license were incompatible with the GPL [29].

A similar exception may be found in relation to the programming language Java. Java is licensed under GPL v2 with Classpath Exception [30]. It is a classic GPL linking exception based on permission of the copyright holder. It consists of the following statement attached to the Java GPL license text: *"As a special exception, the copyright holders of this library give you permission to link this library with independent modules to produce an executable, regardless of the license terms of these independent modules, and to copy and distribute the resulting executable under terms of your choice, provided that you also meet, for each linked independent module, the terms and conditions of the license of that module. An independent module is a module which is not derived from or based on this library."* [30]. Originally, this allowed free software implementations of the standard class library for the Java programming language [20].

Adding special permissions or exceptions to the standard terms of GPL is explicitly permitted by GPL v3. This makes GPL v3 more flexible and license compatible in comparison to GPL v2. *"Additional permissions" are terms that supplement the terms of this License by making exceptions from one or more of its conditions."* [15]. The linking exception to GPL v3, as recommended by the FSF, appears as follows: *"If you modify this Program, or any covered work, by linking or combining it with [name of library] (or a modified version of that library), containing parts covered by the terms of [name of library's license], the licensors of this Program grant you additional permission to convey the resulting work"* [31].

In this respect, it must be noted that adding additional permissions or exceptions to GPL license terms is an exclusive prerogative of the copyright holder. Thus, if a developer builds his program on top of a third party GPL code, he may not add such a linking exception to the GPL license of the whole code, unless he obtained consent to this from all the other copyright holders [31].

A software developer may be motivated to add such linking exceptions to solve GPL-incompatibility issues, which may arise if a GPL program is supposed to run against GPL incompatible programs or libraries, or to allow use of GPL software in software developments, which are not necessarily licensed in a GPL compatible way.

C. Mode of Distribution

Thirdly, the mode of distribution, namely: whether a component is distributed packaged with a GPL dependency or without it, may matter for the application of GPL.

According to the first criterion of OSS, which says that a license must permit distribution of a program either as standalone or as part of *"an aggregate software distribution containing programs from several different sources"* [4], the GPL license allows distributing GPL software *"as a component of an aggregate software"*. As interpreted by the FSF, *"mere aggregation of another work not based on the Program with the Program (or with a work based on the Program) on a volume of a storage or distribution medium does not bring the other work under the scope of this License"* [32]. Such an "aggregate" may be composed of a number of separate programs, placed and distributed together on the same medium, e.g., USB. [32].

The core legal issue here is of differentiating an "aggregate" from other "modified versions" based on GPL software. *"Where's the line between two separate programs, and one program with two parts? This is a legal question, which ultimately judges will decide."* [32]. In the view of the FSF, the deciding factor is the mechanism of communication (exec, pipes, rpc, function calls within a shared address space, etc.) and the semantics of the communication (what kinds of information are exchanged). So, including the modules into one executable file or running modules *"linked together in a shared address space"* would most likely mean *"combining them into one program"*. By contrast, when *"pipes, sockets and command-line arguments"* are used for communication, *"the modules normally are separate programs"* [32].

These observations bring us to the following conclusions. Distributing an independent program together with a GPL program on one medium, so that the programs do not communicate with each other, does not spread the GPL of one program to the other programs. Equally, distributing a program, which has a GPL dependency, separately and instructing the user to download that GPL dependency for himself would release a program from being licensed by GPL. However, distributing a program packaged with a GPL dependency would require licensing the whole software package under GPL, unless exceptions apply.

D. Commercial Distribution

In contrast to the open source licenses, which allow the code to go "closed" in proprietary software "*lost to the open source community*" [12], GPL is aimed to preserve software developments open for the development community. For this reason, GPL does not allow "burying" GPL code in proprietary software products. Against this principle, licensing GPL software in proprietary way and charging royalties is not admissible.

One of the exploitation options for GPL components might be charging fees for distribution of copies, running from the network server as "Software as a Service" or providing a warranty for a fee. For instance, when a GPL program is distributed from the site, fees for distributing copies can be charged. However, *"the fee to download source may not be greater than the fee to download the binary*" [33].

Offering warranty protection and additional liabilities would be another exploitation option. In this regard, GPL allows providing warranties, but requires that provision of warranties must be evidenced in writing, i.e., by signing an agreement. A negative aspect here is that by providing warranties a developer accepts additional liability for the bugs, caused by his predecessors, and assumes "*the cost of all necessary servicing, repair and correction*" [15] for the whole program, including modules provided by other developers. The business model of servicing GPL software has proven to be quite successful, as the Ubuntu [34] and other similar projects, which distribute and provide services for Linux/GNU software, demonstrate.

IV. CONCLUSIONS

In this paper, we have considered some licensing implications, which may arise by the use of open source software. We conclude by way of a case study, showing how the use of OSS may affect licensing of a project component.

In this example, let us consider licensing of a repository for computational models. The repository links, by calling the object code, to the database architecture MySQL, licensed under GPL v2 [35], and a web application Django, licensed under BSD 3-Clause License [36].

We may identify the future (downstream) licensing options for the repository in the following way. GPL v2 considers, "*linking a GPL covered work statically or dynamically with other modules making a combined work based on the GPL covered work. Thus, GNU GPL will cover the whole combination*" [19]. In terms of GPL, a repository, which links to GPL MySQL, qualifies as a work based on a GPL program and must go under GPL. BSD 3-Clause License is a lax software license, compatible with GPL [7]. GPL permits BSD programs in GPL software. Hence, no incompatibility issues with the BSD licensed Django arise. Section 9 GPL v2, applicable to MySQL, allows a work to be licensed under GPL v2 or any later version. This means, a repository, as a work based on GPL v2 MySQL, may go under GPL v3. Hence, GPL v3 has been identified as a license for this repository. The license requirements for distribution are considered next.

A repository may be distributed in source code and/or in object code. Distribution in object code must be supported by either: (a) source code; (b) an offer to provide source code (valid for 3 years); (c) an offer to access source code free of charge; or (d) by peer-to-peer transmission – information where to obtain the source code. If the repository is provided as "Software as a service", so that the users can interact with it via a network without having a possibility to download the code, release of the source code is not required.

In distributing this repository under GPL v3, the developer must include into each source file, or (in case of distribution in an object code) attach to each copy: a copyright notice, a GPL v3 license notice with the disclaimer of warranty and include the GPL v3 license text. If the repository has interactive user interfaces, each must display a copyright and license notice, disclaimer of warranty and instructions on how to view the license.

Django and MySQL, as incorporated into software distribution, remain under BSD and GPL v2, respectively. Here the BSD and GPL v2 license terms for distribution must be observed. It means, all copyright and license notices in the Django and MySQL code files must be reserved. For Django, a copyright notice, the license notice and disclaimer shall be retained in the source files or reproduced, if Django is re-distributed in object code [11]. Distribution of MySQL should be accompanied by a copyright notice, license notices and disclaimer of warranty; recipients should receive a copy of the GPL v2 license. For MySQL, distributed in object code, the source code should be accessible, either directly, or through instructions on how to get it.

As this case study suggests, the use of open source software under copyleft licenses, such as GPL, may be a preferential option for keeping the project components open for development community. On the other hand, if commercial exploitation is intended, the use of open source software under Apache License or MIT or BSD would most likely suit these interests better.

ACKNOWLEDGMENT

The research leading to these results has received funding from the European Union Seventh Framework Programme FP7/2007-2013 under grant agreement No 600841. The author thanks for the helpful comments on this work Prof. Dr. Nikolaus Forgó and Dr. Marc Stauch, Institut für Rechtsinformatik, Leibniz Universität Hannover, Hannover, Germany. Appreciation is also credited to Luis Enriquez A. and his Master Thesis "Dynamic Linked Libraries: Paradigms of the GPL license in contemporary software", which was used in doing this research.

REFERENCES

[1] CHIC, Project, <http://chic-vph.eu/project/> [retrieved: 5 April, 2016].

[2] D. Tartarini, et al, "The VPH Hypermodelling Framework for Cancer Multiscale Models in the Clinical Practice", In G. Stamatakos and D. Dionysiou (Eds): Proc. 2014 6th Int. Adv. Res. Workshop on In Silico Oncology and Cancer Investigation – The CHIC Project Workshop (IARWISOCI), Athens, Greece, Nov.3-4, 2014 (www.6thiarwisoci.iccs.ntua.gr), pp.61-64. (open-access version), ISBN: 978-618-80348-1-5.

[3] F. Rikhtegar, E. Kolokotroni, G.Stamatakos, and P. Büchler, "A Model of Tumor Growth Coupling a Cellular Biomodel with Biomechanical Simulations", In G. Stamatakos and D. Dionysiou (Eds): Proc. 2014 6th Int. Adv. Res. Workshop on In Silico Oncology and Cancer Investigation – The CHIC Project Workshop (IARWISOCI), Athens, Greece, Nov.3-4, 2014 (www.6thiarwisoci.iccs.ntua.gr), pp.43-46. (open-access version), ISBN: 978-618-80348-1-5, pp.43.

[4] Open Source Initiative, Open Source Definition, <http://opensource.org/osd> [retrieved: 6 April, 2016].

[5] Whelan Associates Inc. v. Jaslow Dental Laboratory, Inc., et al, U.S. Court of Appeals, Third Circuit, August 4, 1986, 797 F.2d 1222, 230 USPQ 481.

[6] GNU Operating System, The Free Software Definition, <http://www.gnu.org/philosophy/free-sw.en.html> [retrieved: 6 April, 2016].

[7] GNU Operating System, Various Licenses and Comments about Them, <http://www.gnu.org/licenses/license-list.en.html> [retrieved: 6 April, 2016].

[8] GNU Operating System, What is Copyleft?, <http://www.gnu.org/licenses/copyleft.en.html> [retrieved: 5 April, 2016].

[9] OSI, Licenses by Name, Apache License, Version 2.0, <http://opensource.org/licenses/Apache-2.0> [retrieved: 6 April, 2016].

[10] OSI, Licenses by Name, The MIT License (MIT), <http://opensource.org/licenses/MIT> [retrieved: 5 April, 2016].

[11] OSI, Licenses by Name, The BSD 3-Clause License, <http://opensource.org/licenses/BSD-3-Clause> [retrieved: 6 April, 2016].

[12] A. M. St. Laurent, "Understanding Open Source and Free Software Licensing", O'Reilly, 1 Edition, 2004.

[13] R. T. Nimmer, "Legal Issues in Open Source and Free Software Distribution", adapted from Chapter 11 in Raymond T. Nimmer, The Law of Computer Technology, 1997, 2005 Supp.

[14] GNU General Public License, Version 2 (GPL-2.0), <http://opensource.org/licenses/GPL-2.0> [retrieved: 7 April, 2016].

[15] GNU General Public License, Version 3 (GPL-3.0), <http://opensource.org/licenses/GPL-3.0> [retrieved: 6 April, 2016].

[16] The Linux Kernel Archives, <https://www.kernel.org/pub/linux/kernel/COPYING> [retrieved: 6 April, 2016].

[17] The R Project for Statistical Computing, R Licenses, <https://www.r-project.org/Licenses/> [retrieved: 6 April, 2016].

[18] Mozilla, MPL 2.0 FAQ, <https://www.mozilla.org/en-US/MPL/2.0/FAQ/> [retrieved: 6 April, 2016].

[19] GNU Operating System, Frequently Asked Questions about the GNU Licenses, <http://www.gnu.org/licenses/gpl-faq#GPLStaticVsDynamic> [retrieved: 6 April, 2016].

[20] L. Enriquez, "Dynamic Linked Libraries": Paradigms of the GPL license in contemporary software", EULISP Master Thesis, 2013.

[21] R. Stallman, "Android and Users' Freedom", first published in The Guardian, <http://www.gnu.org/philosophy/android-and-users-freedom.en.html> [retrieved: 6 April 2016].

[22] Hartman Greg Kroat, Linux kernel in a nutshell, O'Reilly, United States, 2007.

[23] Open Source Initiative, Licenses by Name, The GNU Lesser General Public License, version 2.1 (LGPL-2.1), <http://opensource.org/licenses/LGPL-2.1> [retrieved: 6 April, 2016].

[24] Open Source Initiative, Licenses by Name, The GNU Lesser General Public License, version 3.0 (LGPL-3.0), <http://opensource.org/licenses/LGPL-3.0> [retrieved: 6 April, 2016].

[25] The PHP Group, <http://php.net/> [retrieved: 06 April, 2016].

[26] OSI, Licenses by Name, The PHP License 3.0 (PHP-3.0), <https://opensource.org/licenses/PHP-3.0> [retrieved: 7 April, 2016].

[27] Building a LAMP Server, <http://www.lamphowto.com/> [retrieved: 7 April, 2016].

[28] Oracle, Products and Services, MySQL, Overview, <http://www.oracle.com/us/products/mysql/overview/index.html> [retrieved: 7 April, 2016].

[29] MySQL, FOSS License Exception, <https://www.mysql.de/about/legal/licensing/foss-exception//> [retrieved: 7 April, 2016].

[30] GNU Operating System, GNU Classpath, <http://www.gnu.org/software/classpath/license.html> [retrieved: 7 April, 2016].

[31] GNU Operating System, Frequently Asked Questions about the GNU Licenses, <http://www.gnu.org/licenses/gpl-faq#GPLIncompatibleLibs> [retrieved: 6 April, 2016].

[32] GNU Operating System, Frequently Asked Questions about the GNU Licenses, <http://www.gnu.org/licenses/gpl-faq#MereAggregation> [retrieved: 6 April, 2016].

[33] FSF, Frequently Asked Questions about the GNU Licenses, <https://www.gnu.org/licenses/gpl-faq.html#DoesTheGPLAllowDownloadFee> [retrieved: 6 April, 2016].

[34] Ubuntu, <http://www.ubuntu.com/> [retrieved: 6 April, 2016].

[35] MySQL, MySQL Workbench, <http://www.mysql.com/products/workbench/> [retrieved: 6 April, 2016].

[36] Django, Documentation, <https://docs.djangoproject.com/en/1.9/> [retrieved: 6 April, 2016].

Enhancement of Knowledge Resources and Discovery by Computation of Content Factors

Claus-Peter Rückemann
Westfälische Wilhelms-Universität Münster (WWU),
Leibniz Universität Hannover,
North-German Supercomputing Alliance (HLRN), Germany
Email: ruckema@uni-muenster.de

Abstract—**This paper presents a methodology for data description and analysis, the Content Factor (CONTFACT). The Content Factor method can be applied to arbitrary data and content and it can be adopted for many purposes. Normed factors and variants can also support data analysis and knowledge discovery. This paper presents the algorithm, introduces into the norming of Content Factors, and discusses examples and a practical case study and implementation based on long-term knowledge resources, which are continuously in development. The methodology is used for advanced processing and also enables methods like data rhythm analysis and characterisation. It can be integrated with complementary methodology, e.g., classification and allows the application of advanced computing methods. The goal of this research is to create a general and flexible methodology for data description and analysis that can be used with huge structured and even unstructured data resources, allows an automation, and can therefore also be used for long-term multi-disciplinary knowledge.**

Keywords–Data-centric Knowledge Processing; Content Factor (CONTFACT) method; Data Rhythm Analysis; Universal Decimal Classification; Advanced Computing.

I. INTRODUCTION

Information systems handling unstructured as well as structured information are lacking means for data description and analysis, which is data-centric and can be applied in flexible ways. In the late nineteen nineties, the concept of in-text documentation balancing has been introduced with the knowledge resources in the LX Project. Creating knowledge resources means creating, collecting, documenting, and analysing data and information. This can include digital objects, e.g., factual data, process information, and executable programs, as well as realia objects. Long-term means decades because knowledge is not isolated, neither in space nor time. All the more, knowledge does have a multi-disciplinary context.

Therefore, after integration knowledge should not disintegrate, instead it should be documented, preserved, and analysed in context. The extent increases with growing collections, which requires advanced processing and computing. Especially the complexity is a driving force, e.g., in depth, in width, and considering that parts of the content and context may be continuously in development. Therefore, the applied methods cannot be limited to certain algorithms and tools. Instead there are complementary sets of methods.

The methodology of computing factors [1] and patterns [2] being representative for a certain part of content was considered significant for knowledge resources and referred material. Fundamentally, a knowledge representation is surrogate. It enables an entity to determine consequences without forcing an action. For the development of these resources a definition-supported, sortable documentation-code balancing was created and implemented.

The Content Factor (CONTFACT) method advances this concept and integrates a definition-supported sortable documentation-code balancing and a universal applicability. The Content Factor method is focussing on documentation and analysis The Content Factor can contain a digital 'construction plan' or a significant part of digital objects, like sequenced DeoxyriboNucleic Acid (DNA) does for biological objects [3]. Here, a construction plan is what is decided to be a significant sequence of elements, which may, e.g., be sorted or unsorted. Furthermore, high level methods, e.g., "rhythm matching", can be based on methods like the Content Factor.

Classification has proven to be a valuable tool for long-term and complex information management, e.g., for environmental information systems [4]. Conceptual knowledge is also a complement for data and content missing conceptual documentation, e.g., for data based on ontologies used with dynamical and autonomous systems [5].

Growing content resources means huge amounts of data, requirements for creating and further developing advanced services, and increasing the quality of data and services. With growing content resources content balancing and valuation is getting more and more important.

This paper is organised as follows. Section II summarises the state-of-the-art and motivation, Sections III and IV introduce the Content Factor method and an example for the application principle. Section V shows implemented Content Factor examples, explains flags, definition sets, and norming. Section VI provides the results from an implementation case study, showing complementary properties and complex scenarios. Section VII discusses aspects of processing and computation. Sections VIII and IX present and evaluation and main results, summarise the lessons learned, conclusions and future work.

II. STATE-OF-THE-ART AND MOTIVATION

Most content and context documentation and knowledge discovery efforts are based on data and knowledge entities. Knowledge is created from a subjective combination of different attainments, which are selected, compared and balanced against each other, which are transformed, interpreted, and used in reasoning, also to infer further knowledge. Therefore, not all the knowledge can be explicitly formalised.

Knowledge and content are multi- and inter-disciplinary long-term targets and values [6]. In practice, powerful and secure information technology can support knowledge-based works and values. Computing goes along with methodologies, technological means, and devices applicable for universal automatic manipulation and processing of data and information. Computing is a practical tool and has well defined purposes and goals.

Most measures, e.g., similarity, distance and vector measures, are only secondary means [7], which cannot cope with complex knowledge. Evaluation metrics are very limited, and so are the connections resulting from co-occurences in given texts, e.g., even with Natural Language Processing (NLP), or clustering results in granular text segments [8].

Evaluation can be based on word semantic relatedness, datasets and evaluation measures, e.g., the WordSimilarity 353 dataset (EN-WS353) for English texts [9]. The development of Big Data amounts and complexity up to this point show that processing power is not the sole solution [10]. Advanced long-term knowledge management and analytics are on the rise.

Value of data is an increasingly important issue, especially when long-term knowledge creation is required, e.g., knowledge loss due to departing personnel [11]. Current information models are not able to really quantify the value of information. Due to this fact one of the most important assets [12], the information, is often left out [13]. Today a full understanding of the value of information is lacking. For example, free Open Access contributions can bear much higher information values than contributions from commercial publishers or providers.

For numberless application scenarios the entities have to be documented, described, selected, analysed, and interpreted. Standard means like statistics and regular expression search methods are basic tools used for these purposes.

Anyhow, these means are not data-centric, they are volatile methods, delivering non-persistent attributes with minimal descriptive features. The basic methods only count, the result is a number. Numbers can be easily handled but in their solelity such means are quite limited in their descriptiveness and expressiveness.

Therefore, many data and information handling systems create numbers of individual tools, e.g., for creating abstracts, generating keywords, and computing statistics based on the data. Such means and their implementations are either very basic or they are very individual.

The pool of tools requires new and additional methods of more universal and data-centric character – for structured and unstructured data.

New methods should not be restricted to certain types of data objects or content and they should be flexibly usable in combination and integration with existing methods and generally applicable to existing knowledge resources and referenced data. New methods should allow an abstraction, e.g., for the choice of definitions as well as for defined items.

III. The Content Factor

The fundamental method of the Basic Content Factor (BCF), κ_{B} – "Kappa-B" –, and the Normed Basic Content Factor (NBCF), $\overline{\kappa}_{\mathrm{B}}$, can be described by simple mathematical notations. For any elements o_i in an object o, holds

$$o_i \in o \,. \tag{1}$$

The organisation of an object is not limited, e.g., a reference can be defined an element. For κ_{B} of an object o, with elements o_i and the count function c, holds

$$\kappa_{\mathrm{B}}(o_i) = c(o_i) \,. \tag{2}$$

For $\overline{\kappa}_{\mathrm{B}}$ of an object o, for all elements n, with the count function c, holds

$$\overline{\kappa}_{\mathrm{B}}(o_i) = \frac{c(o_i)}{\displaystyle\sum_{i=1}^{n} c(o_i)} \,. \tag{3}$$

All normed κ for the elements o_i of an object o sum up to 1 for each object:

$$\sum_{i=1}^{n} \overline{\kappa}_{\mathrm{B}}(o_i) = 1 \,. \tag{4}$$

For a mathematical representation counting can be described by a set o and finding a result n, establishing a one to one correspondence of the set with the set of 'numbers' $1, 2, 3, \ldots, n$. It can be shown by mathematical induction that no bijection can exist between $1, 2, 3, \ldots, n$ and $1, 2, 3, \ldots, m$ unless $n = m$. A set can consist of subsets. The method can, e.g., be applied to disjoint subsets, too. It should be noted that counting can also be done using fuzzy sets [14].

IV. Application Example

The methodology can be used with any object, independent if realia objects or digital objects. Nevertheless, for ease of understanding the examples presented here are mostly considering text and data processing. Elements can be any part of the content, e.g., equations, images, text strings, and words. In the following example, "letters" are used for demonstrating the application. Given is an object with the sample content of 10 elements:

$$\texttt{A T A H C T O A R Z} \tag{5}$$

For this example it is suggested that `A` and `Z` are relevant for documentation and analysis. The relevant elements, `AAAZ`, in an object of these 10 elements for element `A` means $3/10$ normed so the full notation is

$$\texttt{AAAZ}/10 \text{ with } \overline{\kappa}_{\mathrm{B}}(\texttt{A}) = 3/10 \text{ and } \overline{\kappa}_{\mathrm{B}}(\texttt{Z}) = 1/10 \,. \tag{6}$$

In consequence, the summed value for `AAAZ/10` is

$$\overline{\kappa}_{\mathrm{B}}(\texttt{A}, \texttt{Z}) = 4/10 \,. \tag{7}$$

`AAAZ` in an object of 20 elements, for element `A` means 3/20 normed, which shows that it is relatively less often in this object. $3/22$ for element `A` for this object means this object or an instance in a different development stage, e.g., at a different time or in a different element context. The notation

$$\{i_1\}, \{i_2\}, \{i_3\}, \ldots, \{i_n\}/n \tag{8}$$

of available elements holds the respective selection where $\{i_1\}, \{i_2\}, \{i_3\}, \ldots, \{i_n\}$ refers to the definitions of element groups. Elements can have the same labels respectively values. From this example it is easy to see that the method can be applied independent from a content structure.

V. Content Factor Examples

The following examples (Figures 1, 2, 4, 3, 5) show valid notations of the Normed Basic Content Factor $\overline{\kappa}_{\mathrm{B}}$, which were taken from the LX Foundation Scientific Resources [15]. The LX Project is a long-term multi-disciplinary project to create universal knowledge resources. Application components can be efficiently created to use the resources, e.g., from the Geo Exploration and Information (GEXI) project. Any kind of data can be integrated. Data is collected in original, authentic form, structure, and content but data can also be integrated in modified form. Creation and development are driven by multifold activities, e.g., by workgroups and campaigns. A major goal is to create data that can be used by workgroups for their required purposes without limiting long-term data to applications cases for a specific scenario. The usage includes a targetted documentation and analysis. For the workgroups, the Content Factor has shown to be beneficial with documentation and analysis. There are countless fields to use the method, which certainly depend on the requirements of the workgroups. For the majority of use cases, especially, selecting objects and comparing content have been focus applications. With these knowledge resources multi-disciplinary knowledge is documented over long time intervals. The resources are currently already developed for more than 25 years. A general and portable structure was used for the representation.

```
CONTFACT:20150101:MS:{A}{A}{G}{G}{G}/2900
CONTFACT:20150101:M:{A}:=Archaeology|Archeology
CONTFACT:20150101:M:{G}:=Geophysics
```

Figure 1. NBCF $\overline{\kappa}_{\mathrm{B}}$ for an object, core notation including the normed CONTFACT and definitions, braced style.

The Content Factor can hold the core, the definitions, and additional information. The core is the specification of κ_{B} or $\overline{\kappa}_{\mathrm{B}}$. Definitions are assignments used for the elements of objects, specified for use in the core.

Here, the core entry shows an International Standards Organisation (ISO) date or optional date-time code field, a flag, and the CONTFACT core. The definitions hold a date-time code field, flag, and CONTFACT definitions or definitions sets as shown here. Definition sets are groups of definitions for a certain Content Factor. The following examples show how the definition sets work.

```
CONTFACT:20150101:MS:AAG/89
CONTFACT:20150101:M:A:=Archaeology|Archeology
CONTFACT:20150101:M:G:=Geophysics
```

Figure 2. NBCF $\overline{\kappa}_{\mathrm{B}}$ for an object, core notation including the normed CONTFACT and definitions, non-braced style.

```
CONTFACT:20150101:MU:A{Geophysics}{Geology}/89
CONTFACT:20150101:M:A:=Archaeology|Archeology
CONTFACT:20150101:M:{Geophysics}:=Geophysics|
  Seismology|Volcanology
CONTFACT:20150101:M:{Geology}:=Geology|
  Palaeontology
```

Figure 3. NBCF $\overline{\kappa}_{\mathrm{B}}$ for an object, core notation including the normed CONTFACT and definitions, mixed style.

```
CONTFACT:20150101:MU:{Archaeology}{Geophysics}/120
CONTFACT:20150101:M:Archaeology:=Archaeology|
  Archeology
CONTFACT:20150101:M:Geophysics:=Geophysics
```

Figure 4. NBCF $\overline{\kappa}_{\mathrm{B}}$ for an object, core notation including the normed CONTFACT and definitions, multi-character non-braced style.

```
CONTFACT:20150101:MU:vvvvaSsC/70
CONTFACT:20150101:M:v:=volcano
CONTFACT:20150101:M:a:=archaeology
CONTFACT:20150101:M:S:=Solfatara
CONTFACT:20150101:M:s:=supervolcano
CONTFACT:20150101:M:C:=Flegrei
```

Figure 5. NBCF $\overline{\kappa}_{\mathrm{B}}$ for an object from a natural sciences collection, multi-case non-braced style.

Definitions can, e.g., be valid in braced, non-braced, and mixed style. Left values can have different labels, e.g., uppercase, lowercase, and mixed style can be valid. Figure 6 shows an example using Universal Decimal Classification (UDC) notation definitions.

```
CONTFACT:20150101:MS:{UDC:55}{UDC:55}/210
CONTFACT:20150101:M:{UDC:55}:=Earth Sciences. Geological
  sciences
```

Figure 6. NBCF $\overline{\kappa}_{\mathrm{B}}$ for an object from a natural sciences collection, UDC notation definitions, braced style.

Conceptual knowledge like UDC can be considered in many ways, e.g., via classification and via description.

A. Flags

Content Factors can be associated with certain qualities. Sample flags, which are used with core, definition, and additional entries are given in Table I.

Table I. Sample flags used with CONTFACT entries.

Purpose	*Flag*	*Meaning*
Content Factor quality	U	Unsorted
	S	Sorted
Content Factor source	M	Manual
	A	Automated
	H	Hybrid

The CONTFACT core entries can have various qualities, e.g., unsorted (U) or sorted (S). Unsorted means in the order in which they appear in the respective object. Sorted means in a different sort order, which may also be specified. CONTFACT entries can result from various workflows and procedures, e.g., they can be created on manual base (M) or on automated base

(A). If nothing else is specified the flag refers to the way object entries were created. Content Factor quality refers to core entries, source also refers to the definitions and information.

The Content Factor method provides the specified instructions. The required features with an implementation can, e.g., implicitly require large numbers of comparisons, resulting in highly computationally intensive workflows on certain architectures. It is the choice of the user to weighten between the benefits and the computational efforts, and potentially to provide suitable environments.

B. *Definition sets*

Definition sets for object elements can be created and used very flexibly, e.g., word or string definitions. Therefore, a reasonable set of elements can be defined for the respective purpose, especially:

- Definition sets can contain appropriate material, e.g., text or classification.
- Groups of elements can be created.
- Contributing elements can be subsummarised.
- Definition sets can be kept persistent and volatile.
- Definition set elements can be weighted, e.g., by parameterisation of context-sensitive code growth.
- Context sensitive definition sets can be referenced with data objects.
- Content can be described with multiple, complementary definition sets.
- Any part of the content can be defined as elements.

The Content Factors can be computed for any object, e.g., for text and other parts of content. Nevertheless, the above definition sets for normed factors are intended to be used with one type of elements.

C. *Normed application*

$\overline{\kappa}_{\mathrm{B}}$ is a normed quantity. Norming is a mathematical procedure, by which the interesting quantity (e.g., vector, operator, function) is modified by multiplication in a way that after the norming the application of respective functionals delivers 1. The respective $\overline{\kappa}_{\mathrm{B}}$ Content Factor can be used to create a weighting on objects, e.g., multiplying the number of elements with the respective factor value.

VI. IMPLEMENTATION

The implementation has been created for the primary use with knowledge resources' objects (`lxcontfact`). This means handling of any related content, e.g., documentation, keywords, classification, transliterations, and references. The respective objects were addressed as Content Factor Object (CFO) (standard file extension `.cfo`) and the definition sets as Content Factor Definition (CFD) (standard file extension `.cfd`).

A. *Case study: Computing complementation and properties*

The following sequence of short examples shows a knowledge resources object (Figure 7), and three pairs of complementary CONTFACT definition sets and the according $\overline{\kappa}_{\mathrm{B}}$ computed for the knowledge resources object and respective definition sets (Figures 8 and 9; 10 and 11; 12 and 13).

```
object A        %-GP%-XX%---: object A              [A, B, C, D, O]:
                %-GP%-EN%---:                       A B C D O
                %-GP%-EN%---:                       A B C D O
                %-GP%-EN%---:                       A B C D O
                %-GP%-EN%---:                       A B C D O
                %-GP%-EN%---:                       A B C D O
```

Figure 7. Artificial knowledge resources object (LX Resources, excerpt).

The right parts are entry and keywords. Here, the algorithm can count in object entry name (right "object A"), keywords (in brackets), and object documentation (lower right block).

```
% (c) LX-Project, 2015, 2016
{A}:=\bA\b
{O}:=\bO\b
```

Figure 8. CONTFACT definition set 1 of 3 (LX Resources, excerpt).

The definition set defines {A} and {O}. The definitions are case sensitive for this discovery. We can compute $\overline{\kappa}_{\mathrm{B}}$ (Figure 9) according to the knowledge resources object and definition set.

```
CONTFACT:BEGIN
CONTFACT:20160117-175904:AU:{A}{A}{O}{A}{O}{A}{O}{A}{O}{A}{O}{A}{O}/32
CONTFACT:20160117-175904:AS:{A}{A}{A}{A}{A}{A}{A}{O}{O}{O}{O}{O}{O}/32
CONTFACT:20160117-175904:M:{A}:=\bA\b
CONTFACT:20160117-175904:M:{O}:=\bO\b
CONTFACT:20160117-175904:M:STAT:OBJECTELEMENTSDEF=2
CONTFACT:20160117-175904:M:STAT:OBJECTELEMENTSALL=32
CONTFACT:20160117-175904:M:STAT:OBJECTELEMENTSMAT=13
CONTFACT:20160117-175904:M:STAT:OBJECTELEMENTSCFO=.40625000
CONTFACT:20160117-175904:M:STAT:OBJECTELEMENTSKWO=2
CONTFACT:20160117-175904:M:STAT:OBJECTELEMENTSLAN=1
CONTFACT:20160117-175904:M:INFO:OBJECTELEMENTSOBJ=object A
CONTFACT:20160117-175904:M:INFO:OBJECTELEMENTSDCM=(c) LX-Project, 2015, 2016
CONTFACT:20160117-175904:M:INFO:OBJECTELEMENTSMTX=LX Foundation Scientific
 Resources; Object Collection
CONTFACT:20160117-175904:M:INFO:OBJECTELEMENTSAUT=Claus-Peter R\"uckemann
CONTFACT:END
```

Figure 9. NBCF $\overline{\kappa}_{\mathrm{B}}$ computed for knowledge resources object and definition set 1 (LX Resources, excerpt).

The result is shown in a line-oriented representation, each line carrying the respective date-time code for all the core, statistics, and additional information. The second complementary set (Figure 11) defines {B} and {D}.

```
% (c) LX-Project, 2015, 2016
{B}:=\bB\b
{D}:=\bD\b
```

Figure 10. CONTFACT definition set 2 of 3 (LX Resources, excerpt).

```
CONTFACT:BEGIN
CONTFACT:20160117-175904:AU:{B}{D}{B}{D}{B}{D}{B}{D}{B}{D}{B}{D}/33
CONTFACT:20160117-175904:AS:{B}{B}{B}{B}{B}{B}{D}{D}{D}{D}{D}{D}/33
CONTFACT:20160117-175904:M:{B}:=\bB\b
CONTFACT:20160117-175904:M:{D}:=\bD\b
CONTFACT:20160117-175904:M:STAT:OBJECTELEMENTSDEF=2
CONTFACT:20160117-175904:M:STAT:OBJECTELEMENTSALL=33
CONTFACT:20160117-175904:M:STAT:OBJECTELEMENTSMAT=12
CONTFACT:20160117-175904:M:STAT:OBJECTELEMENTSCFO=.37500000
...
```

Figure 11. NBCF $\overline{\kappa}_{\mathrm{B}}$ computed for knowledge resources object and definition set 2 (LX Resources, excerpt).

The resulting $\overline{\kappa}_{\mathrm{B}}$ is shown in the excerpt (Figure 12).

```
% (c) LX-Project, 2015, 2016
{C}:=\bC\b
```

Figure 12. CONTFACT definition set 3 of 3 (LX Resources, excerpt).

The third complementary set (Figure 13) defines {C}.

```
CONTFACT:BEGIN
CONTFACT:20160117-175905:AU:{C}{C}{C}{C}{C}{C}/32
CONTFACT:20160117-175905:AS:{C}{C}{C}{C}{C}{C}/32
CONTFACT:20160117-175905:M:{C}:=\bC\b
CONTFACT:20160117-175905:M:STAT:OBJECTELEMENTSDEF=1
CONTFACT:20160117-175905:M:STAT:OBJECTELEMENTSALL=32
CONTFACT:20160117-175905:M:STAT:OBJECTELEMENTSMAT=6
CONTFACT:20160117-175905:M:STAT:OBJECTELEMENTSCFO=.18750000
...
```

Figure 13. NBCF $\overline{\kappa}_{\mathrm{B}}$ computed for knowledge resources object and definition set 3 (LX Resources, excerpt).

The sum of all elements considered for $\overline{\kappa}_{\mathrm{B}}$ by the respective CONTFACT algorithm in an object is 100 percent. Here, the overall number of

- definitions is $2 + 2 + 1 = 5$,
- elements is 32,
- matches is $13 + 12 + 6 = 31$.

The sum of aggregated $\overline{\kappa}_{\mathrm{B}}$ values for all relevant elements results in $0.40625000 + 0.37500000 + 0.18750000 + 1/32 = 1$.

B. Case study: Complex resources and discovery scenario

The data used here is based on the content and context from the knowledge resources, provided by the LX Foundation Scientific Resources [15]. The LX knowledge resources' structure and the classification references [16] based on UDC [17] are essential means for the processing workflows and evaluation of the knowledge objects and containers.

Both provide strong multi-disciplinary and multi-lingual support. For this part of the research all small unsorted excerpts of the knowledge resources objects only refer to main UDC-based classes, which for this part of the publication are taken from the Multilingual Universal Decimal Classification Summary (UDCC Publication No. 088) [18] released by the UDC Consortium under the Creative Commons Attribution Share Alike 3.0 license [19] (first release 2009, subsequent update 2012).

The excerpts (Figures 14, 15, 16), show a CFO from the knowledge resources a CFD and the computed CONTFACT.

```
Vesuvius [Volcanology, Geology, Archaeology]:
         (lat.) Mons Vesuvius.
         (ital.) Vesuvio.
         Volcano, Gulf of Naples, Italy.
         Complex volcano (compound volcano). Stratovolcano, large cone (Gran
          Cono).
         ...
         The most well known antique settlements at the Vesuvius are \lxidx{
          Pompeji}, \lxidx{Herculaneum}, and \lxidx{Stabiae}.
         s. also seismology, phlegra, Solfatara
         %%IML: keyword: volcano, Vesuvius, Campi Flegrei, phlegra, scene of
          fire, Pompeji, Herculaneum, volcanic ash, lapilli, catastrophe,
          climatology, eruption, lava, gas ejection, Carbon Dioxide
         %%IML: UDC:[911.2+55]:[57+930.85]:[902]"63"(4+37+23+24)=12=14
         ...
         Object:              Volcanic material.
         Object-Type:         Realia object.
         Object-Location:     Vesuvius, Italy.
         Object-FindDate:     2013-10-00
         Object-Discoverer:   Birgit Gersbeck-Schierholz, Hannover, Germany.
         Object-Photo:        Claus-Peter Rückemann, Minden, Germany.
         %%IML: media: YES 20131000 {LXC:DETAIL--M-} {UDC:(0.034)(044)770}
          LXDATASTORAGE://...img_3824.jpg
         %%IML: UDC-Object:[551.21+55]:[911.2](37+4+23)=12
         %%IML: UDC: 551.21        :: Vulcanicity. Vulcanism. Volcanoes. Eruptive
          phenomena. Eruptions
         %%IML: UDC: 55            :: Earth Sciences. Geological sciences
         %%IML: UDC: 911.2         :: Physical geography
```

Figure 14. Knowledge resources object (geosciences collection, LX, excerpt).

Labels, language fields, and spaces were stripped. A knowledge object can contain any items required, e.g., including storing data, documentation, classification, keywords, algorithms, references, implementations, in any languages and representations, allowing support tables and algorithms. Examples of application scenarios for the Content Factor method range from libraries, natural sciences and archaeology, statics, architecture, risk coverage, technology to material sciences [20].

```
% (c) LX-Project, 2009, 2015
{Ve}:=Vesuvius
{Vo}:=\b[Vv]olcano
{Po}:=Pompe[ji]i
{UDC:55}:=Geology
{UDC:volcano}:=UDC.*\b911\b.*\b55\b
```

Figure 15. CONTFACT definition set (geosciences collection, LX, excerpt).

The definition sets can contain anything required for the definitions and additional information for the respective Content Factor implementation, e.g., definitions of elements and groups as well as comments. The left side defines the element used in the Content Factor and the right side states the matching element components. Left value and right value are separated by ":=" for an active definition.

```
CONTFACT:BEGIN
CONTFACT:20160130-235804:AU:{Ve}{Vo}{UDC:55:geology}{Ve}{Ve}{Vo}{Vo}{Vo}{Vo}{Vo
 }{Vo}{Vo}{Ve}{Ve}{Po}{Ve}{Po}{Ve}{Ve}{Ve}{Vo}{Vo}{Vo}{Vo}{Vo}{UDC:volcano}{Vo}{
 Vo}/319
CONTFACT:20160130-235804:AS:{Po}{Po}{UDC:55:geology}{UDC:volcano}{Ve}{Ve}{Ve}{Ve
 }{Ve}{Ve}{Ve}{Ve}{Ve}{Vo}{Vo}{Vo}{Vo}{Vo}{Vo}{Vo}{Vo}{Vo}{Vo}{Vo}{Vo}{Vo}{Vo}{
 Vo}/319
CONTFACT:20160130-235804:M:{Ve}:=Vesuvius
CONTFACT:20160130-235804:M:{Vo}:=\b[Vv]olcano
CONTFACT:20160130-235804:M:{Po}:=Pompe[ji]i
CONTFACT:20160130-235804:M:{UDC:55:geology}:=Geology
CONTFACT:20160130-235804:M:{UDC:volcano}:=UDC.*\b911\b.*\b55\b
CONTFACT:20160130-235804:M:STAT:OBJECTELEMENTSDEF=5
CONTFACT:20160130-235804:M:STAT:OBJECTELEMENTSALL=319
CONTFACT:20160130-235804:M:STAT:OBJECTELEMENTSMAT=28
CONTFACT:20160130-235804:M:STAT:OBJECTELEMENTSCFO=.09180304
CONTFACT:20160130-235804:M:INFO:OBJECTELEMENTSDCM=(c) LX-Project, 2009, 2015
...
CONTFACT:END
```

Figure 16. NBCF $\overline{\kappa}_{\mathrm{B}}$ computed for knowledge resources object and definition set (geosciences collection, LX Resources, excerpt).

The left value can include braces (e.g., curly brackets) in order to support the specification and identification of the left value. The right value can include common representations of pattern specification. The result of which can be seen from the computed CONTFACT.

The example patterns follow the widely used Perl (Practical Extraction and Report Language) regular expressions [21], e.g., `\b` for word boundaries and `[...]` and multiple choices of characters at a certain position.

C. Case study: Rhythm matching and core sequences

As soon as Content Factors have been computed for an object the patterns can be compared with pattern of other objects. The Content Factor method allows to compare the occurrences of relevant elements in objects in many ways. The following example shows the "rhythm matching" method for two computed unsorted CONTFACT core sequences (Figures 18, 19) for an object and a definition set (Figure 17).

```
% (c) LX-Project, 2009, 2015, 2016
{Am}:=\b[Aa]mphora
{Ce}:=[Cc]eramic
{Gr}:=\b[Gg]reek\b
{Pi}:=[Pp]itho[is]
{Ro}:=\b[Rr]oman\b
{Tr}:=[Tt]ransport
{Va}:=[Vv]ases
```

Figure 17. Example of CONTFACT definition set, geoscientific and archaeological resources (LX Resources, excerpt).

```
CONTFACT:20160101-215751:AU:{Am}{Gr}{Ce}{Ro}{Am}{Gr}{Am}{
Am}{Va}{Pi}{Tr}/474
```

Figure 18. CONTFACT rhythm matching: Computed core for same object (before modification) and definition set (LX Resources, excerpt).

```
CONTFACT:20160101-231806:AU:{Am}{Gr}{Ce}{Ro}{Am}{Gr}{Am}{
Am}{Va}{Pi}{Tr}{Ce}{Ce}{Tr}{Tr}{Ce}{Pi}{Am}/488
```

Figure 19. CONTFACT rhythm matching: Computed core for same object (after modification) and definition set (LX Resources, excerpt).

The comparison shows that relevant passages were appended to the object (italics font). Relevant regarding the rhythm matching means relevant from the object and definition set. Even short sequences like `{Am}{Gr}{Ce}` and even when sorted like `{Am}{Ce}{Gr}` can be relevant and significant in order to compute factors and identify and compare objects. The Content Factor method does not have built-in or intrinsic limitations specifying certain ways of further use, e.g., with comparisons and analysis.

Unsorted CONTFACT are more likely to describe objects and quality, including their internal organisation. Sorted CONTFACT tend to describe objects by their quantities, with reduced focus on their internal organisation.

Objects with larger amount of documentation maybe candidates for unsorted CONTFACT. Objects, e.g., with factual, formalised content maybe candidates for sorted CONTFACT. Combining several methods in a workflow is possible.

Anyhow, the further use of the CONTFACT core, e.g., sorting the core data for a certain comparison, is a matter of application and purpose with respective data.

VII. Processing and Computation

A. Scalability, modularisation, and dynamical use

The algorithms can be used for single objects as well as for large collections and containers, containing millions of entries each. The computation routines allow a modularised and dynamical use.

The parts required for an implementation computing a Content Factor can be modularised, which means that not only a Content Factor computation can be implemented as a module but even core, definitions, and additional parts can be computed by separate modules.

A sequence of routine calls used for examples in this case study shows the principle and modular application of respective functions (Figure 20).

The modules create an entity for the implemented Content Factor (begin to end). They include labels, date, unsorted elements and so on as well as statistics and additional information.

```
contfactbegin
contfact
contfactdate
contfacttype
contfactelementsu
contfactref
contfactsum
...
contfactdef
...
contfact
contfactdate
```

```
contfacttypestat
contfact_stat_mat_u_lab
contfact_stat_mat_u
...
contfact
contfactdate
contfacttypeinfo
contfact_info_obj_lab
contfact_info_obj
...
...
contfactend
```

Figure 20. Sequence of modular CONTFACT routines for `lxcontfact` implementation (LX Resources, excerpt).

Application scenarios may allow to compute Content Factors for many objects in parallel. Content Factors can be computed dynamically as well as in batch mode or "pre-computed". Content Factors can be kept volatile as well as persistent. Everything can be considered a set, e.g., an object, a collection, and a container. Therefore, an implementation can scale from single on the fly objects to millions of objects, which may also associated with pre-computed Content Factors.

B. Parallelisation and persistence

There is a number of modules supporting computation based on persistent data, e.g., in collections and containers. The architecture allows task parallel implementations for multiple instances as well as highly parallel implementations for core routines. Examples are collection and container decollators, collection and container slicers, collection and container atomisers, formatting modules, and computing modules for (intermediate) result matrix requests.

Content Factor data can easily be kept persistent and dynamically. The algorithms and workflows allow the flexible organisation of data locality, e.g., central locations and with compute units, e.g., in groups or containers.

VIII. Evaluation

The case study has shown that the formal description can be implemented very flexibly and successful (`lxcontfact`). Content Factors can be computed for any type of data. The Content Factor is not limited to text processing or even NLP, term-frequencies, and statistics. It has been successfully used with long term knowledge resources and with unstructured and dynamical data. The Content Factor method can describe arbitrary data in a unique form and supports data analysis and knowledge discovery in many ways, e.g., complex data comparison and tracking of relevant changes.

Definition sets can support various use cases. Examples were given from handling single characters to string elements. Definitions can be kept with the Content Factor, together with additional Content Factor data, e.g., statistics and documentation. Any of this Content Factor information has been successfully used to analyse data objects from different sources. The computation of Content Factors is non invasive, the results can be created dynamically and persistent. Content Factors can be automatically computed for elements and groups of large data resources. The integration with data and knowledge resources can be kept non invasive to least invasive, depending on the desired purposes. Knowledge objects, e.g., in collections and containers, can carry and refer to complementary information and knowledge, especially Content Factor information, which can be integrated with workflows, e.g., for discovery processes.

The benefits and usability may depend on the field of application and the individual goals. The evaluation refers to the case context presented, which allows a wide range of freedom and flexibility. The benefits for the knowledge resources are additional means for documentation of objects. In detail, the benefits for the example workflows were improved data-mining pipelines, due to additional features for comparisons of objects, integrating developing knowledge resources, and creating and developing knowledge resources. In practice, the computation of Content Factors has revealed significant benefits for the creation and analysis of large numbers of objects and for the flexibility and available features for building workflows, e.g., when based on long-term knowledge objects. In addition, creators, authors, and users of knowledge and content have additional means to express their views and valuation of objects and groups of objects. From the computational point of view, the computation of Content Factors can help minimise the recurrent computing demands for data.

IX. Conclusion

This paper introduced a methodology for data description and analysis, the Content Factor (CONTFACT) method. The paper presents the formal description and examples, a successful implementation, and a practical case study. It has been shown that the Content Factor is data-centric and can describe and analyse arbitrary data and content, structured and unstructured. Data-centricity is even emphasized due to the fact that the Content Factor can be seamlessly integrated with the data. The data locality is most flexible and allows an efficient use of different computing, storage, and communication architectures.

The method can be adopted for many purposes. The Content Factor method has been successfully applied for knowledge processing and analysis with long-term knowledge resources, for knowledge discovery, and with variable data for system operation analysis. It enables to specify a wide range of precision and fuzziness for data description and analysis and also enables methods like data rhythm analysis and characterisation, can be integrated with complementary methodologies, e.g., classifications, concordances, and references. Therefore, the method allows weighting data regarding significance, promoting the value of data. The method supports the use of advanced computing methods for computation and analysis with the implementation. The computation and processing can be automated and used with huge and even unstructured data resources. The methodology allows an integrated use with complementary methodologies, e.g., with conceptual knowledge like UDC. It will be interesting to see various Content Factor implementations for individual applications, e.g., dynamical classification and concordances. Future work concentrates on advanced analysis and automation for different application scenarios, e.g., object comparisons, multi-lingual discovery, and concordance discovery.

Acknowledgements

We are grateful to the "Knowledge in Motion" (KiM) long-term project, Unabhängiges Deutsches Institut für Multidisziplinäre Forschung (DIMF), for partially funding this implementation, case study, and publication and to its senior scientific members, especially to Dr. Friedrich Hülsmann, Gottfried Wilhelm Leibniz Bibliothek (GWLB) Hannover, to Dipl.-Biol. Birgit Gersbeck-Schierholz, Leibniz Universität Hannover, and to Dipl.-Ing. Martin Hofmeister, Hannover, for fruitful discussion, inspiration, practical multi-disciplinary case studies, and the analysis of advanced concepts. We are grateful to all national and international partners in the GEXI cooperations for their constructive and trans-disciplinary support.

References

[1] C.-P. Rückemann, "Advanced Content Balancing and Valuation: The Content Factor (CONTFACT)," Knowledge in Motion Long-term Project, Unabhängiges Deutsches Institut für Multidisziplinäre Forschung (DIMF), Germany; Westfälische Wilhelms-Universität Münster, Münster, 2009, Project Technical Report.

[2] C.-P. Rückemann, "CONTCODE – A Code for Balancing Content," Knowledge in Motion Long-term Project, Unabhängiges Deutsches Institut für Multidisziplinäre Forschung (DIMF), Germany; Westfälische Wilhelms-Universität Münster, Münster, 2009, Project Technical Report.

[3] F. Hülsmann and C.-P. Rückemann, "Content and Factor in Practice: Revealing the Content-DNA," KiM Summit, October 26, 2015, Knowledge in Motion, Hannover, Germany, 2015, Project Meeting Report.

[4] C.-P. Rückemann, "Integrated Computational and Conceptual Solutions for Complex Environmental Information Management," in The Fifth Symposium on Advanced Computation and Information in Natural and Applied Sciences, Proceedings of The 13th International Conference of Numerical Analysis and Applied Mathematics (ICNAAM), September 23–29, 2015, Rhodes, Greece, Proceedings of the American Institute of Physics (AIP). AIP Press, 2015, ISSN: 0094-243X, (in press).

[5] D. T. Meridou, U. Inden, C.-P. Rückemann, C. Z. Patrikakis, D.-T. I. Kaklamani, and I. S. Venieris, "Ontology-based, Multi-agent Support of Production Management," in The Fifth Symposium on Advanced Computation and Information in Natural and Applied Sciences, Proceedings of The 13th International Conference of Numerical Analysis and Applied Mathematics (ICNAAM), September 23–29, 2015, Rhodes, Greece, Proceedings of the American Institute of Physics (AIP). AIP Press, 2015, ISSN: 0094-243X, (in press).

[6] C.-P. Rückemann, F. Hülsmann, B. Gersbeck-Schierholz, P. Skurowski, and M. Staniszewski, Knowledge and Computing. Post-Summit Results, Delegates' Summit: Best Practice and Definitions of Knowledge and Computing, September 23, 2015, The Fifth Symposium on Advanced Computation and Information in Natural and Applied Sciences, The 13th International Conference of Numerical Analysis and Applied Mathematics (ICNAAM), September 23–29, 2015, Rhodes, Greece, 2015.

[7] O. Lipsky and E. Porat, "Approximated Pattern Matching with the L_1, L_2 and L_∞ Metrics," in 15th International Symposium on String Processing and Information Retrieval (SPIRE 2008), November 10–12, 2008, Melbourne, Australia, ser. Lecture Notes in Computer Science (LNCS), vol. 5280. Springer, Berlin, Heidelberg, 2008, pp. 212–223, Amir, A. and Turpin, A. and Moffat, A. (eds.), ISSN: 0302-9743, ISBN: 978-3-540-89096-6, LCCN: 2008938187.

[8] G. Ercan and I. Cicekli, "Lexical Cohesion Based Topic Modeling for Summarization," in Proceedings of The 9th International Conference on Computational Linguistics and Intelligent Text Processing (CICLing 2008), February 17–23, 2008, Haifa, Israel, ser. Lecture Notes in Computer Science (LNCS), vol. 4919. Springer, Berlin, Heidelberg, 2008,

pp. 582–592, Gelbukh, A. (ed.), ISSN: 0302-9743, ISBN: 978-3-540-78134-9, LCCN: 2008920439, URL: http://link.springer.com/chapter/10.1007/978-3-540-78135-6_50 [accessed: 2016-01-10].

[9] G. Szarvas, T. Zesch, and I. Gurevych, "Combining Heterogeneous Knowledge Resources," in Proceedings of The 12th International Conference on Computational Linguistics and Intelligent Text Processing (CICLing 2011), February 20–26, 2011, Tokyo, Japan, ser. Lecture Notes in Computer Science (LNCS), vol. 6608 and 6609. Springer, Berlin, Heidelberg, 2011, pp. 289–303, Gelbukh, A. (ed.), ISSN: 0302-9743, ISBN: 978-3-642-19399-6, DOI: 10.1007/978-3-642-19400-9, LCCN: 2011921814, URL: http://link.springer.com/chapter/10.1007/978-3-642-19400-9_23 [accessed: 2016-01-10].

[10] A. Woodie, "Is 2016 the Beginning of the End for Big Data?" Datanami, 2016, January 5, 2016, URL: http://www.datanami.com/2016/01/05/is-2016-the-beginning-of-the-end-for-big-data/ [accessed: 2016-01-10].

[11] M. E. Jennex, "A Proposed Method for Assessing Knowledge Loss Risk with Departing Personnel," VINE: The Journal of Information and Knowledge Management Systems, vol. 44, no. 2, 2014, pp. 185–209, ISSN: 0305-5728.

[12] R. Leming, "Why is information the elephant asset? An answer to this question and a strategy for information asset management," Business Information Review, vol. 32, no. 4, 2015, pp. 212–219, ISSN: 0266-3821 (print), ISSN: 1741-6450 (online), DOI: 10.1177/0266382115616301.

[13] "The (Unknown) Value of Information (in German: Der (unbekannte) Wert von Information)," library essentials, LE_Informationsdienst, Dez. 2015 / Jan. 2016, 2015, pp. 10–14, ISSN: 2194-0126, URL: http://www.libess.de [accessed: 2016-01-10].

[14] B. Kosko, "Counting with Fuzzy Sets," IEEE Transactions on Pattern Analysis and Machine Intelligence, vol. PAMI-8, no. 4, Jul. 1986, pp. 556–557, ISSN: 0162-8828, DOI: 10.1109/TPAMI.1986.4767822.

[15] "LX-Project," 2016, URL: http://www.user.uni-hannover.de/cpr/x/rprojs/en/#LX (Information) [accessed: 2016-01-01].

[16] C.-P. Rückemann, "Enabling Dynamical Use of Integrated Systems and Scientific Supercomputing Resources for Archaeological Information Systems," in Proc. INFOCOMP 2012, Oct. 21–26, 2012, Venice, Italy, 2012, pp. 36–41, ISBN: 978-1-61208-226-4.

[17] "UDC Online," 2015, URL: http://www.udc-hub.com/ [accessed: 2016-01-01].

[18] "Multilingual Universal Decimal Classification Summary," 2012, UDC Consortium, 2012, Web resource, v. 1.1. The Hague: UDC Consortium (UDCC Publication No. 088), URL: http://www.udcc.org/udcsummary/php/index.php [accessed: 2016-01-01].

[19] "Creative Commons Attribution Share Alike 3.0 license," 2012, URL: http://creativecommons.org/licenses/by-sa/3.0/ [accessed: 2016-01-01].

[20] F. Hülsmann, C.-P. Rückemann, M. Hofmeister, M. Lorenzen, O. Lau, and M. Tasche, "Application Scenarios for the Content Factor Method in Libraries, Natural Sciences and Archaeology, Statics, Architecture, Risk Coverage, Technology, and Material Sciences," KiM Strategy Summit, March 17, 2016, Knowledge in Motion, Hannover, Germany, 2016.

[21] "The Perl Programming Language," 2016, URL: https://www.perl.org/ [accessed: 2016-01-10].

GRChat: A Contact-based Messaging Application for the Evaluation of Information Diffusion

Enrique Hernández-Orallo, David Fernández-Delegido, Andrés Tomás, Jorge Herrera-Tapia, Juan-Carlos Cano, Carlos T. Calafate, Pietro Manzoni
Departamento de Informática de Sistemas y Computadores. Universitat Politècnica de València. Spain.
emails: ehernandez@disca.upv.es, daferde1@fiv.upv.es, antodo@upv.es, jorherta@doctor.upv.es,
{jucano, calafate, pmanzoni}@disca.upv.es

Abstract—**Contact-based messaging applications establish a short-range communication directly between mobile devices, storing the messages in the devices in order to achieve a full dissemination of such messages. When a contact occurs, the mobile devices interchange their stored messages, following a epidemic diffusion. No messages are sent or stored in servers. In order to evaluate the diffusion of messages among mobile devices based on opportunistic contacts, we developed GRChat, an Android application that uses Bluetooth as near-by communication protocol. We present some results about the efficiency of peer-to-peer message diffusion depending on message size and devices distance.**

Keywords–Opportunistic networks; Contact-based Messaging; Performance Evaluation; Epidemic diffusion

I. Introduction

Routing protocols for opportunistic communication environments enable the storing, carrying, and forwarding of information between mobile devices [1]. Based on this technology, Mobile Social Networking in Proximity (MSNP) [2], is defined as a wireless peer-to-peer network of opportunistically connected nodes that use proximity as the social relationship. This condition allows the establishment of local communication channels that can be used for applications, such as information sharing, advertisement, disaster and rescue operations, gaming, etc. For example, FireChat (developed by Open Garden) is a successful contact-based messaging application.

Contact-based messaging applications work as follows (see figure 1): Each mobile device is a node with an application that notifies and present to the user any received messages for the subscribed groups. The application is also cooperative: it must store all messages and performs the diffusion of such messages to other nearby nodes. Each node has a limited buffer where it can store the messages obtained from other nodes. When two nodes establish a pair-wise connection, they exchange all messages they have in their buffers, and check whether some of the newly received messages are suitable for notification to the user. Message spreading is based on epidemic diffusion, a concept similar to the spreading of infectious diseases, when an infected node (the one that has a message) contacts another node to infect it (transmit the message). Epidemic routing obtains the minimum delivery delay at the expense of increased local buffer usage and transmission count.

To evaluate the performance of contact-based messaging applications we have developed our own app: the *GRChat*. GRChat is an Android app that can establish connection between two or more phones and transmit data and images using bluetooth. With this app, we can evaluate several aspects that can affect the message diffusion performance, such as local buffer management, message interchange protocol, message time-to-live, power consumption, etc. Several sample screenshots of the GRChat app are shown in figure 2. It has two operating modes: normal and benchmarking. In normal mode, it works like a messaging app where the user can watch previous messages/images and write new ones. When the user pushes the send button, GRChat connects to any near-by devices in order to send this new message, as shown in figure 2a (and just in case, it also can receive new messages). When a device gets a new message it also tries to connect to other devices in order to complete the diffusion of the message. The results of sending and receiving several messages are shown in figure 2b. When no messages are sent, the application is periodically searching for near-by devices in order to automatically interchange messages. The benchmarking mode (see screenshot in figure 2c) is for evaluating the setup and transmission times. In this mode, one of the devices iteratively sends a number of messages or images with a predetermined size for measuring the delivery times of a bunch of messages.

The experience shows that contact-based messaging applications seem to be operative in open places with a moderate-high density of persons (greater than 0.05 people per m^2). Furthermore, analytical and simulation models show that information diffusion have a strong dependence on contact patterns, but also on message size [3] [4]. One of the key issues for performance evaluation is determining the contact setup time between two devices and the practical transmission bandwidth. These values will clearly depend on several factors such as the distance between mobile devices and network congestion. Thus, in this paper we focus our experiments in message interchange performance for obtaining contact and message delivery times depending on devices distance.

On the following section we detail the experiments and results for obtaining the delivery time, ending the paper with the conclusions section.

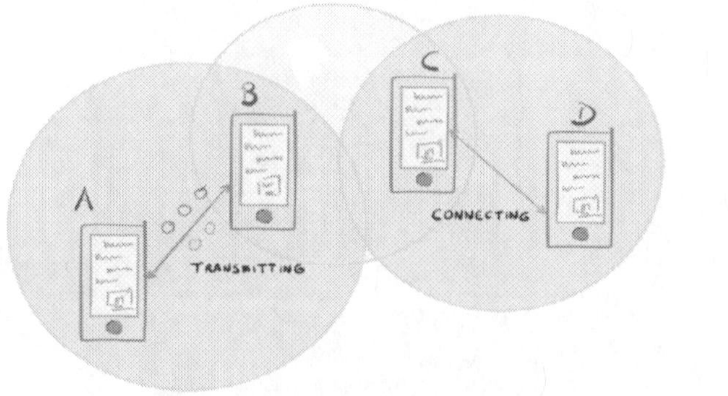

Figure 1. Opportunistic diffusion of messages.

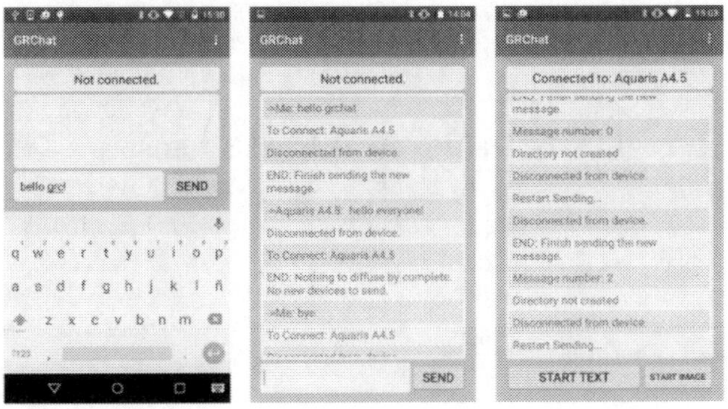

(a) (b) (c)

Figure 2. Several screenshots of the GRChat App.

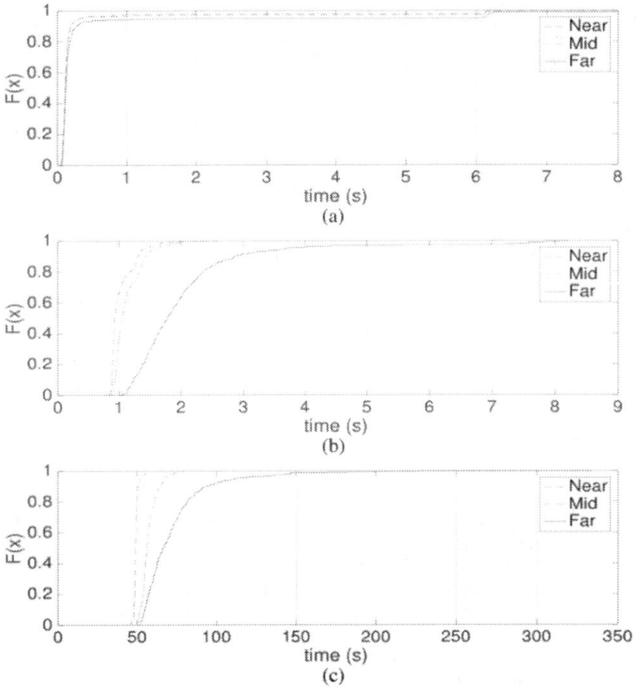

Figure 3. Cumulative distribution plots of the delivery times for different message sizes a) 375B; b) 109KB, c) 11MB

II. Experimental results

The goal of the following experiments was to obtain the message delivery time (i.e. the time needed to transmit a message) depending on message size, evaluating the impact on the performance of the relative distance between the devices. The mobile devices used on the experiments were two BQ Aquarius M4.5 smartphones using Android Version Lollipop API 22 with the following hardware characteristics: ARMv7 988Mhz processor, 938MB of RAM, GPU ARM Mali-T720 and Bluetooth 4.0.

The experiments consisted on sending 500 messages from one device to another one. Every message sending comprises three steps: the device connection or pairing, the message transmission and finally the end of the connection, so the message delivery times reported include both connection and transmission times. Three message sizes were considered: a short text message (375 Bytes), a low-resolution picture or photo (109 KB), and a short video or high resolution picture (11 MB). Regarding the separation of the devices, three different distances are considered: near (10 cm), mid (5m) and far (10m). The cumulative distribution function plot (cdf) of the packet delivery time for the different message sizes are shown in figure 3, and a resume of the main statistics is on table I. We can see that, shorter messages have a high variability due mainly to the connection time, which have less impact on larger messages. The results for near and mid distance are very similar. When the distance is far (larger than the practical bluetooth range, that is 7m), the mean delivery time increases especially for shorter messages, due to connection and retransmission problems, affecting seriously the performance of the diffusion protocol. From these delivery times, we can estimate the connection time and the practical bandwidth: when the devices are close, the mean connection time is about 0.35s and the bandwidth is 1.8Mbps; when the devices are distant the connection time is increased to 5.8s and the bandwidth is reduced to 1.5Mbps.

TABLE I. Message delivery times. All values in seconds.

	mean	min	max	Q1	Q3
375B					
Near (10cm)	0.30	0.04	12.42	0.09	0.14
Mid (5m)	0.26	0.06	9.35	0.10	0.14
Far (10m)	0.60	0.05	62.13	0.09	0.16
109KB					
Near (10cm)	1.03	0.85	2.56	0.90	1.07
Mid (5m)	1.13	0.76	2.33	0.97	1.13
Far (10m)	2.05	1.01	8.20	1.45	2.24
11MB					
Near (10cm)	49.37	45.43	56.75	48.66	49.71
Mid (5m)	57.35	49.62	80.17	54.10	59.60
Far (10m)	72.68	51.21	333.86	58.51	77.95

III. Conclusions

This paper briefly describes the GRChat app and the experiments performed for obtaining the connection and message delivery times. In conclusion, as expected, these times are seriously affected when devices are distant. The obtained values are planned to be used in simulations and models as the one detailed in [3]. Also, as a future work, we plan to perform more experiments regarding buffer and message transmission strategies.

Acknowledgments

This work was supported by *Generalitat Valenciana*, Spain (Grant AICO/2015/113).

References

[1] L. Pelusi, A. Passarella, and M. Conti, "Opportunistic networking: data forwarding in disconnected mobile ad hoc networks," Communications Magazine, IEEE, vol. 44, no. 11, November 2006, pp. 134–141.

[2] Y. Wang, A. Vasilakos, Q. Jin, and J. Ma, "Survey on mobile social networking in proximity (MSNP): approaches, challenges and architecture," Wireless Networks, vol. 20, no. 6, 2014, pp. 1295–1311.

[3] E. Hernandez-Orallo, J. Herrera-Tapia, J.-C. Cano, C. Calafate, and P. Manzoni, "Evaluating the impact of data transfer time in contact-based messaging applications," Communications Letters, IEEE, vol. 19, no. 10, Oct 2015, pp. 1814–1817.

[4] C. S. De Abreu and R. M. Salles, "Modeling message diffusion in epidemical DTN," Ad Hoc Networks, vol. 16, May 2014, pp. 197–209.

Density-Aware Multihop Clustering for Irregularly Deployed Wireless Sensor Networks

Sangil Choi and Sangman Moh
Dept. of Computer Engineering
Chosun University
Gwangju, South Korea
E-mail: wo566@naver.com, smmoh@chosun.ac.kr

***Abstract*—In wireless sensor networks (WSNs), reducing energy consumption in battery-operated sensor nodes is very important for prolonging network lifetime. In this paper, a density-aware multihop clustering (DAMC) protocol is proposed for irregularly deployed WSNs to reduce energy consumption. Every node determines the probability that it becomes a cluster head (CH) based on the node density around itself and, thus, CHs are distributed evenly over the network and every cluster has almost the same coverage area. And excessively redundant nodes are turned into sleep mode to save energy. Then, a multi-level tree in each cluster is constructed for low-energy multihop transmissions. In DAMC, the network lifetime can be significantly prolonged because the unnecessary redundant sensing and transmissions are reduced remarkably and the multihop transmissions are used rather than single-hop transmissions in clusters. The performance study shows that the proposed DAMC outperforms the conventional clustering protocols in terms of network lifetime.**

Keywords-Wireless sensor network; irregular deployment; multihop clustering; energy consumption; network lifetime.

I. Introduction

Wireless sensor networks (WSNs) are widely used for various applications such as environment monitoring, logistics, target tracking, military fields, home networks, and industrial diagnosis [1]. A WSN consists of many battery-powered sensor nodes that sense their surroundings and send the sensed data to a sink node or base station. In many WSNs, the batteries are difficult to replace and, even if replaceable, the replacement cost is very high [2]. Thus, reducing energy consumption in sensor nodes is very important for prolonging network lifetime.

In WSNs, routing is the process of forwarding data gathered by sensor nodes to the sink or base station. A WSN consists of a lot of sensor nodes, and it is inefficient for all the sensor nodes to send their sensed data to the single sink node or base station directly. Instead, the sensor nodes are grouped as clusters, and every sensor node sends its sensed data to its cluster head (CH). Then, the CHs send the aggregated data to the sink. Such a hierarchical routing is energy-efficient compared to the flat routing that each sensor delivers data sensed by itself to the sink directly.

The typical hierarchical routing or clustering protocols are low energy adaptive clustering hierarchy (LEACH) [3], low-energy adaptive cluster hierarchy centralized (LEACH-C) [4], hybrid, energy-efficient distributed (HEED) [5], base station controlled dynamic clustering protocol (BCDCP) [6], threshold sensitive energy-efficient sensor network protocol (TEEN) [7], hybrid protocol for efficient routing and comprehensive information retrieval in wireless sensor networks (APTEEN) [8], tree-based clustering (TBC) [9], and balanced clustering algorithm (BCA) [10]. The well known LEACH is the pioneer clustering protocol in WSNs, and TBC is the most advanced clustering scheme for uniformly deployed WSNs. The recently developed BCA is a single-hop clustering scheme targeted for irregularly deployed WSNs. The existing clustering algorithms will be reviewed in more detail in Section II.

In many applications such as environment monitoring, sensor nodes can be irregularly deployed due to some limited condition. For example, when the sensors nodes are deployed over a mountain area by a helicopter, there is the possibility that they may be irregularly deployed. Such an irregularly deployed WSN, the sensing area or coverage area of each cluster varies region by region, i.e., there are many small-area clusters in dense regions and a few large-area clusters in sparse regions. In BCA [10], equal-size clustering is achieved even in irregularly deployed WSNs and the excessively redundant nodes are turned into sleep mode to save energy and to prolong network lifetime. In BCA, however, the single-hop transmission from sensor nodes to their CH needs more energy consumption compared to multihop transmission in a cluster because transmission power is exponentially increased with distance. On the other hand, TBC [9] implements a multi-level tree within a cluster enabling multihop transmission, but it does not take the irregular deployment into consideration resulting in severely conflicted transmissions and unnecessary energy consumption in dense regions.

In this paper, a density-aware multihop clustering (DAMC) protocol is proposed for irregularly deployed sensor networks to reduce energy consumption and prolong network lifetime. The node density in this paper is defined as the number of nodes within the node's sensing range divided by the node's sensing area. During the initial network configuration, every node calculates the node density and determines the probability that it becomes a CH based on the node density so that CHs are distributed evenly over the network area and every cluster has almost the same coverage area. Excessively redundant nodes are turned into sleep mode to save energy. Then, a multi-level tree in each cluster is constructed for low-energy multihop transmissions. In the proposed DAMC, the network lifetime can be significantly prolonged because the unnecessary redundant sensing and transmissions are reduced remarkably and the multihop transmissions are used rather than single-hop transmissions in clusters.

According to the simulation results, the proposed DAMC outperforms the conventional clustering protocols by up to 70 percent in terms of network lifetime in the given simulation setting. The network lifetime in our performance study is defined as the time duration until half of the sensor nodes die due to the energy depletion of battery.

The rest of this paper is organized as follows: In the following section, the existing clustering protocols are reviewed in detail. In Section III, the operating principles and characteristics of the proposed DAMC protocol are discussed step by step. In Section IV, the performance of DAMC is evaluated via extensive computer simulation and compared to the conventional schemes. Finally, the paper is concluded in Section V.

II. RELATED WORKS

For more than a decade, many clustering algorithms based on randomness have been studied. Since the pioneer clustering protocol LEACH was introduced [3], more advanced clustering algorithms have been proposed so far [4]-[10]. In this section, they are reviewed with respect to major characteristics and improvements.

A. LEACH

In the LEACH protocol [3], each round consists of set-up phase and steady-state phase. Clusters are formed during the set-up phase, and the sensed data are periodically delivered to the sink through CHs during the steady-state phase.

In LEACH, CHs are elected probabilistically every round. Every sensor node generates a random number between zero and one and, then, it becomes a CH if the generated number is less than the calculated threshold value. For a node n, the threshold value $T(n)$ at the r-th round is calculated by

$$T(n) = \begin{cases} \dfrac{p}{1 - p(r \bmod \frac{1}{p})}, & \text{if } n \in G \\ 0, & \text{otherwise} \end{cases} \tag{1}$$

where the given parameter p is the probability that a sensor node becomes a CH and G is the set of sensor nodes that have not been chosen as a CH for $1/p$ rounds. If a node n has not been chosen as a CH for the last $1/p$ rounds, $T(n)$ is calculated by (1) and, if the generated random number is less than $T(n)$, the node becomes a CH at the current round; otherwise, $T(n)$ is zero and the node n is not elected as a CH at the current round.

Once CHs are chosen according to the above procedure, every CH broadcasts that it has becomes a CH. Then, sensor nodes send a join message to the nearest CH based on the received signal strength of the broadcast messages.

In the steady-state phase after cluster formation, sensor nodes send the sensed data to their CHs periodically in accordance with the TDMA (Time Division Multiple Access) schedule assigned by their CHs. CHs aggregate the received data and send the aggregated data to the sink node.

Such a series of procedural steps are repeated every round. That is, the CHs are rotated per round because they consume more energy than normal sensor nodes. This makes all the nodes consume energy as evenly as possible, resulting in increased network lifetime. However, when sensor nodes are irregularly deployed over the network area, the balanced energy consumption is not possible due to unbalanced clustering.

B. TBC

In the TBC protocol, a multi-level tree is constructed in a cluster, in which the CH is the root node [9]. The CH is elected in the same manner as in the LEACH protocol. The broadcast and join messages are also similar to those in LEACH, which are sent by CHs and normal sensor nodes, respectively. Unlike LEACH, however, the location information of the sensor node is included in the join message.

By receiving the join messages from sensor nodes, the CH finds the farthest sensor node, and the distance between the CH and the farthest sensor node is denoted as d_{max}. The maximum distance d_{max} is divided by the tree depth α, where α is also called tree height or the maximum level of the tree. Therefore, the average transmission distance d_{avg} between the node and its parent node in the tree can be represented by

$$d_{avg} = \frac{d_{\max}}{\alpha}. \tag{2}$$

The CH is at level 0 in the tree and member nodes are at the specific level according to the distance from the CH. Figure 1 shows an example of constructing a tree in TBC when α is 3. Once the cluster is divided into α concentric circles as shown in Figure 1, each sensor node selects an upper-level node with the minimum distance from the node itself as its parent node. Finally, a single tree is generated.

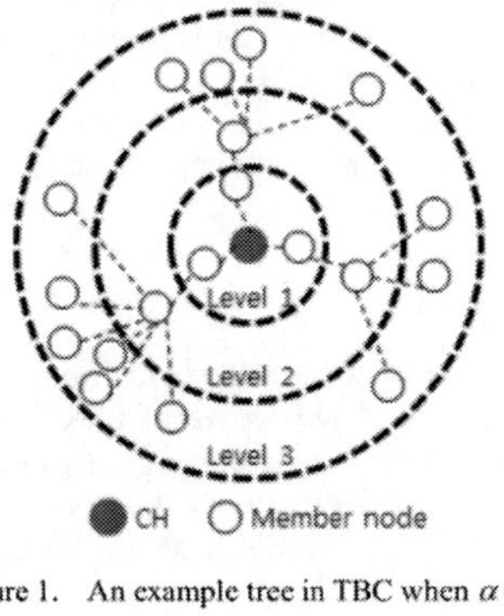

Figure 1. An example tree in TBC when $\alpha = 3$.

In a cluster, the multihop transmission through the multi-level tree from sensor nodes to the CH reduces energy consumption in comparison to single-hop transmission because transmission power is exponentially increased with distance. Also, the energy consumption is distributed over the network. As in LEACH, however, the unbalanced clustering causes unbalanced energy consumption over the network if sensor nodes are irregularly deployed. In addition, if there is an error or failure at the parent node, the messages from its children nodes cannot be delivered.

C. BCA

In the BCA protocol [10], every cluster area is almost the same even when sensor nodes are deployed irregularly over the network area. The balanced clustering is achieved by electing the CH on the basis of relative node density. For a node *n*, the relative node density *D(n)* is given by dividing node density by network density, where the node density is the ratio of the number of nodes within the node's sensing range over the node's sensing area and the network density is the ratio of the total number of nodes in the network over the network area. Therefore, *D(n)* can be represented by

$$D(n) = \frac{F/(\pi R^2)}{N/A} = \frac{F/N}{\pi R^2/A}, \quad (3)$$

where F is the number of nodes within the node's sensing range, N is the total number of nodes in the network, R is the sensing range, and A is the network area.

The CH is selected according to a new threshold taking the *D(n)* into consideration. That is, for a node *n*, the new threshold value $\tilde{T}(n)$ at the r-th round is calculated by

$$\tilde{T}(n) = T(n) + \frac{mT(n)}{N}\left(\frac{1}{D(n)} - 1\right), \quad (4)$$

where *T(n)* is the same threshold value calculated in (1), N is the total number of nodes in the network, and m is the number of living nodes in the network.

In the region where the node density is high, $\tilde{T}(n)$ is decreased compared to *T(n)* and, thus, a less number of CHs are selected every round. This results in balanced clustering even when sensor nodes are irregularly deployed. After cluster formation, if the number of nodes in a cluster exceeds the average number of nodes per cluster in the network, the randomly chosen excessive nodes in the cluster are remained sleep every round. That is, the nodes not included in clusters in dense regions are remained sleep every round. However, when sensor nodes are regularly deployed in the network area, BCA incurs extra overhead for calculating the node density unnecessarily.

D. Other Clustering Protocols

LEACH-C [4] is a centralized version of LEACH. That is, the base station elects cluster heads and forms clusters. All nodes in the network send a message including position and residual energy information to the base station. Based on the information, the base station selects cluster heads and divides all nodes to the clusters. Then, the base station broadcasts the information of clusters to all the nodes which are deployed in the network area.

HEED [5] uses some values which take into account the nodes residual energy for cluster formation. A node with more residual energy can be elected as a cluster head for prolonging network lifetime. If candidates for the cluster head have the same residual energy, then their transmission costs are compared.

In BCDCP [6], the complex calculations are assigned to the base station as in LEACHC. In cluster formation, base station elects a candidate set of cluster heads to determine cluster heads. In this scheme, cluster heads send aggregated messages to the base station on a multi-hop basis without direct transmission.

In TEEN [7], sensor nodes manage the threshold data reactively. The process which excludes the threshold value is equal to LEACH. The cluster formation process in TEEN is the same as that in LEACH. After cluster formation, cluster heads transmit the parameters of the data, the hard threshold (HT) value, and the soft threshold (ST) value to their member nodes. All nodes collect and transmit data when the value exceeds the HT value first. After exceeding HT, nodes collect and transmit data only when the measured data exceeds ST.

APTEEN [8] combines the advantages of LEACH and TEEN. As a hybrid protocol, APTEEN unites the data transmission according to the threshold value of TEEN and the periodic data transmission of LEACH. After cluster formation, the cluster heads transmit the threshold value and parameters that include the TDMA schedule time to the member nodes.

More recently, some works on clustering have been reported in the literature [11-13] even though they do not achieve a major quantum jump. They mainly focus on the improvement of energy efficiency because the energy efficiency is one of the most important design criteria for prolonging network lifetime in battery-operated wireless sensor networks. In addition, they do not take the irregular deployment of sensor nodes into consideration yet.

III. DENSITY-AWARE MULTIHOP CLUSTERING

In this section, the operating principles and characteristics of the proposed DAMC protocol are discussed in detail. CH selection, sleep node selection, tree construction, and sensing and data transmission are presented step by step. As in TBC [9], it is assumed that each node has the location information of itself and it can adjust its transmission power depending on the distance to its receiver.

A. Cluster Head Selection

For density-aware clustering in an irregularly deployed WSN, DAMC considers the node density for cluster formation as in BCA [10]. As mentioned in Section I, the node density in this paper is defined as the number of nodes within the node's sensing range divided by the node's sensing area. During the initial network configuration just after network deployment, every sensor node calculates the node density and determines the probability that it becomes a

CH based on the node density. As a result, CHs are distributed evenly over the network area. This means that every cluster has almost the same coverage area.

The number of CHs is decided in accordance with the probability that a sensor node becomes a CH. Usually, the probability is initially set up when sensor nodes are deployed. Just after CHs are probabilistically chosen, every CH broadcasts that it has become a CH. Each sensor node can receive multiple broadcast messages from multiple CHs and calculate their received signal strength. Then, each sensor node sends a join message to the nearest CH based on the received signal strength of the broadcast messages. By doing so, cluster membership is determined and every sensor node belongs to a cluster. However, the number of nodes in a cluster varies cluster by cluster because the node density differs region by region in the irregularly deployed WSN.

B. Sleep Node Selection

Immediately after CHs are selected, some nodes in densely populated clusters should be turned into sleep mode to reduce unnecessary energy consumption and severely conflicted transmissions in densely deployed regions. That is, if the number of nodes in a cluster exceeds the average number of nodes per cluster in the network, the randomly chosen excessive nodes in the cluster remain in sleep mode. The sleep nodes are randomly chosen every round.

As a matter of fact, the number of sleep nodes in a cluster is recalculated depending on the number of living nodes as the number of dead nodes is increased over time. That is, the number of sleep node in a cluster, $\widetilde{S}(u,m)$, is calculated by

$$S(u,m) = u - \frac{m}{c} \qquad (5)$$

and

$$\widetilde{S}(u,m) = \begin{cases} \left\lceil \dfrac{S(u,m)\times m}{N} \right\rceil, & \text{if } S(u,m) > L \\ 0, & \text{otherwise} \end{cases} \qquad (6)$$

where u is the number of nodes in a cluster, m is the number of living nodes in the network, c is the expected number of clusters, N is the total number of nodes in the network, and L is the minimum number of living nodes in a cluster for network operation.

After the CH selects the sleep nodes randomly, it broadcasts the identifiers of sleep nodes to all member nodes. Then, the sleep nodes go into sleep mode during the round.

C. Tree Construction

For multihop clustering of the selected member nodes without sleep nodes in a cluster, a multi-level tree is constructed in a cluster as in [9], in which the CH is the root node. When each sensor node sends a join message to the nearest CH during CH selection, the location information of the sensor node is also included in the join message. Once the cluster is divided into α concentric circles by the CH, where α is tree height, the CH informs its active members of the necessary information for parent node selection. Then, each sensor node selects an upper-level node with the minimum distance from the node itself as its parent node. After tree construction, the CH broadcasts the TDMA schedule to all the active member nodes. Figure 2 shows an example tree composed of 16 active nodes in a 20-node cluster when tree height (α) is set to 3.

The multi-level tree can reduce energy consumption significantly because a series of multihop short-distance transmissions consume much less energy than a single-hop long-distance transmission. Note here that the transmitted signal is usually attenuated in inversely proportional to the fourth power of the distance. Figure 3 shows examples of cluster formation in an irregularly deployed WSN, in which four clustering schemes of LEACH, TBC, BCA and the proposed DAMC are compared schematically. In the figure, the nodes labeled S are sleep nodes in the densely populated clusters. The sleep nodes are randomly chosen every round.

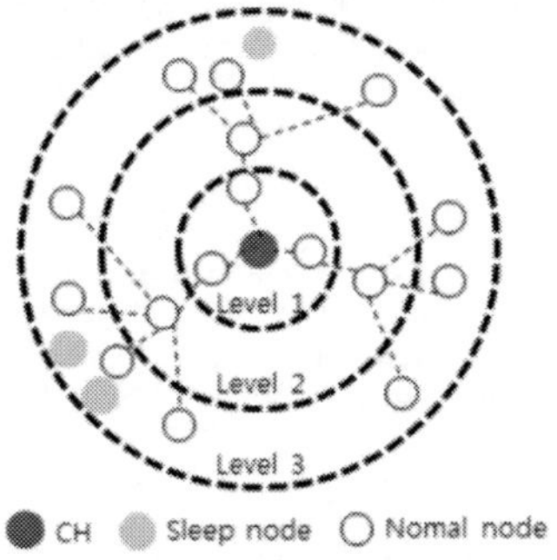

Figure 2. An example tree of 16 active nodes ($\alpha = 3$).

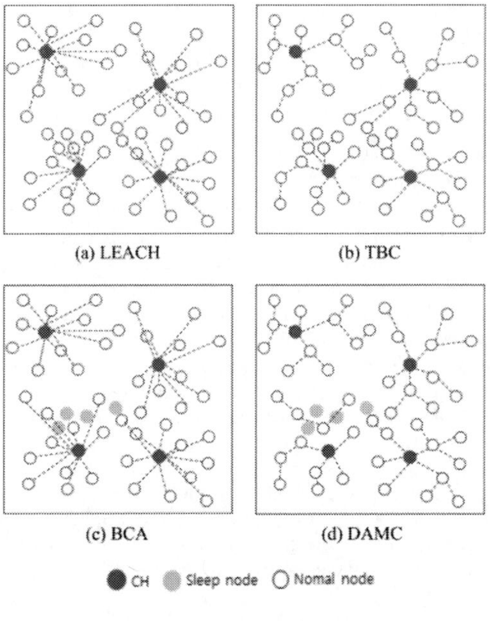

Figure 3. Examples of cluster formation in an irregularly deployed WSN.

D. *Data Gathering and Transmission*

After the cluster formation including tree construction, sensor nodes send the sensed data to their CHs periodically in accordance with the TDMA schedule. Each CH aggregates the received data and sends the aggregated data to the sink node by using the CSMA (Carrier Sense Multiple Access) protocol. Once a multihop cluster is formed, the data gathering and transmission are repeated in rounds as shown in Figure 4. In the figure, the back-slashed boxes and the subsequent gray boxes indicate the communications from cluster members to their CHs and the communications from CHs to the sink node, respectively. It should be also noted that the node density detection is carried out only once at the beginning, but the cluster formation is done in every round.

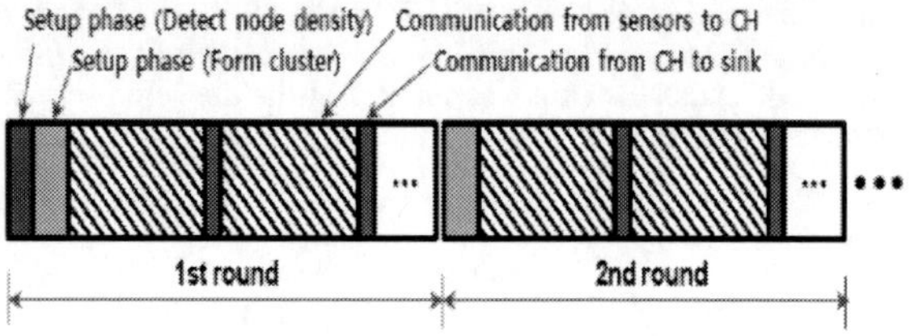

Figure 4. Rounds of the proposed DAMC.

In summary, the energy consumption in DAMC can be significantly reduced, resulting in prolonged network lifetime, because the unnecessary redundant sensing and transmissions are reduced remarkably and the low-energy multihop transmissions are used instead of single-hop transmissions from sensor nodes to CH in a cluster.

IV. PERFORMANCE EVALUATION

In this section, the performance of DAMC is evaluated via computer simulation using Matlab and compared to the conventional clustering schemes of LEACH [3], TBC [9] and BCA [10]. As described earlier, the popular LEACH is a pioneer protocol in clustering for WSNs, TBC is the most advanced clustering scheme for uniformly deployed WSNs, and the recently developed BCA is a single-hop clustering scheme targeted for irregularly deployed WSNs.

A. *Simulation Environment*

In our simulation, 200 sensor nodes are deployed over the network area of 100 × 100 m^2. The sink node (or base station) is fixed at the location (125, 75), and the initial energy of each senor node is set to 2 J. In our simulation, two irregular deployments are experimented: (i) 100 nodes are deployed in the region of 50 × 50 m^2 and the other 100 nodes are deployed in the other regions and (ii) 100 nodes are deployed in the region of 25 × 25 m^2 and the other 100 nodes are deployed in the other regions. Figure 5 shows the two irregular deployments of 200 nodes for simulation.

In our experiment, the energy consumption model [14] is as follows: The free space (*fs*) model is used if the distance is less than a threshold d_0; otherwise, the multipath (*mp*) model is used. Hence, when transmitting k bits of a message along with distance d, the energy consumption can be calculated by

$$E_{Tx}(k,d) = E_{Tx-elec}(k) + E_{Tx-amp}(k,d) = \begin{cases} kE_{elec} + k\varepsilon_{fs}d^2, & \text{if } d < d_0 \\ kE_{elec} + k\varepsilon_{mp}d^4, & \text{otherwise} \end{cases} \tag{7}$$

where d_0 is set to 87 m as in [9]. The energy consumption for receiving k bits of data is calculated by

$$E_{Rx}(k,d) = E_{Rx-elec}(k) = kE_{elec}. \tag{8}$$

In (7) and (8), E_{elec} is the radio electronics energy depending on digital coding, modulation, filtering and spreading of the signal. ε_{fs} and ε_{mp} are constant values for the amplifier energy depending on the distance to the receiver and acceptable bit-error rate.

The parameters used in our simulation are summarized in Table 1. In the table, E_{sense} is the energy consumption required for sensing and E_{da} is the energy consumption for data aggregation. The simulations were performed 100 times for each experiment and the mean value of results was used as the simulation results.

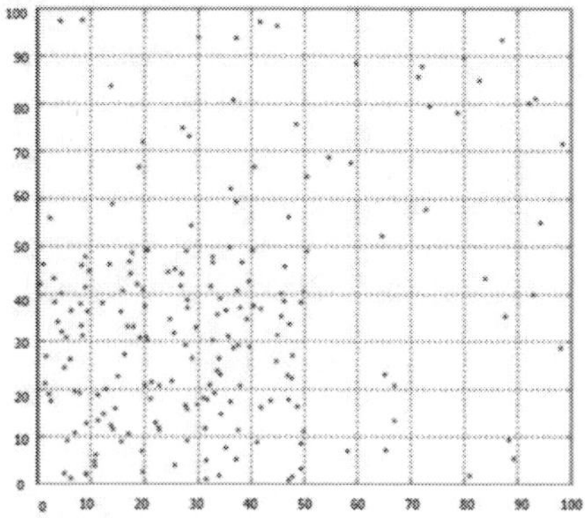

(a) 100 nodes are deployed in the region of 50 × 50 m2.

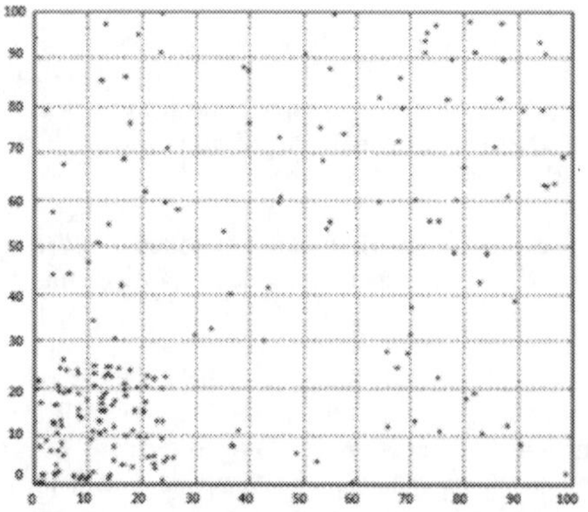

(b) 100 nodes are deployed in the region of 25 × 25 m^2.

Figure 5. Two irregular deployments of 200 nodes for simulation..

TABLE I. SIMULATION PARAMETER.

Parameter	Value
Network area	100 × 100 m2
Location of sink	(125, 75)
Number of nodes	200
Number of clusters	10
Initial energy	2 J
Esense	5 nJ/bit
Eda	5 nJ/bit
Eelec	50 nJ/bit
Efs	10 pJ/bit/m2
Emp	0.00013 pJ/bit/m4
Sensing range	10 m
Maximum transmission range	136 m

B. Simulation Results and Discussion

In our performance study, the network lifetime is extensively evaluated it is the most important metric in WSNs. The network lifetime in our performance study is defined as the time duration until half of the sensor nodes die due to the energy depletion of battery. So, the number of living nodes is observed with respect to round progress.

Figures 6 and 7 show the number of living nodes per round for the two scenarios of irregular deployment described in Section IV-A. From the two figures, it is clearly shown that the proposed DAMC outperforms the three conventional schemes of LEACH, TBC and BCA. In the first deployment that 100 nodes are deployed in the region of 50 × 50 m^2 and the other 100 nodes are deployed in the other regions, the network lifetime is 26 to 57 percent longer than the others. In the second deployment that 100 nodes are deployed in the region of 25 × 25 m^2 and the other 100 nodes are deployed in the other regions, the network lifetime is 26 to 70 percent longer than the others. That is, it can be easily inferred that the improvement is better and better as the irregularity increases.

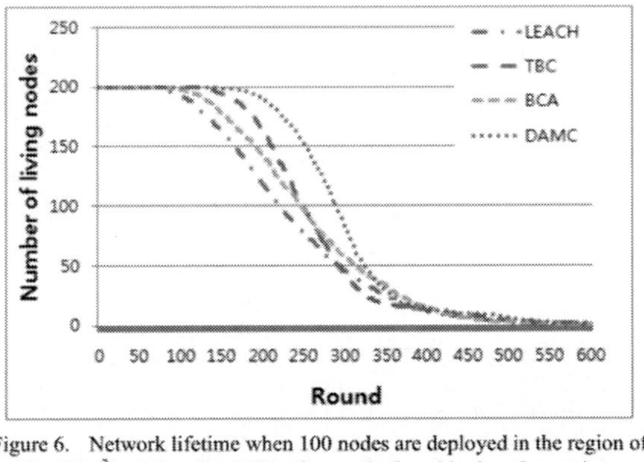

Figure 6. Network lifetime when 100 nodes are deployed in the region of 50 × 50 m^2 and the other 100 nodes are deployed in the other regions.

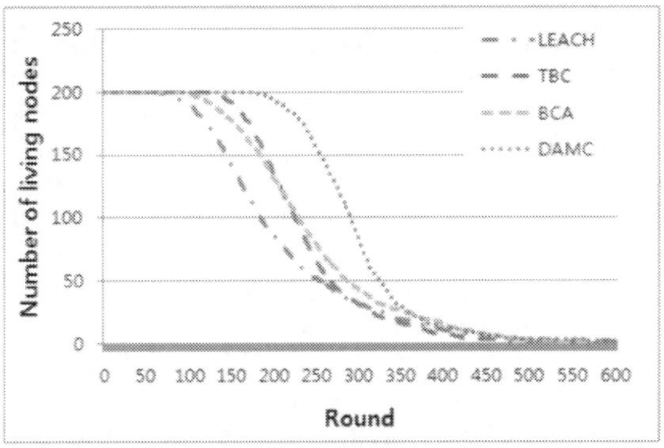

Figure 7. Network lifetime when 100 nodes are deployed in the region of 25 × 25 m^2 and the other 100 nodes are deployed in the other regions.

Among the four clustering schemes, LEACH shows the worst performance in our simulation. The comparative performance of TBC and BCA depends on the irregularity. When the irregularity is relatively low, the performance difference of them is not significant. With high irregularity, however, BCA obviously outperforms TBC as shown in the two graphs. The proposed DAMC always outperforms the other three protocols.

In the proposed DAMC, the network lifetime is remarkably prolonged. CHs are distributed evenly over the network area and every cluster has almost the same coverage area. Excessively redundant nodes are turned into sleep mode to save energy. That is, the unnecessary redundant sensing and transmissions are significantly reduced. In addition, a multi-level tree in each cluster reduces energy further thanks to low-energy multihop transmissions.

V. CONCLUSIONS

In this paper, an energy-efficient clustering protocol called DAMC for irregularly deployed WSNs has been proposed, in which the local node density and the multi-level tree structure are exploited in every cluster. During cluster formation, excessively redundant nodes are turned into sleep mode to avoid unnecessary redundant sensing and transmissions. And the multi-level tree in each cluster enables low-energy multihop transmissions rather than long single-hop transmissions. Such effects result in significantly low energy consumption and prolonged network lifetime in DAMC. The performance study has shown that the proposed DAMC outperforms the conventional clustering protocols in terms of network lifetime. As possible future works, we are going to devise a more efficient tree in a cluster and evaluate various scenarios of irregular deployment with specific probability distributions.

ACKNOWLEDGMENT

This research was supported in part by Basic Science Research Program through the National Research Foundation of Korea (NRF) funded by the Ministry of Education (NRF-2013R1A1A2011744). Correspondence should be addressed to Dr. Sangman Moh (smmoh@chosun.ac.kr).

References

[1] L. Dan, K. D. Wong, H. H. Yu, and A. M. Sayeed, "Detection, Classification, and Tracking of Targets," IEEE Signal Processing Magazine, Vol. 19, No. 2, Mar. 2002, pp. 17-29.

[2] Asaduzzaman and H. Y. Kong, "Energy Efficient Cooperative LEACH Protocol for Wireless Sensor Networks," Jounal of Communications and Networks, Vol. 12, No. 4, 2010, pp. 358-365.

[3] W. R. Heinzelman, A. Chandrakasan, and H. Balakrishnan, "Energy-efficient Communication Protocols for Wireless Microsensor Networks," Proc. of the Hawaii International Conference on Systems Sciences, Vol. 2, 2010, pp. 10-19.

[4] W. B. Heinzelman, A. P. Chandrakasan, and H. Balakrishnan, "An Application-Specific Protocol Architecture for Wireless Microsensor Networks," IEEE Transactions on Wireless Communications, Vol. 1, No. 4, 2002, pp. 660-670.

[5] O. Younis and S. Fahmy, "HEED: A Hybrid, Energy-Efficient, Distributed Clustering Approach for Ad Hoc Sensor Networks," IEEE Transactions on Mobile Computing, Vol. 3. No. 4, 2004, pp. 366-379.

[6] S. D. Muruganathan, D. C. F. Ma, R. I. Bhasin, and A. O. Fapojuwo, "A Centralized Energy-Efficient Routing Protocol for Wireless Sensor Networks," IEEE Radio communications, Vol. 43, No. 3, 2005, pp. S8-S13.

[7] A. Manjeshwar and D. Agrawal, "TEEN: A Routing Protocol for Enhanced Efficiency in Wireless Sensor Networks," Proc. of 15th Int. Parallel and Distributed Processing Symposium, 2001, pp. 2009-2015.

[8] A. Manjeshwar and D. P. Agrawal, "APTEEN: A Hybrid Protocol for Efficient Routing and Comprehensive Information Retrieval in Wireless Sensor Networks," Proc. of Int. Parallel and Distributed Processing Symposium, 2002, pp. 195-202.

[9] K. T. Kim, C. H. Lyu, S. S. Moon, and H. Y. Yoon, "Tree-Based Clustering (TBC) for Energy Efficient Wireless Sensor Networks," Proc. of IEEE 24th Int. Conf. on Advanced Information Networking and Applications Workshop, 2010, pp. 680-685.

[10] H. Shin, S. Moh, I. Chung, and M. Kang, "Equal-Size Clustering for Irregularly Deployed Wireless Sensor Networks," Wireless Personal Communications, Vol. 82, No. 2, 2014, pp. 995-1012.

[11] J.-S. Lee and W.-L. Cheng, "Fuzzy-Logic-Based Clustering Approach for Wireless Sensor Networks Using Energy Predication," IEEE Sensors Journal, Vol. 12, No. 9, 2012, pp. 2891-2897.

[12] K. Li and K. A. Hua, "Mobility-Assisted Distributed Sensor Clustering for Energy-Efficient Wireless Sensor Networks," Proc. of 2013 IEEE Global Communications Conference (Globecom 2013), 2013, pp. 316-321.

[13] L. Xu, G. M. P. O'Hare, and R. Collier, "A Balanced Energy-Efficient Multihop Clustering Scheme for Wireless Sensor Networks," Proc. of 7th IFIP Wireless and Mobile Networking Conference (WMNC 2014), 2014, pp. 1-8.

[14] W. Bo, H. Y. Hu, and F. Wen, "An Improved LEACH Protocol for Data Gathering and Aggregation in Wireless Sensor Networks," Proc. of 2008 Int. Conf. on Computer and Electrical Engineering, 2008, pp. 398-401.

An Enhanced IEEE 802.11 RSSI Measurement Compensation Method Using Kalman Filter

Jingjing Wang, Jun Gyu Hwang, Giovanni Escudero, Joon-Goo Park
School of Electronics Engineering
Kyungpook National University
Daegu, Republic of Korea
email: wjj0219@naver.com, cjstk891015@naver.com, gioescudero@gmail.com, jgpark@knu.ac.kr

***Abstract*— With the development of indoor positioning technology, the demand for accurate positioning is getting higher. Moreover, location determination technologies especially for indoor environments are getting a lot of attention. For more accurate positioning, the more accurate distance information should be determined. Existing distance determination methods using Received Signal Strength Indicator (RSSI) measurements are mostly processed by simple averaging. That has some limitations to remove variable noise sources. In this paper, we adopt Kalman filter to get more accurate distance information from RSSI measurements. Our proposed method improves distance measurement accuracy about 68.3% and 41.8%, respectively.**

Keywords- RSSI; Kalman filter.

I. INTRODUCTION

In the era of mobile internet services, Location Based Service (LBS) is one of key-role playing mobile services. Therefore, the position information of human or objects are getting more attention. At present, people can have position information from GNSS(Global Navigation Satellite System), A-GPS(Assisted GPS), TC-OFDM technology. Ultrasonic technology, Radio Frequency Identification technology (RFID), geomagnetic positioning technology, etc. [1][2].

In outdoor environments, satellite navigation system such as GPS is the most reliable and accurate positioning system. However, almost 80 % of our ordinary daily life is executed in indoor environments. Therefore, we need an indoor positioning method showing stable and accurate performance just like outdoor GPS.

Now, there are various indoor positioning methods using infrared, ultrasonic, Bluetooth, RFID, UWB and WLAN, etc. We can find out the common development trends of indoor positioning methods in 4 aspects.

Aspect 1: Positioning accuracy improvement (nearing to that of GPS)

Aspect 2: Positioning efficiency improvement

Aspect 3:.Cost Reduction of indoor positioning signal coverage.

Aspect 4: Fusion with outdoor positioning technology (for seamless positioning)

Hence, we focus on indoor positioning method based on IEEE802.11 WLAN, which is the most widely spread wireless communication network.

In Section II, we propose an RSSI measurement compensation method using Kalman filters. Simulation results and concluding remarks are given in Sections III and IV, respectively.

II. PROPOSED METHOD

In this paper, We propose a IEEE802.11 RSSI measurement compensating method for more precise indoor positioning by adopting Kalman filter.

A. RSSI Attenuation Model

The Received Signal Strength Indicator (RSSI) defines a measurement of RF energy and its unit is dBm. The RSSI is decreased exponentially as the distance from an AP (Access Point) is increased. Because of these characteristics, in this paper we used an RSSI attenuation model and it is given as [3][4]

$$\mathrm{RSSI[dBm]} = -10n\log_{10}\frac{d}{d_0} + A \quad (1)$$

$$\mathrm{d[m]} = 10^{\frac{\mathrm{RSSI}-A}{-10n}} \quad (2)$$

In (1), n is the attenuation factor, parameter A is the offset which is the measured RSSI value at a reference point (usually 1m) apart from the AP, and d is the distance from AP. These parameters reflect the indoor propagation environments. RSSI is a sensitive measurement which can be significantly affected by the environment. Fig. 1 shows that RSSI measurements are attenuated by log scale as distances are increased.

In common situations, many factors can affect the RSSI value such as furniture, walls and pedestrians, etc. These factors can produce scattering signals and a multipath effect. Thus, it can result in positioning error. In order to reduce positioning error, proper parameter determination is necessary.

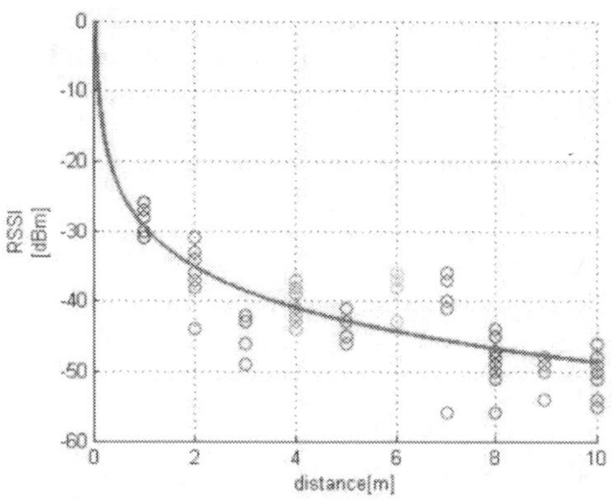

Figure 1. RSSI Attenuation according to the Elapsed Distance

B. Kalman Filter

Linear system state equation and measurement equation is as follows:

$$x(k+1) = F(k)x(k) + G(k)u(k) + v(k) \quad (3)$$

$$z(k+1) = H(k)x(k+1) + \omega(k+1) \quad (4)$$

x(k) represents a state vector at time k. F(k) and G(k) are state matrix and input matrix, respectively. $v(k)$ means process noise at time k. z(k) represents an output vector at time k. H(k) is measurement matrix. $\omega(k+1)$ means measurement noise at time k+1.

Kalman filtering procedures are made up of two processes such as prediction and state update [5]. Firstly, we predict state, measurement and covariance. After that, we calculate Kalman gain using predicted information at first step. Finally, we update state estimate and state covariance using Kalman gain.

$$\hat{x}(k+1|k) = F(k)\hat{x}(k|k) + G(k)u(k) \quad (5)$$

$$\hat{z}(k+1|k) = H(k)\hat{x}(k+1|k) \quad (6)$$

$$P(k+1|k) = F(k)P(k|k)F(k)' + Q(k) \quad (7)$$

$$Q(k) = E[v(k)v(k)'] \quad (8)$$

$$H(k+1)P(k+1|k)H(k+1)' \quad (9)$$

$$R(k) = E[w(k)w(k)'] \quad (10)$$

$$v(k+1) = z(k+1) - \hat{z}(k+1|k) \quad (11)$$

$$W(k+1) = P(k+1|k)H(k+1)'S(K+1)^{-1} \quad (12)$$

$$\hat{x}(k+1|k+1) = \hat{x}(k+1|k) + W(k+1)v(k+1) \quad (13)$$

$$P(k+1|k+1) = P(k+1|k) - W(k+1)S(k+1)W(k+1)' \quad (14)$$

$\hat{x}(k+1|k)$ represents state estimate at time k+1 given measurements until time k. $\hat{x}(k+1|k+1)$ represents state estimate at time k+1 given measurements until time k+1. $\hat{z}(k+1|k)$ represents measurement estimate at time k+1 given measurements until time k. P(k + 1|k) means error covariance matrix at time k given measurements until time k. Q(k) and R(k) are the covariance matrix of process noise and measurement noise, respectively. W(k) is the optimal Kalman gain.

We define state vector x(k) with RSSI(k) and d(k), where RSSI(k) is the RSSI measurement at time k and d(k) is distance at time k. We made F(k), G(k) from the RSSI attenuation model given by Eq. (1) and Eq. (2). H(k) is defined as in (19).

$$x(k) = \begin{bmatrix} RSSI(k) \\ d(k) \end{bmatrix} \quad (16)$$

$$F(k) = \begin{bmatrix} 1 & \frac{10nlog_{10}d(k)}{d(k)} \\ 0 & 1 \end{bmatrix} \quad (17)$$

$$G(k) = \begin{bmatrix} \frac{-10nlog_{10}(d(k)+u(k))}{u(k)} \\ 1 \end{bmatrix} \quad (18)$$

$$H(k) = [1 \quad 0] \quad (19)$$

III. SIMULATION RESULTS

We assume the Kyungpook National University IT-1 building's first floor as simulation environments. This building has attenuation factor *n* which is 2.7. The process noise $v(k)$ is modeled uniform distribution. It has zero mean and 0.01 variance. Measurement noise $\omega(k)$ is modeled as Gaussian. It has zero mean and 2.12 variance. In this paper, we consider two simulation situations: one is regular step situation and the other is random step. Fig 2 is sectional view of Kyungpook National University IT-1 building

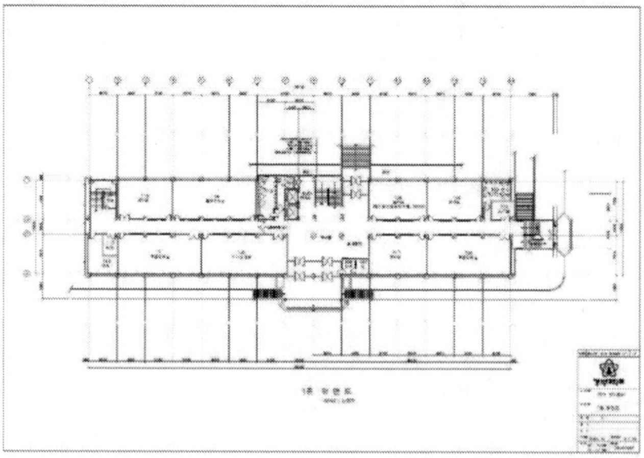

Figure 2. Kyungpook National University IT-1 Building (First Floor)

In this simulation, we symbolize Measurement as existing distance determination method, which decides RSSI measurement at a point by averaging multi epoch RSSI measurements at the point. Also, we symbolize Estimation as the proposed distance calculation method.

Existing method (Measurement) determines the distance of a point by averaged multi epoch RSSI measurements around the point. On the other hand, Proposed method (Estimation) determines the distance of a point by Kalman filtered each epoch RSSI measurement around the point.

A. *Regular Step Situation*

Regular step situation means a movement with 0.1m distance in every second from 1m to 10m. Fig. 3 shows the regular step situation which goes away from AP, regularly.

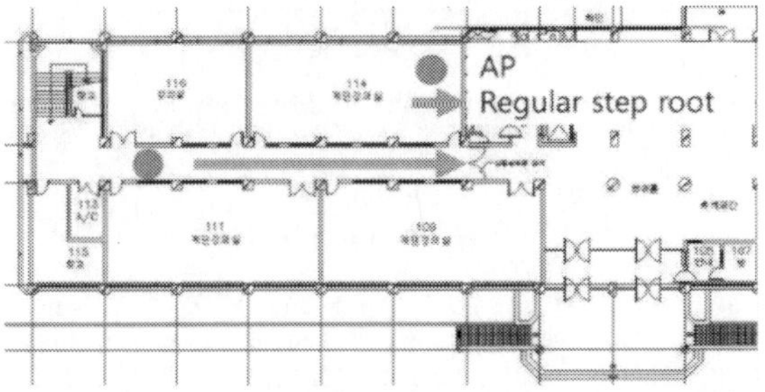

Figure 3. Regular Step Situation

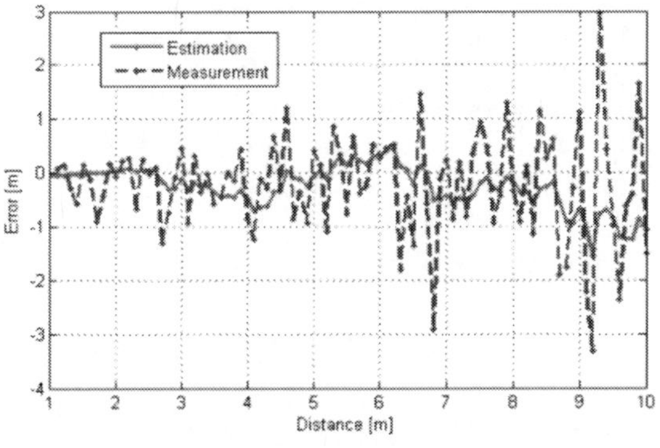

Figure 4. Distance Error of Measurem ent and Estimation (Regular step)

Fig. 4 shows distance errors of Measurement and Estimation. The green line (Estimation) is closer to the zero line more than the blue line. For random step situation, the distance errors and variances of Measurement and Estimation are given in Table I, respectively.

TABLE I. DISTANCE ERROR OF MEASUREM ENT AND ESTIMATION(REGULAR STEP)

	Error [m]	Variance
Measurement	0.82	0.69
Estimation	0.26	0.08

The distance error of the proposed method (Estimation) is less than that of existing one (Measurement) by 0.56m. It means that for regular step situation, the proposed method (Estimation) will produce 68.3% less distance error, compared with existing method (Measurement).

B. *Random Step Situation*

Random step situation means a movement with random distance in every second. This random distance is modelled as Gaussian with 0 mean and 1.2 variance. Fig. 5 shows the random step situation which describes wandering around AP within 10m.

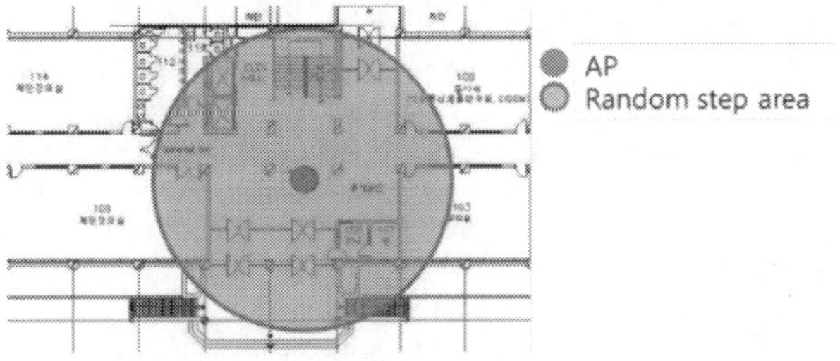

Figure 5. Random Step Situation

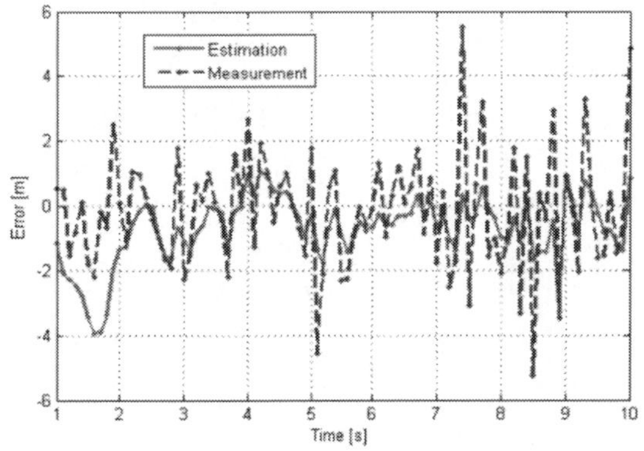

Figure 6. Distance Errors of Measurement and Estimation(

Fig. 6 shows distance errors of Measurement and Estimation. The blue line is distance error from Measurement. The green line is distance error from Estimation. The green line is closer to the zero line than the blue line. For random step situation, the distance errors and variances of Measurement and Estimation are given in Table II, respectively.

TABLE II. DISTANCE ERROR OF MEASUREM ENT AND ESTIMATION(RANDOM STEP)

	Error [m]	Variance
Measurement	1.84	3.56
Estimation	1.07	0.92

The distance error of the proposed method (Estimation) is less than that of existing one (Measurement) by 0.77m. It also means that for random step situation, the proposed method (Estimation) will produce 41.8% less distance error, compared with existing method (Measurement).

IV. CONCLUSIONS

In this paper, we proposed an RSSI measurement compensation method using Kalman filter to reduce the calculated distance errors, which results in a more accurate indoor positioning. By estimating the noises in RSSI measurements using Kalman filter, we can compensate the estimated noises from RSSI measurements and calculate more precise distance information, which results in a more precise positioning.

Simulation results for the two representative situations, regular step situation and random step one, show that the distance error of the proposed method (Estimation) can be improved over that of the existing method (Measurement) by 68.3% and 41.8%, respectively.

For future works, we are trying to classify indoor environments in more detail. Attenuation factor (n) and offset (A) of RSSI attenuation log model are dominantly dependent on applied environments. The RSSI attenuation log model, which is adapted to real indoor environment, will provide more accurate distance information.

ACKNOWLEDGMENTS

This work has been supported by the National GNSS Research Center program of Defense Acquisition Program Administration and Agency for Defense Development.

REFERENCES

[1] Liu, Hui, Houshang Darabi, Pat Banerjee, Jig Liu. "Survey of wireless indoor positioning techniques and systems." Systems, Man, and Cybernetics, Part C: Applications and Reviews, IEEE Transactions on 37.6 (2007): 1067-1080

[2] Bensky, Alan. Wireless positioning technologies and applications. Artech House, 2007

[3] Sinwoo Park, Dowoo Park, A sol Kim, Jinhyung Park, Seunghae Kim, and Joo Goo Park, "A Study on enhanced indoor localization method through IEEE 802.11 signal strength measurement" KSII The first International Conference on Internet (ICONI) 2009, December 2009

[4] Seokhun Shin and Joon goo Park. "Improved IEEE 802.11 RSSI attenuation log model by weighted fitting method" Journal of Institute of Control, Robotics and Systems(ICROS) on 21.1 2011, 70-75

[5] Bar-Shalom, Yaakov, X. Rong Li, and Thiagalingam Kirubarajan. Estimation with applications to tracking and navigation: theory algorithms and software. John Wiley & Sons, 2004.

Modeling and Analysis of Inter-Satellite Link based on BeiDou Satellites

Chaofan Duan, Jing Feng, XinLi Xiong
Institute of Meteorology and Oceanography
PLA University of Science and Technology
Nanjing, China
E-mail: jfeng@seu.edu.cn

Xiaoxing Yu
Department of Information and Networks
TELECOM Paris Tech (ENST)
Paris, France
E-mail: yu@telecom-paristech.fr

Abstract—**According to the development planning of BeiDou Navigation Satellite System (BDS), a triple-layered satellite network architecture serving as relay satellite is studied. On this basis, the spatial information system of satellite network architecture is analyzed; the satellite network dynamic topology model is established. The geometrical properties of inter-satellite links (ISLs) are studied deeply with comparing the encounter duration of satellites in different orbits. Having analyzed the simulation results by Satellite Tool Kit (STK), the connectivity features of the ISLs were acquired, and topology structure evolution laws of satellite network were also obtained. The simulation result shows that adopting IGSO satellites as relay satellites enables better stability of elevation angle, which is convenient to trace the antenna of satellite and establish high quality links. Moreover, full-time ISLs could be established by using MEO satellites serve as relay satellites and is able to ensure that at least 15 inter satellite links could be established.**

Keywords-satellite relay; dynamic topology model; encounter duration; inter-satellite link.

I. INTRODUCTION

Due to the Earth's curvature and the linear propagation characteristics of radio waves, for observation satellites at low Earth orbit, the transmission efficiency (ratio of real-time transmission time and satellite on orbit time) is being in an extremely low state. The expansion of base station can not fundamentally solve the problem [1].

Artificial Earth Satellite can be divided into several types considering its orbit altitude, as low Earth orbit (LEO) satellite, medium Earth satellite (MEO) and geostationary Earth orbit satellite (GEO). Relay satellites are generally GEO satellites, and the information between the user spacecraft and the Earth station is transmitted by it. Its favorable geometric position solves the above problems effectively, which makes it has many advantages such as good real-time performance and high coverage. This greatly improves the transmission efficiency of LEO observation satellites.

BeiDou Navigation Satellite System plans to build 5 satellites in GEO, 27 satellites in MEO and 3 in inclined geosynchronous satellite orbit (IGSO) [2]. The system will be able to provide a powerful autonomous navigation and positioning service when it is completely deployed. The abundant satellite resources of the BeiDou could be used in relay services, which will greatly shorten the delay of satellite data transmission.

The key technology of the BeiDou satellite as data relay service is the establishment of inter-satellite links. However, due to the complexity and dynamic characteristics of the satellite network topology, inter-satellite link (ISL) handoff problem becomes more serious [3]. No matter it is a multi-layer satellite network, or a single-layer satellite network, the relative motion between satellites on different orbital planes, leads to the change of ISL is more frequent, and thus brings serious challenges for the design of network protocols [4]. Therefore, ISL design is an essential part of satellite network research, since it affects the overall performance of the network. Z. Wang proposed the positional relationship and the necessary conditions using two satellites to establish a permanent ISL [4]. Liu proposed the theoretical formula of the ISL performance of non-geostationary Earth orbit (NGEO), and analyzed the variation law of ISL performance with the change of constellation parameters [5]. Gao made a thorough study on satellite network geometry model, and deduced the equation of link distance and elevation angle [6]. Based on the analysis of the geometric parameters between LEO and MEO satellite layer, L. Wang proposed an analytical formula of ISL spatial geometry parameters with time variation [7]. However, these studies did not take into account the effect of relay satellites in different orbit altitude. We proposed triple-layered satellite network architecture based on BeiDou Navigation Satellite System, and analyzed inter-satellite connectivity and elevation angle to investigate the possibility of BDS satellites serving as relay satellites in this paper.

The rest of the article is structured as follows: In section II, the network architecture of BeiDou Navigation Satellite System is studied and dynamic topology network model is proposed; in section III, a comparison is discussed among satellites of different orbits to serve as relay satellites; in section IV, the performance of BeiDou Navigation Satellite System is analyzed. Finally, the conclusion and future work are given in section V.

II. ANALYSIS AND MODELING OF SPACE INFORMATION SYSTEM STRUCTURE

The topology of Spatial Information System is the basis of information exchange and sharing, and it is also the primary problem to be faced by dynamic network topology. In this section, a triple-layered MEO/IGSO/GEO satellite network architecture serving as relay satellites based on BeiDou Navigation Satellite System is studied firstly, and the spatial information system of satellite network architecture is analyzed.

A. *Structure Analysis of Spatial Information System*

The space segment of BeiDou Navigation Satellite System is constituted of MEO group satellites, IGSO satellites and GEO satellites. The spatial information system can be regarded as triple-layered satellite network structure shown in Figure 1. It is composed of the MEO constellation, IGSO constellation, GEO constellation and ground stations. Ground stations communicate with each other via wired networks.

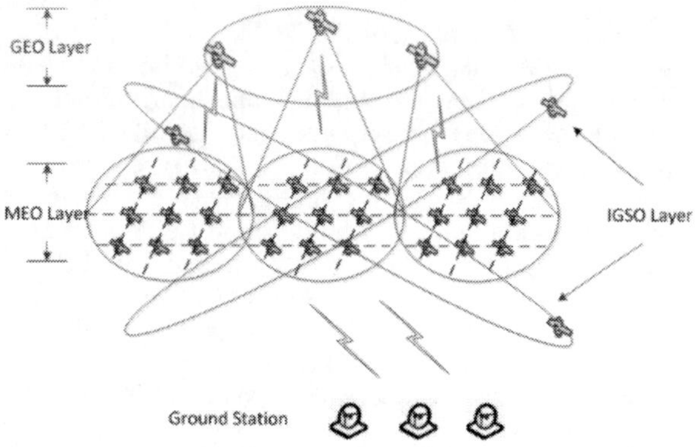

Figure 1. Satellite network structure with MEO / IGSO / GEO

According to the design of BeiDou satellite constellation, the whole spatial information systems can be divided into three satellite layers.

- GEO layer. Geosynchronous orbit lies directly over the equator and the satellite in the orbit is relatively stationary to the Earth. GEO satellite network has advantages over fewer switching, simple control of satellite tracking and global coverage. Suppose the total number of satellites in GEO layer is N_G, single GEO satellite is expressed as G_i, $i=1,2,\cdots N_G$.
- IGSO layer. IGSO was designed primarily to meet the needs of the information transmission for Polar areas. IGSO satellites have the same orbital altitude as GEO satellites; therefore they possess the same orbital period as the Earth's rotation period. IGSO constellation possesses a high efficiency use of the regional constellation, ranging between GEO and MEO. Suppose the total number of IGSO satellites is N_I, single IGSO satellite is expressed as I_i, $i=1,2,\cdots N_I$.
- MEO layer. The visibility time of single MEO satellite up to 1h ~ 2h. Although the two-hop transmission delay is longer than LEO satellite, concerning the entire length of the inter-satellite links, on-board processing ability and other factors, the delay performance of MEO constellation may be better than LEO constellation. Relative to LEO constellation, MEO constellation owns a lower switching probability, reduced Doppler Effect, simplified space control system and antenna tracking system. Suppose the total number of MEO satellites is N_M, single MEO satellite is expressed as M_i, $i=1,2,\cdots N_M$. Triple-layer satellite network maintains three types of full-duplex links.

Inter satellite link is the foundation of satellite communication, and ground station establishes a data link connection to the satellite when it is in the coverage of the satellite.

B. *Dynamic Topology Modeling of Spatial Information System*

The body of BeiDou Navigation Satellite System is 27 MEO satellites, which are distributed in 3 orbital planes according to the walker constellation. Assuming that the configuration code of a Walker constellation is N / P / F, which respectively corresponds to the number of satellites, orbital plane number and phase factor [8]. Configuration code of MEO constellation in BeiDou Navigation Satellite System is: 27/3/1, that is, there are three orbital planes, each of which has nine satellites, and the phase factor is 1. The right ascension and angular distance of the ascending node are described by (1), in the equation i represents the number of plane while j represents the number of satellite in one orbit plane.

$$\begin{cases} \Omega_{ij} = \dfrac{360}{P}(i-1) & (i=1,2,\cdots,P) \\ u_{ij} = \dfrac{360P}{N}(j-1) + \dfrac{360}{N}F(i-1) & (j=1,2,\cdots\dfrac{N}{P}) \end{cases} \tag{1}$$

According to trajectory equations of circular orbit satellite in ECI coordinates, the trajectory equation of satellite in the space described as Equation (2) could be deduced via geometric analysis of orbital dynamics and spherical geometry [9].

$$\varphi = \arcsin[\sin(i)\sin(\theta)] \tag{2}$$

$$\lambda = \Omega_0 + \arctan[\cos(i)\tan(\theta)] + \begin{cases} -180^\circ(-180^\circ \le \theta \le -90^\circ) \\ 0^\circ(-90^\circ \le \theta \le 90^\circ) \\ 180^\circ(90^\circ \le \theta \le 180^\circ) \end{cases} \tag{3}$$

In Equation (3), φ, λ represent satellite latitude and longitude on the celestial sphere; θ represents the angular distance of the ascending node; γ_0 represents the initial phase of the satellite; ω represents the angular velocity of the satellite rotation around the Earth; Ω_0 represents satellite

Right Ascension of Ascending Node (RAAN); i represents the orbital inclination angle.

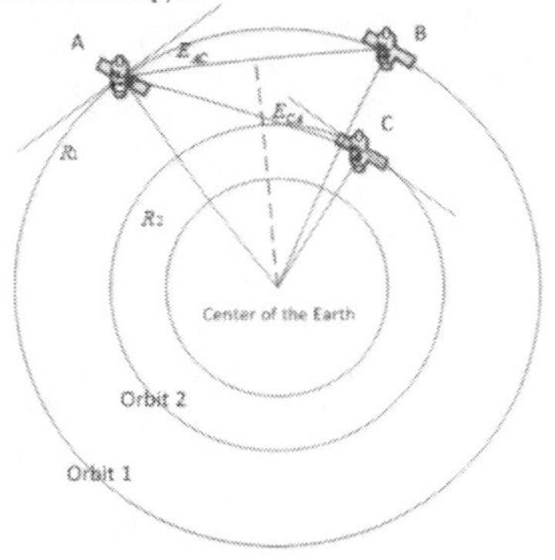

Figure 2. Link length and visibility schematic

As shown in Figure 2, A and B are two satellites lie in the same orbital altitude, and satellite C lies in a lower orbit, the link between satellite A and B is intra-plane ISL, while the link between satellite A and C is a cross-layer link, inter-plane ISL. Distance between satellites can be calculated through spherical geometry, and the distance of intra-plane ISL is deduced by(4).

$$d_{AB} = \sqrt{2}R_1\sqrt{1-\cos\angle AOB} \tag{4}$$

Specially, when A and B are two adjacent satellites in the walker constellation, the distance equation is transformed into (5).

$$d_{AB} = \sqrt{2}R_1\sqrt{1-\cos\frac{2\pi P}{N}} \tag{5}$$

The distance of inter-plane ISL is:

$$d_{AC} = \sqrt{R_1^2 + R_2^2 - 2R_1R_2\cos\angle AOC} \tag{6}$$

$\angle AOC$ and $\angle AOB$ can be calculated according to the latitude and longitude of the two satellites [10], and the representation of $\angle AOB$ is described as (7).

$$\angle AOB = \arcsin[\sin(\varphi_A)\sin(\varphi_B) + \cos(\varphi_A)\cos(\varphi_B)\cos(\lambda_A - \lambda_B)] \tag{7}$$

Elevation angle is of great significance for inter-satellite data transmission, since with the elevation increases, multipath and shadowing problems will be eased so that the quality of the ISL is improved. Transient elevation angle E_{AC} and E_{CA} can be expressed as (8) and (9).

$$E_{AC} = \arccos[\frac{R_2\sin(\theta)}{d_{AC}}] \tag{8}$$

$$E_{CA} = \arccos[\frac{R_1\sin(\theta)}{d_{AC}}] \tag{9}$$

Multi-layer satellite ISL connectivity is determined by the running status of satellites, at the same time, the Earth and the atmosphere covered the ISL, so orbit altitude and satellite distribution should be taken into consideration when designing satellite constellation, making it possible to obtain more inter satellite visible time. In judging whether the Earth will obstruct to the ISL, the ISL protection clearance should be taken into consideration as well [9]. Assuming that H is the protection clearance, and d is the distance between ISL and the center of the Earth, to meet the satellite ISL is not covered, H and d should satisfy (10).

$$d \geq R + H \tag{10}$$

Among them, R is the radius of the earth.

III. Topology Network Simulation and Analysis

In the simulation experiment, BeiDou satellites are selected as the relay satellites; the monitoring satellite lies in low Earth orbit is selected as the access satellite; three ground stations, Beijing, Sanya and Mudanjiang are selected as data receive station. A comparison is discussed among satellites of different orbits to serve as relay satellites in the possibility of link establishment and elevation angle.

A. GEO Satellites as Relay Satellite

Geostationary satellite lies in high orbit position, and its relative position is stable regardless of the Earth's movement, its relatively static properties make it possible for GEO satellite to serve as a data relay satellite. As is shown in Figure 3, the visibility between GEO satellites and three ground stations is permanent, so only the visibility between LEO and GEO satellites needs to be considered, then we can determine the feasibility of the inter satellite link.

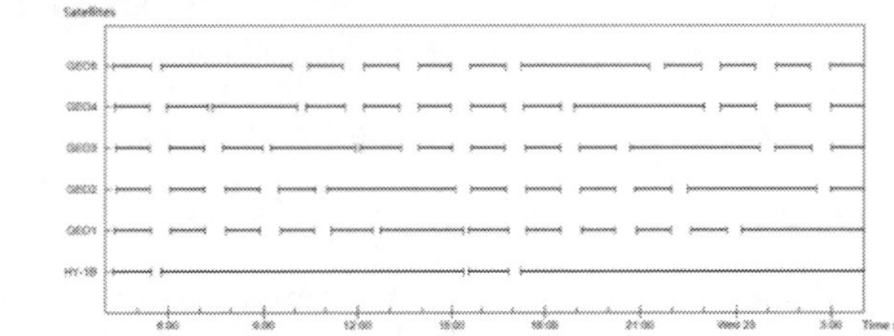

Figure 3. LEO satellite - GEO satellite visibility

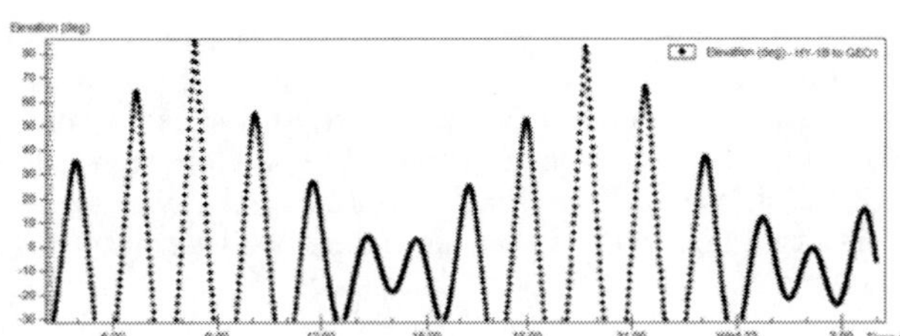

Figure 4. Elevation Angle between LEO satellite and GEO satellite

In Figure 3, LEO satellite can establish a long time inter satellite link with GEO satellites. Total coverage time between LEO and GEO satellites is 82341s, accounting for 95.30% of the total time, and each of 5 GEO satellites has a long time visibility, the shortest time is 64317s, accounting for 74.50% of the total time. GEO satellites are able to establish more permanent connection to the LEO satellite. For the most of time, more than one GEO satellite exists in the visibility range of the LEO satellite, the selection between satellites depends on the visibility time in order to reduce handover. Due to the high orbital position, inter-satellite links do not exist between GEO satellites. The elevation angle between LEO satellite and single GEO satellite is shown in Figure 4, changes periodically.

B. *IGSO Satellite as Relay Satellite*

IGSO satellite shares the same orbit altitude with GEO satellite. Different from GEO satellites, due to the orbital plane is inclined; its star point track on the Earth surface is ‘8’ shaped, and this kind of satellite make up for the deficiency of the GEO satellite’s incomplete coverage in polar areas. Adopting IGSO satellite as a relay satellite, single satellite cannot achieve full-time coverage to the ground station, but 3 satellites working together can achieve full-time coverage; Figure 5 shows the visibility between LEO satellite and IGSO satellites.

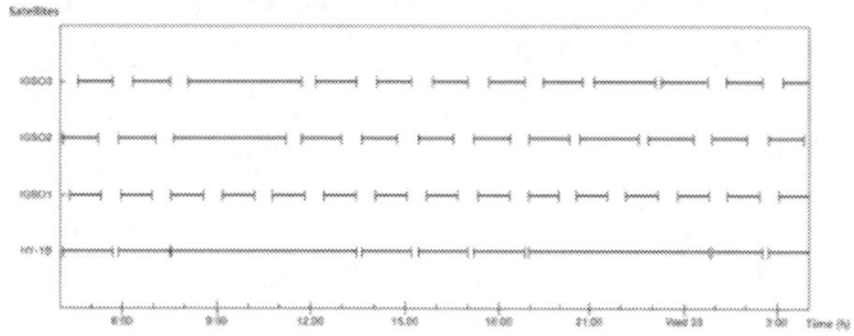

Figure 5. LEO satellite - IGSO satellite visibility

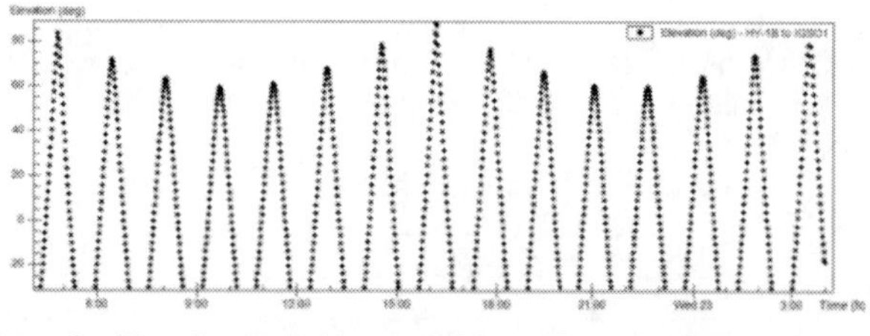

Figure 6. Elevation Angle between LEO satellite and IGSO satellite

As is shown in Figure 5, total coverage time between LEO and IGSO satellites is 81485 s, accounting for 94.31% of the total time. Due to the business characteristics of observation satellite, data from Polar Regions is particularly significant. IGSO satellites can provide data relay services for blind area [11], where GEO satellite failed to provide total coverage in polar areas. However, as is shown in Figure 6, the elevation angle between LEO satellite and single IGSO satellite stays in a high level compared changes with GEO satellites, which is benefit to the establishment of high-quality ISLs.

C. *MEO Satellites as Relay Satellite*

The problem will be more complicated when the MEO satellite group serves as relay satellites. Two types of ISLs, intra-plane ISL and inter-plane ISL exist in MEO constellation, intra plane ISL connecting satellites within the same orbit and inter-plane ISL connecting satellites in adjacent orbits [12].

1) Analysis of ISLs in MEO constellation

In circular orbit satellite constellation, the distance between adjacent satellites is constant within same obit plane; but the length of inter-plane ISL is alterable periodically according to the satellite network topology. Figure 7 shows the distance of intra-plane ISL and inter-plane ISL if Sat_{ij} is used to denote the orbit number of the satellite j in plane i.

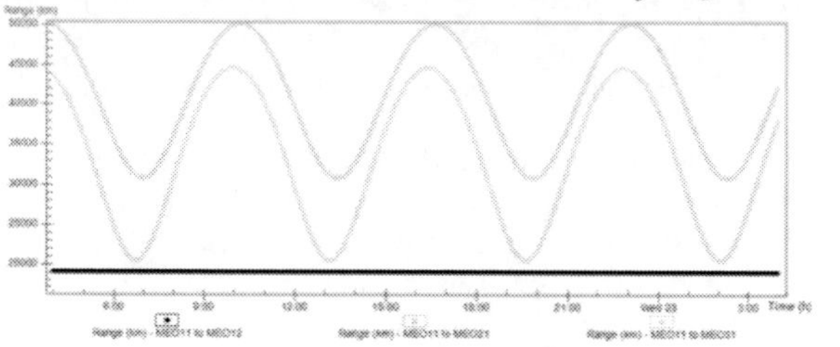

Figure 7. MEO-MEO ISLs analysis

As is shown in Figure 7, the distance between Sat_{11} and Sat_{12} is stable, about 19088 km, and the distance between Sat_{11} and Sat_{21} changes periodically, the distance between satellites is different because of the existence of phase factor and the inclination of the orbit. Multi-ISLs could be established while the visibility is constrained, but this will greatly increase the system cost and receive low profits. In the existing satellite system, only the Iridium constellation [13] uses ISL technology: two intra-plane ISLs and two inter-plane ISLs. The Iridium system using polar orbit satellite constellation, which makes inter-plane ISLs stable, and satellite antenna tracking can be realized reliably.

2) Visibility analysis bewteen MEO satellite group and LEO satellite

The same with IGSO satellite, single MEO satellite could not cover ground stations at any time, but MEO satellite group working together can achieve full-time coverage. In the MEO constellation, satellites are evenly distributed in 3 orbital planes. The visibility analysis between LEO satellite and satellites in one orbital plane can represent the whole constellation. Figure 8 shows the visibility between LEO satellite and MEO satellites in one orbital plane.

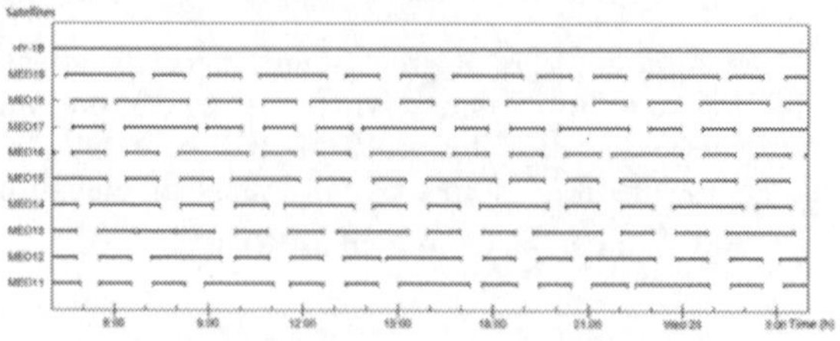

Figure 8. LEO satellite - MEO satellite visibility

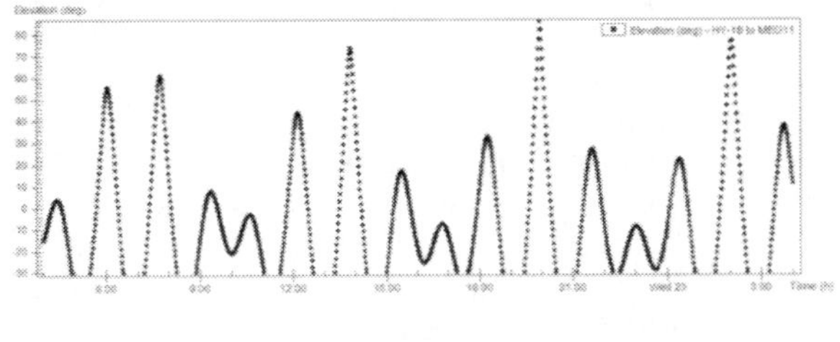

Figure 9. Elevation Angle between LEO satellite and MEO satellite

As is shown Figure 8, due to the shelter of the Earth, full-time ISL could not be established between LEO satellite and single MEO satellite, but for one orbit plane in the MEO satellite constellation, full-time ISL could be established, and be able to ensure that at least 5 MEO satellites in the LEO visibility range and this number goes up to 15 for the whole constellation.

Figure 9 shows the elevation angle between LEO satellites and MEO satellites, and the angle stays in low level for the most of time compared with GEO satellites. Moreover, MEO satellites do not possess the strong ability as GEO satellite, complicated antenna tracking technology and strong communication ability are required.

IV. PERFORMANCE ANALYSIS

In this section, the experiment parameters are given firstly, and then the performance of relay satellites in different orbits is analyzed especially in satellite connectivity.

A. *Data Trasmission Without Relay Satellite*

The BeiDou satellite constellation consists of 5 GEO satellites and 30 non-GEO satellites, which contains 27 MEO satellites and 3 IGSO satellites. 27 MEO satellites are evenly distributed on three orbit planes, and every 9 satellites are evenly distributed in an orbit; the monitoring satellite lies in low orbit, as a data collecting satellite. Specific parameters are shown in Table I.

TABLE I. SATELLITE ORBIT PARAMETER

Orbit type	LEO	MEO	IGSO	GEO
Altitude (km)	973	21528	35786	35786
Inclination Angle(degree)	99.34	55	-	0
Period (s)	6626.17	46393.9	86170.5	86170.5
Satellite Number	1	27	3	5
Orbit Number	1	3	3	1
Phase factor	-	1	-	-

Figure 10 shows the visibility between LEO satellite and ground stations, as we can see from the figure, the visible time between the satellite and the ground station is very short. The time for LEO satellite to cover ground stations is 9023 s, accounting for 10.44% of the total time, and in the rest of the time, the link is failed to establish. So, for a long period of time, data could not be transmitted to the ground station, and the satellite needs to transmit the data to ground stations until the satellite cross the border again. In this situation, limited resources of the satellite will be occupied and the burden on satellite will be increased when the satellite cross the border again.

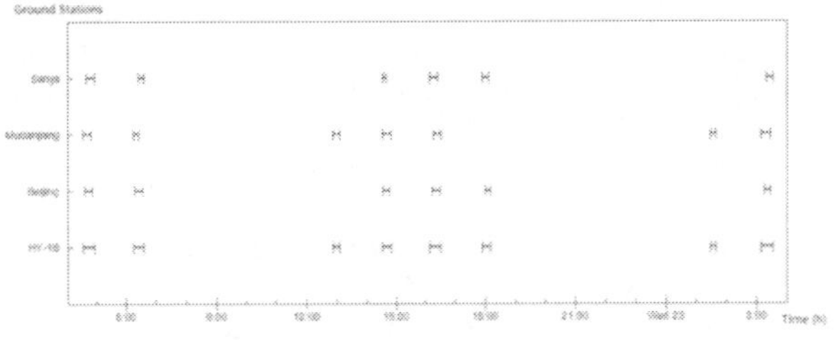

Figure 10. LEO satellite- Ground visibility

From the visibility analysis between LEO satellite and ground stations, it is concluded that only the satellite and the ground station satisfy visibility conditions, inter satellite link could be established. However, the establishment of the inter satellite link is related to the quality of the channel, the antenna elevation and so on, so the visibility between the satellite and the ground station is the necessary condition for the inter satellite link. At the same time, observation satellites are mostly polar orbiting satellites, whose running speed are fast and orbital altitude are relatively low. From Figure 10, we can see that covering time of three ground stations is relatively concentrated, which is due to geography, political and other factors limit the choice of the ground station's location. In a lot of spare time, satellite data cannot be transmitted in real time, meanwhile, due to characteristics of satellite service, launching a large number of satellites will greatly increase the cost of system.

B. *Data Trasmission with Relay of BeiDou Satellites*

Through the analysis of the previous sections, it is concluded that using BeiDou navigation satellite system as the relay of observation satellites can greatly reduce the latency of satellite data transmission, and can achieve the timely transmission of satellite data in the absence of new ground stations. Due to the fact that relay satellites could achieve full-time coverage to the ground stations, the feasibility of data transmission depends on the visibility time between satellites. In this paper, we mainly discuss single layer satellites serving as relay satellites, since multi-layer relay satellites would perplex the problem and increase the system cost. Table II shows the result of analysis and comparisons by using GEO satellites, IGSO satellites, MEO satellites as relay satellites respectively.

TABLE II. RELAY SATELLITE PERFORMANCE ANALYSIS

Relay satellite	Non	GEO	IGSO	MEO
Connectivity	10.44%	95.30%	94.31%	100%
Visible number	-	0-5	0-3	15
Routing hops	-	1	1	indefinite
Technical difficulty	low	medium	high	high
System cost	low	medium	medium	high

The model we proposed focuses on the link distance and elevation angle, and these two factors are fundamental for link establishment. Surely, more factors should be considered when judging whether the link could be established, such as perturbation of the orbit, antenna tracking, etc. And these should be considered in a more complicated model.

From the perspective of the feasibility of establishing a link, GEO, IGSO and MEO satellites can provide long-term visibility. So, the use of relay satellites can solve the problem that LEO satellite could not transfer data to ground stations when it's not in the visibility zones.

When GEO or IGSO satellites serve as relay satellites, the transmission delay will be large, since the distance of ISL is long. Therefore, for real-time data transmission, MEO satellites will be better choice. However, in the current BeiDou satellite system network architecture, the link bandwidth of ISLs is rather small and can't meet the acquirement of large-scale data transmission. Compared to MEO satellites, the number of GEO and IGSO satellites is small and only one hop that we can have data transmitted to the ground stations, the routing control is rather simple; on the contrary, this problem becomes complex when MEO satellites serving as relay satellites since there are more than one ISLs could be established between satellites at the same time. The satellite to be selected is under a series of criterions such as to choose the satellite with the greatest elevation angle to possess the best communication quality; the longest service time to minimize handoff times, etc. It will involve a series of more complex problems of satellite handoff.

Experimental results indicate that the proportion of satellite visibility rises to 95.30% when GEO satellites serve as relay satellites. The GEO satellite has been widely used as a relay satellite around the world, due to its high orbit altitude and complex on-board processing capability; adopting IGSO satellites to serve as relay satellites solves the problem that GEO satellite has blind areas around Polar Regions; choosing MEO satellites serve as relay satellites could provide a full-time relay service. The number of visible satellites is 15 at least, so we can choose the best among them to achieve better service. Yet choosing MEO satellites as relay satellites faces many difficulties including complicated antenna tracking technology, complex on-board processing capability, and high system cost.

V. CONCLUSION AND FUTURE WORK

BeiDou Navigation Satellite System is one of the most important navigation satellite systems in the world, and will provide global coverage in the future. Due to the limited space resources the new satellite has to be limited launching. So make use of existing satellites to complement new functions is a feasible solution. In this paper, the Inter-Satellite Link based on BeiDou satellites is analyzed. Firstly, the network architecture of spatial information system studied, and the dynamic network topology model is proposed. Then, by simulation the running of BeiDou satellites, the connectivity features of ISLs were acquired. Meanwhile, the topology structure's evolution laws of satellite network and a selection suggestion of relay satellites were also obtained by analyzing the simulation results. We will explore the more practical computing model of link distance by tracing and research handoff algorithm of ISL in MEO constellation to choose the optimal satellite to achieve acceptable relay performance in future work.

ACKNOWLEDGMENT

Scientific issues of this study come from Nature Fund of Science of China with grant No. 61371119.

REFERENCES

[1] R. Stampfl and A. Jones, "Tracking and Data Relay Satellites" IEEE Trans 1 on Aerospace and Electronic System, vol.6, No.3, 1970, pp. 276 - 289.

[2] H. Wu, Z. Li, H. Liu, and M. Zhang, "Analysis and Countermeasure on Working Status of International Standard for the Satellite Navigation System," Geomatics World, Vol.21, No.6, pp.35-42, doi: 10.3969/j.issn. 1672-1586 (2014) 06-0035-08.

[3] I. F. Akyildiz, H. Uzunalio, and M. D. Bender, "Handover management in Low Earth Orbit (LEO) satellite networks," Mobile Networks and Applications, vol.4, 1999, pp.301-310.

[4] Z. Wang, P. Wang, X. Gu, and Q. Guo, "Research on design of permanent inter-satellite-links in satellite networks," Journal on Communications, vol. 27, Aug 2006, pp. 129-133.

[5] G. Liu and S. Wu, "Study on the ISLs' Characteristics of Non-Geostationary Satellite Communication System," Systems Engin- eering and Electronics, vol.24, No.1, 2001, pp.105-109.

[6] L. Gao, H.Zhao and T.Jiang, "Modeling and Simulation for Dynamic Topology Network of SIS," Journal of System Simulation, vol.18, Aug.2006, pp.69-72.

[7] L. Wang, N. Zhang, Y. Wang, H. Chu, and H. Li, "Geometric Characters of Inter Satellite Links Between MEO Layer and LEO Layer in MEO/LEO Networks," Chinese Space Science and Technology, Feb.2004

[8] L. Fan and Y. Zhang, "Research on the ISL Building Rules and the Optimization Design of Walker Constellation," Flight dynamics,vol.25, 2007, pp:93-96.

[9] Z. Yin, L. Zhang, and X. Zhou, "Performance analysis of inter-layer ISLs in triple-layered LEO/HEO/GEO satellite networks," Computer Engineering and Applications, vol.46, Dec.2010, pp. 9-13, doi:10.3778/j.issn.1002-8331.2010.12.003

[10] L. Gao, H. Zhao, and J. Jiang, "Modeling and Simulation for Dynamic Topology Network of SIS," Journal of System Simulation, vol.18, Aug.2006 pp:69-72.

[11] J. Wang. "Proposal for Developing China. s Data Relay Satellite System," Spacecraft Engineering, vol.20, No.2, Feb. 2011.

[12] P. K. Chowdhury, M. Atiquzzaman, and W. Ivancic, "Handover Schemes In Satellite Networks: State of the Art and Future Research Directions", IEEE Communications Surveys & Tutorials • 4th Quarter 2006, vol. 8, NO. 4

[13] S. R. Pratt, R. A. Raines, "An Operational and performance overview of the Iridium Low Earth Orbit satellite system," IEEE CommunicationsSurveys •2th Quarter 1999, vol.2, NO.2, pp:2-10.

A RESTful Sensor Data Back-end for the Internet of Things

Antti Iivari and Jani Koivusaari
VTT Technical Research Centre of Finland Ltd
Oulu, Finland
email: antti.iivari@vtt.fi, jani.koivusaari@vtt.fi

***Abstract*—As rapidly increasing amounts of smart communicating objects with sensing capabilities are generating raw measurement and observation data, scalable back-ends are needed to collect, store, marshal and process that influx of machine-generated data into actionable information. The data constantly flowing out from these embedded devices is very periodic and structured in nature, referred to as machine-generated data, beginning with a timestamp of some sort and then consisting of designated fields, such as measurement values, ranges and tags. Furthermore, as wireless sensing devices are in many cases battery operated and resource constrained, a mode of operation can be assumed where the device transmits measurement data at specific intervals between which it preserves power by sleeping or idling. This is only one of the reasons why a RESTful approach that has been more commonly associated with the World Wide Web, could be appropriate when dealing with the challenges brought forth by the Internet of Things (IoT) revolution. In this paper, initial findings concerning a proof-of-concept back-end implementation are presented in addition to discussing the benefits and technologies related to a RESTful approach in building a scalable sensor data back-end for the Internet of Things.**

Keywords-IoT; Sensor; Back-end; Data; REST.

I. INTRODUCTION

Today a rapidly increasing amount of smart communicating objects with sensing capabilities are generating raw measurement and observation data that in order to be useful, must be collected, stored, marshalled and processed in a back-end of some sort. This onslaught of small interconnected embedded devices and the messages they are transmitting is commonly referred to as the Internet of Things (IoT) [1]. Typically, the kind of data constantly flowing out from such systems is very periodic and structured in nature, referred to as machine-generated data [2], beginning with a timestamp of some sort and then consisting of designated fields, such as measurement values, ranges and tags Furthermore, as wireless sensing devices are in many cases battery operated and resource constrained, a mode of operation can be assumed where the device transmits measurement data at specific intervals between which it preserves power by sleeping or idling. This is only one of the reasons why a RESTful approach [3], which has been more commonly associated with the worldwide web, is appropriate when dealing with the systems and devices in an IoT context.

Representational state transfer, or REST [3], is a software architectural style for designing distributed systems and it is used for the World Wide Web. When distributed systems and services conform to the constraints of REST they can be called "RESTful". RESTful systems virtually always communicate via the Hypertext Transfer Protocol (HTTP) with the standard HTTP commands (GET, POST, PUT, DELETE). REST has gained widespread acceptance across the Web as an easier-to-use, resource-oriented alternative to more complex approaches such as SOAP or WSDL. When considering a RESTful approach for constrained very low-power sensor devices, the CoAP protocol is particularly interesting, as it is designed to interface with HTTP and the Web while meeting specialized requirements such as very low overhead and multicast support. In essence, CoAP aims to provide a more compact version of HTTP/REST with additional features optimized for M2M and IoT applications. As a reliable and scalable back-end solution is a requirement for most IoT-type applications where large amounts of rapidly streaming machine-generated data from multiple sources needs to be handled and stored for later processing, a RESTful approach for implementing such a back-end is discussed in this paper. The goal of the work described in this paper is to design and deploy a REST-style HTTP/POST -interface and enable IoT devices to communicate towards the backend as effortlessly as possible.

The paper is organised as follows: In Section II the most important characteristics of protocols and data formats for the Internet of Things are discussed, while Section III outlines the key building blocks of a sensor data back-end solution. Section IV presents the prototype implementations before we summarize and discuss some future work items in Section V.

II. MACHINE-GENERATED DATA FROM SMART CONNECTED OBJECTS

In order to build and design a viable back-end solution for reliably handling large amounts of machine-generated IoT data, the characteristics of such systems must be studied and understood. For the purposes of the work presented in this paper, there are two key facets of sensor data that must be considered. First is the format of the represented sensor data itself. Second is the message protocol with which this machine-generated data is transmitted. Some of the most common examples of sensor data formats in current systems are listed as follows:

- JSON: JavaScript Object Notation is a lightweight data-interchange format for storing and exchanging

data. It is easy to read and write by both humans and machines. While JSON is a text-based format and language independent, it is originally a subset of the JavaScript programming language.
- CSV: Basic comma separated values are by far the simplest and most rudimentary of commonly used sensor data formats.
- XML: Extensible Markup Language (XML) is essentially a set of rules for encoding documents in a format which is readable for both man and machine. XML also acts as a basis for some M2M protocols [4], such as XMPP and BitXML.

Similarly, the most essential messaging protocols [5] employed in application layer transfer of machine-generated data and IoT-type data transfer are listed below:
- Hypertext Transfer Protocol: HTTP the tried and true RESTful HTTP over TCP very familiar to us all from the web service world, is a particularly attractive option for constrained IoT devices, when considering the almost universal availability and compatibility of the legacy HTTP-stack on various platforms.
- Message Queuing Telemetry Transport: MQTT is a lightweight publish/subscribe based message protocol especially well-suited for running on limited computational power and lean network connectivity.
- Constrained Application Protocol: CoAP aims to be a generic web protocol for the special requirements of constrained sensor environments while easily integrating with HTTP and existing web technologies with a very low overhead.

It should be noted that any technologies related to the REST software architectural style, such as CoAP and HTTP, were given special consideration during this work, as RESTful architectures are clearly a promising and common approach employed in many contemporary IoT-platforms and sensor data platforms. The CoAP interaction model is similar to the client/server model of HTTP as a CoAP request is equivalent to that of HTTP and is sent by a client to request a resource. However, unlike HTTP, CoAP deals with these interchanges asynchronously over a lighter datagram-oriented transport such as UDP. Furthermore, employing RESTful APIs will also give the advantage of easy integration with existing web services and other popular http-based platforms.

III. Internet of Things on the Back-end

Raw sensor data in and of itself, consisting of measurement values or observational data corresponding to a short time-frame, is rarely useful or informative in an immediate or direct manner. Typically the data is transmitted to an application back-end to be marshalled and processed into something useful for the application at hand. The back-end consists of an interface (such as REST) to act as the collector towards which the sensing devices communicate either directly or via a gateway device [6].

In a typical IoT scenario, in addition to the embedded intercommunicating smart objects (the "things"), we have the server-side functionality where the actual application specific logic and data processing takes place. This is referred to as the back-end. The back-end usually consists of three main parts: a server, an application, and a database. In order to make the server, application, and database communicate with each other, server-side languages like PHP, Ruby, Python and JavaScript are employed, and database tools like MySQL or PostgreSQL are needed to find, save, or change data and serve it back to the users (either man or machine) of the service. MySQL is an open-source relational database management system (RDBMS) and one of the most popular ones used in modern web-applications. MySQL is also the database of choice prototype work discussed in this paper.

A. *Representational State Transfer for IoT*

In technical terms REST, or Representational State Transfer [3], is an architectural style for building networked applications. It is based on a stateless, client-server communications protocol and is almost always heavily tied to the HTTP protocol. Representational State Transfer (or REST) has become a widely accepted alternative software architecture approach for developing scalable web services. So called RESTful systems adhering to this principle communicate with each other simply by using the standard Hypertext Transfer Protocol (HTTP) with GET, POST, PUT and DELETE -queries. The basic idea is that simple HTTP is used to make resource calls between machines, instead of using complicated mechanisms such SOAP to connect services. This is essentially the same method that any web browser today uses to retrieve (GET) data and web pages from the internet and send (POST) input by the user to the remote server.

The benefits of REST from an IoT perspective are easily apparent, as it is a relatively lightweight approach to building intercommunicating services while also being fully-featured in the sense that there are not many things that can be done with Web Services that can't be realized with a RESTful software architecture in one way or another. Furthermore, REST itself is not a "standard" as there will never be a formal W3C specification for REST, for example. A concrete implementation of a RESTful distributed service always follows the following four key design principles:
- Resources expose easily understood directory structure-like URIs.
- Transfer JSON or XML to represent data.
- Messages use HTTP methods explicitly (GET, POST, PUT, DELETE).
- Based on stateless interactions. No client context information is stored on the server between requests.

While discussing the back-end prototype for a conditions monitoring system in the next section of this paper, it is important to note that the goal in this case is not to implement a fully functional REST-based architecture or interface strictly adhering to the specification. Instead, the approach is to design and deploy a REST-like HTTP/POST -

web interface to enable the sensing devices to communicate towards the backend as effortlessly as possible, as devices such as these sensors are often extremely resource constrained, not only in terms of processing power and memory, but also in terms of network capabilities and battery reserves. This has the added benefit of enabling any communication capable device, regardless of other operational or hardware characteristics, to push their measurement or log data towards the back-end by simply sending HTTP/POST-messages to the known address of the server. Formulating a HTTP-compliant POST message with the data included in the header as a payload is a simple matter and computationally light-weight operation. Some of the main benefits of implementing a RESTful service for the Internet of Things are as follows:

- Platform-independency
- Language-independency
- Standards-based (e.g. HTTP)
- Easy to work with firewalls

Utilizing RESTful architectures in the context of IoT or M2M applications is nothing new in and of itself. Indeed, others have successfully designed approaches for such systems before [7][8] based on REST.

IV. The RESTful prototype implementations

During this work, a proof-of-concept pilot system has been established to measure, collect and store sensor data for the purpose of monitoring the conditions of an inhabited building. This paper focuses solely on the technical matters and preliminary findings concerning the back-end implementation, while the pilot system as a whole is left as the subject matter for another publication. In this section, the overall structure, main technological components and the chosen RESTful approach employed for the sensor data back-end system are outlined. It should also be noted that a simple but effective JSON-based sensor data format was designed at VTT for the purposes of this work.

A. *The traditional LAMP-stack*

First version of the RESTful sensor back-end was built on top of the traditional LAMP-stack [9]. The so called LAMP stack has become the tried and true basis for web-based applications now for two decades and the software components that make up the stack can be found in any of the default software repositories in most major Linux distributions. A standard LAMP stack consists of the following technologies: Linux as the underlying operating system, Apache as the Web server, MySQL as the relational database and PHP as the object-oriented scripting language. The components of LAMP are individually freely available Open Source Software, making them very attractive to potential users eliminating the need to purchase expensive commercial tools. The open licences make it possible for anyone to develop and distribute software based on the LAMP-stack without any licensing efforts or payments. The source code for any of the components in LAMP can be accessed by anyone, thus making it significantly easier to find faults and apply bug fixes, giving the users of the stack a degree of flexibility that is usually not available in comparable commercial alternatives.

While each of the technologies included in the LAMP stack are powerful and useful already in their own right, they are often used together and their compatibility towards each other has therefore been extended numerous times in the past to create a truly powerful and versatile platform for web-based applications. For these reasons, the LAMP stack was utilized as the key enabler and technological basis for the first prototype implementation of the back-end solution within the conditions monitoring prototype system. The PHP-based REST-interface for sensor data capturing implemented in the context of the prototype also includes support for HTTP Basic authentication as a relatively simple access control technique to ensure an elementary level of security in the exchange of measurement information. From the point of view of the sensor devices, applying HTTP basic authentication is also a very light-weight approach, as no handshakes, costly encryption calculations or similar procedures are required prior the transmission of data.

As discussed in the previous chapter, one of the key building blocks of a sensor data back-end is the database for storing the time-series data. The widely used and popular MySQL database, also used in the prototype discussed here, as a part of a web-based solution, works very well in combination with a number of modern programming languages (such as PERL, C, C++, Java, JavaScript and PHP) and various software development frameworks. From all of these languages, PHP is still the most popular one because of its convenience and capabilities in the domain of web-based application development. PHP provides a number of useful modules to access the MySQL databases and to manipulate data records and settings inside the database.

B. *First prototype*

To outline the structure of the LAMP-based first version of the prototype, a diagram illustrating the main components is given in Figure 1.

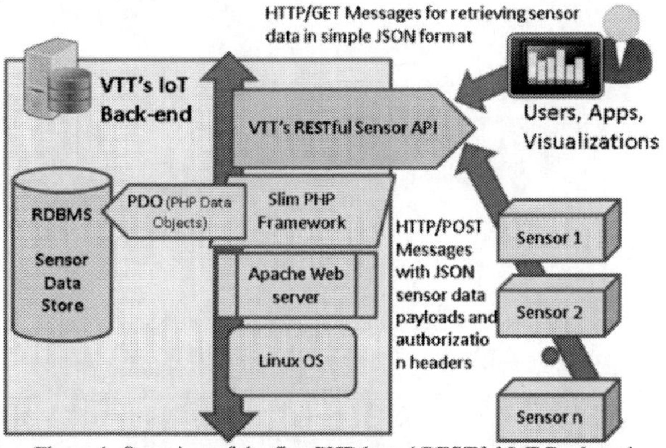

Figure 1. Overview of the first PHP-based RESTful IoT Back-end prototype.

Convenient and easily deployable interoperation with MySQL technology and the aforementioned capabilities geared towards web-applications and services led to the choosing of PHP as the programming language to implement the required REST-like functionalities in the first version of the IoT back-end prototype. The PHP-functionalities were implemented by utilizing slimPHP [10], which is an open-source micro-framework designed for rapid development of responsive web applications and REST APIs with lots of useful functionalities built-in such as URL-routing and middleware architecture.

A REST –interface was programmed for storing and retrieving JSON-based sensor data payloads sent through standard HTTP GET and POST –messages. The sensor data is stored into a relational MySQL database.

C. The Node.js environment

Node.js is an open source JavaScript-based platform built on top of Google Chrome's JavaScript V8 Engine [11]. As it provides an event-driven architecture and a non-blocking I/O API making it very lightweight and efficient it is especially suitable for building data-intensive real-time applications that are scalable and run across distributed devices. Node.js facilitates the creation of highly scalable servers without using threading by using a simplified model of event-driven programming and providing a rich library of various usable JavaScript modules greatly simplifying the development of distributed applications. In the following, some of the key benefits of Node.js for IoT applications are listed.

- Fast code execution due to the underlying Google Chrome's V8 JavaScript Engine.
- The event driven asynchronous API ensures that the server never needs to wait for an API to return data.
- Highly scalable single threaded event mechanism scales better to a larger number of requests than traditional servers.
- Released under the open source MIT license.

D. Second prototype

The Node.js platform enables the developer to discard the traditional and somewhat cumbersome, LAMP-stack altogether while still providing excellent modules and built-in capabilities for development and interacting with various database technologies such as MySQL, as shown in Figure 2.

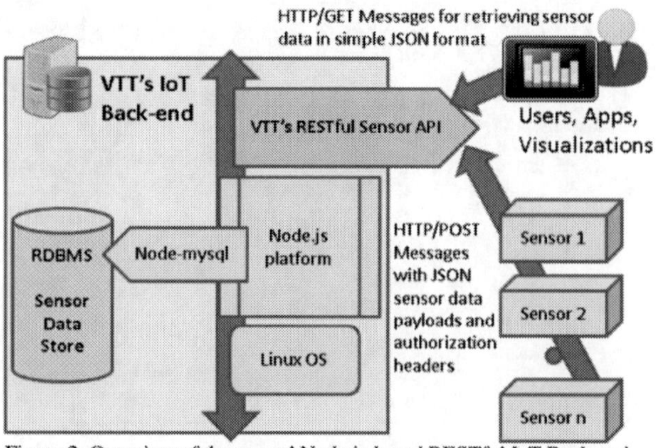

Figure 2. Overview of the second Node.js-based RESTful IoT Back-end prototype.

The potential of the platform for IoT-style application quickly becomes apparent, and as such, a second improved experimental version was built for this work by utilizing the more modern and scalable Node.js-platform. Functionalities in the second version of the back-end prototype correspond closely to the first version, but the scalability and maintainability of the system became superior. The data model for storing the sensor data from IoT devices into the database was also redesigned for the second version of the prototype system.

In addition to Node.js, some additional modules were employed for the implementation; with the most important one to mention being the Express framework [12], a flexible and minimalistic application framework for rapid development of HTTP-based web applications.

V. CONCLUSIONS

A RESTful approach for managing the rapidly incoming streams of machine-generated data in modern IoT systems is indeed a viable one. By harnessing modern software tools for web application development and server side application platforms, building scalable back-ends for the Internet of Things becomes more fluent and productive. When experimenting with the potential of these various technologies more familiar from the web-application world, it can be concluded that there is a lot of untapped potential for managing machine-generated sensor data and exploiting the true information value of the Internet of Things revolution. Scalability, security, reliability and easy deployment are just some of the observed benefits. In this paper, we have presented the first phases of the implementation work for a RESTful sensor data back-end.

The SlimPHP micro-framework proved to be an excellent tool in alleviating many of the problems and concerns with plain PHP-code or the heavier full-scale PHP frameworks, but as running PHP as the back-end code still required separate underlying Web server (such as Apache) there is a degree of cumbersomeness that can't be overcome with the LAMP-stack. The Node.js platform provided a flexible and dexterous alternative when implementing various features and interfaces for the second version of the prototype back-end. With the Node.js platform as a basis, superior flexibility and agility, in both deployment and maintaining phases, when compared to the standard LAMP-stack could be observed. Furthermore, due to the asynchronous and event driven nature of the Node.js technology, it is also expected to scale better for larger number of requests.

Some items are left altogether as next steps for the following phases of the work and future publications. Further comparisons and quantitative measurements on the performance and scalability of these back-end technologies are one topic of future interest. Enhanced security features for data privacy and system robustness are another item considered as next steps. Also, comparing the suitability of different database technologies as the amount of incoming sensor data starts nearing Big Data –volumes and different processing engines for data analytics become necessary, is another topic left for future work.

Acknowledgments

The research from DEWI project (www.dewi-project.eu) leading to these results has received funding from the ARTEMIS Joint Undertaking under grant agreement n° 621353 and from TEKES.

References

[1] J. Gubbi, R. Buyya, S. Marusic, and M. Palaniswami, "Internet of things (IoT): A vision, architectural elements, and future directions" Future Generation Computer Systems, vol. 29, no. 7, pp. 1645 – 1660, 2013.

[2] K. Monash, "Examples and definition of machine-generated data", URL: http://www.dbms2.com/2010/12/30/examples-and-definition-of-machine-generated-data/ [retrieved: April, 2016]

[3] L. Richardson and S. Ruby, Restful Web Services, 1st ed. O'Reilly Media, May 2007.

[4] A. Iivari, T. Väisänen, M. Ben Alaya, T. Riipinen & T. Monteil, "Harnessing XMPP for Machine-to-Machine Communications & Pervasive Applications" Journal of Communications Software & Systems, Vol. 10 Issue 3, 2014, pp.163-178.

[5] V. Karagiannis, "A survey on application layer protocols for the internet of things." Transaction on IoT and Cloud Computing 3.1, 2015, pp.11-17.

[6] J. Latvakoski et al., "A survey on M2M Service Networks", Computers , vol.2, 2014, pp.130 - 173.

[7] W. Colitti, K. Steenhaut, N. De Caro, B. Buta and V. Dobrota, "REST Enabled Wireless Sensor Networks for Seamless Integration with Web Applications," Mobile Adhoc and Sensor Systems (MASS), 2011 IEEE 8th International Conference on, Valencia, 2011, pp. 867-872.

[8] D. Guinard, V. Trifa and E. Wilde, "A resource oriented architecture for the Web of Things," Internet of Things (IOT), 2010, Tokyo, 2010, pp. 1-8.

[9] G. Lawton, "LAMP lights enterprise development efforts", Computer, 2005, 9: 18-20.

[10] V. Vaswani, "Create REST applications with the Slim micro-framework" URL: http://www.ibm.com/developerworks/library/x-slim-rest/ [retrieved: April, 2016]

[11] J. R. Wilson, Node.js the right way. Pragmatic Programmers, 2014.

[12] A. Mardan, Pro Express. js: Master Express. js: The Node. js Framework For Your Web Development. Apress, 2014.

Advanced Simulations of RNA-based Biological Nanostructures

Shyam Badu
MS2Discovery Interdisciplinary Institute
Wilfrid Laurier University
Waterloo, ON, Canada N2L 3C5

Roderick Melnik
MIRI, Wilfrid Laurier University
Waterloo, ON, Canada N2L 3C5, and
BCAM, Bilbao, Basque Country, Spain
Email: rmelnik@wlu.ca

Sanjay Prabhakar
MS2Discovery Interdisciplinary Institute
Wilfrid Laurier University
Waterloo, ON, Canada N2L 3C5

Abstract—**We present a methodology and the results of numerical simulations of complex biological polymeric molecular nanostructures, whose major components consist of ribonucleic acids (RNAs). The case where such nanostructures are considered in fluids, e.g. physiological solutions, is also reported. The developed methodology is based on molecular dynamics and our efficient coarse graining algorithms applied to such structures. We discuss such important characteristics as the radius of gyration, root mean square deviation, and radial distribution function in the application to RNA nanotubes, consisting of a number nanorings, studied in the previous works. Among other things, we provide insight into typical distributions of various ions around the RNA nanotubes as a function of time within a distance of a few angstroms from their surface.**

Keywords–Coarse-Graining Algorithms; Ribonucleic Acid Nanostructures; Molecular Dynamics; Scaffolding; Medical Biology; High Performance Computing.

I. Introduction

Modelling complex systems such as biological polymers is necessarily closely connected with advanced high performance computing. The task is becoming even more challenging when biological polymeric nanostructures are considered. Such structures have a range of current and potential therapeutic and other biomedical applications [1]. By now we know that the stability of the ribonucleic acid (RNA) assemblies is higher than that of the DNA self assembled nanoparticles in fluidic solutions [2], [3], and that different shape RNA molecules are available to form RNA building blocks and their complexes with other biomolecules [4], [5], [6]. Here our main focus is on such RNA nanostructures constructed with six helical building blocks of either one or two types (RNAI/RNAII). They consist of a number of nanorings linked together via base pairing hydrogen bonds, forming RNA nanotubes which may operate in the applications mentioned above in fluidic physiological solutions.

II. Computational Models, Methodology, and Main Results

Given the computational complexity of the problem at hand and its multiscale character, it is necessary to develop efficient coarse-graining procedures for molecular dynamics simulations of these structures [7]. To do that, we use the Boltzmann inversion method. The force matching is based on the objective function of the parameter α:

$$Z(\alpha) = Z_F(\alpha) + Z_c(\alpha), \tag{1}$$

$$Z_F(\alpha) = \left(3\sum_{k=1}^{M} N_k\right)^{-1} \sum_{k=1}^{M}\sum_{i=1}^{N_k} |F_{ki}(\alpha) - F_{ki}^0|^2, \tag{2}$$

$$Z_C(\alpha) = \sum_{r=1}^{N_C} W_r|A_r(\alpha) - A_r^0|^2. \tag{3}$$

The parameters α defined in the above equations (1) -(3) are calculated by matching the forces obtained by using the first-principles calculations of the several configurations of the molecular system and the classical potentials. Notations in (1) - (3) are as follows: the integer M in Z_F (the force objective function) is the number of configurations, N_k is the number of atoms in the k-th configuration and $F_{ki}(\alpha)$ is the force on the ith atom in the kth configuration which is obtained from the parametrization of α, and the F_{ki}^0 is the corresponding reference force obtained from the first principles calculations. In the constraint objective function Z_C the quantities $A_r(\alpha)$ are also physical parameters obtained from parametrization, A_r^0 are experimental values or the values calculated from the first principles methods and W_r is the weight factor. The force objective function defined in equation (1) is minimized for given α to calculate the classical force parameters by using the force and physical quantities obtained from *ab initio* calculations.

The entire system is integrated in time where the potential uses the CHARMM force field. The compatibility of this force field for this type of biological system was tested earlier [8], [9], demonstrating that the results are close to experiments.

We have performed all-atom molecular dynamics simulations of RNA nanotubes by using the CHARMM27 force field implemented in the NAMD package as it was done for the nanoring [10], [11]. The modeling of the nanotube, visualization and the analysis of the simulation outputs have been performed using the software visual molecular dynamics (VMD).

The RNA-nanotube was solvated in a water box where the distance from the surface of the nanocluster to the wall is slightly larger than the cut off radius used in the molecular dynamics simulation. In order to make the system neutral we have added ions, depending on the size of the nanotube (e.g., for a 4-ring nanotube we had 1254 ions). The resulting system has been first simulated at constant temperature and pressure using the NAMD software package. The temperature in the system has been controlled by using Langevin's method with

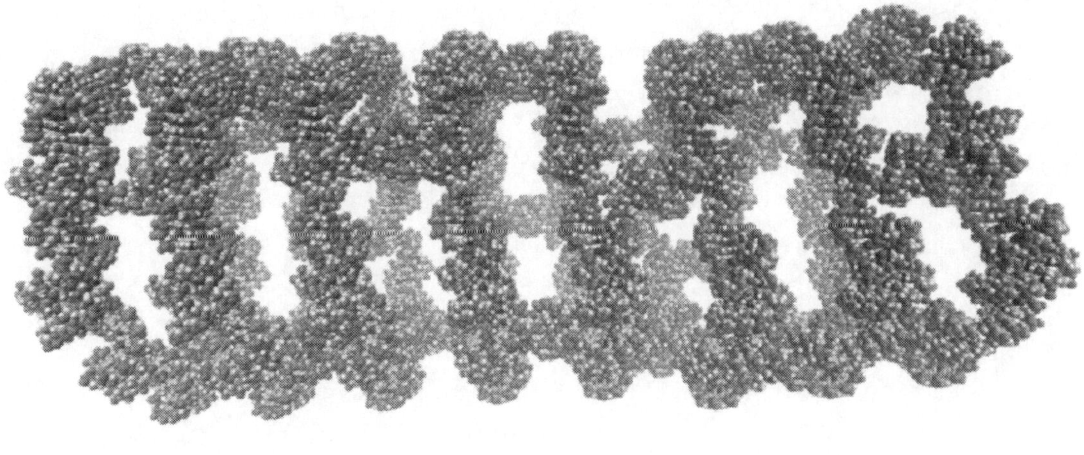

Figure 1. Three-dimensional structure on 8-ring nanotube modeled by using VMD

damping η = 5 ps^{-1}. For adding chemical bonds between the segments in the nanoclusters we have used the topotools available in the VMD. A typical RNA nanotube is shown in the figure above, where 8 nanorings were used (we modeled currently up to 20). The tails used to connect the RNA nanorings are the double strand RNAs with the length of 22 nucleotides. The chemical bonds between the ring and the links are mediated through the phosphorous of the phosphate group in the ring and the oxygen in the sugar ring of the corresponding link or vice versa. Using NAMD, we optimized the chemical bonds added between different segments of the RNA nanoclusters. We analyzed the obtained results for the variation of the energy and temperature as a function of simulation time, as well as the number of ions around the RNA nanotube within the distance of 5 $\AA$ at different temperatures, the number of bonds per basepairs, the radius of gyration and the root mean square deviation (RMSD) at two temperatures, 310K and 510K. The results corresponding to variations of the parameters are similar to the results obtained for the other nanoclusters described in our earlier studies [10], [11]. The radial distribution functions have been calculated for our RNA nanotubes for phosphorous-phosphorous, phosphorous-water, phosphorous-sodium and phosphorous-chlorine. For example, from the P-P RDF analysis, we have concluded that there are three well-pronounced peaks around the same positions at it was observed for other nanoclusters studied in our earlier paper [11]. These peaks actually show the first, second and third nearest neighbours of the phosphorous atom respectively. Similar analyses were carried out for other RDFs (e.g., P-OH2, etc). The results for larger RNA nanotubes have shown that the nature of solvation and the ionic distribution during the molecular dynamics simulation is similar to those found in the case of the smaller nanotubes (e.g., we studied earlier 3- and 4- ring nanotubes). Finally, it is worthwhile mentioning that the phenomenon of self stabilization, first reported in [10], has also been observed in this case.

III. Conclusion

Complex RNA-based biological nanostructures have been analyzed with molecular dynamics simulations based on the developed coarse-graining procedures. Main characteristics, such as the root mean square deviation, radius of gyration, number of hydrogen bonds per basepair, ion accumulation around the tube, and the radial distribution functions, have been calculated. The results may be useful for the development of new drug delivery procedures, scaffolding, and other biomedical applications.

Acknowledgments

Authors are grateful to the NSERC and CRC Programs for their support, as well as to SHARCNET, and R. M. is thankful also to the Bizkaia Talent Grant under the Basque Government through the BERC 2014-2017 program.

References

[1] H. Cui, T. Muraoka, A.G. Cheetham, and S.I. Stupp, "Self-assembly of giant peptide nanobelts", Nano Lett., vol. 9, no. 3, 2009, pp. 945–951.

[2] W.W. Grabow and L. Jaeger, "RNA self-assembly and RNA nanotechnology", Acc. Chem. Res., vol. 47, no. 6, 2014, pp. 1871–1880.

[3] K.A. Afonin, W. Kasprzak, E. Bindewald, P.S. Puppala, A.R. Diehl, K.T. Hall, T.J. Kim, M.T. Zimmermann, R.L. Jernigan, L. Jaeger, and B.A. Shapiro, "Computational and experimental characterization of RNA cubic nanoscaffolds", Methods, vol. 67, no. 2, 2014, pp. 256–265.

[4] M. Anokhina, S. Bessonov, Z. Miao, E. Westhof, K. Hartmuth, and R. Lhrmann, "RNA structure analysis of human spliceosomes reveals a compact 3D arrangement of snRNAs at the catalytic core", The EMBO Journal, vol. 32, no. 21, 2013, pp. 2804–2818.

[5] E. Osada, Y. Suzuki, K. Hidaka, H. Ohno, H. Sugiyama, M. Endo, and H. Saito, "Engineering RNA-Protein Complexes with Different Shapes for Imaging and Therapeutic Applications", ACS Nano, vol. 8, no. 8, 2014, pp. 8130–8140.

[6] N.B. Leontis and E. Westhof, "Self-assembled RNA nanostructures", Science, vol. 345, 2014, pp. 732-733.

[7] M. Paliy, R. Melnik, and B.A. Shapiro, "Coarse-graining RNA nanostructures for molecular dynamics simulations", Phys. Biol., vol. 7, no. 3, 2010, 036001, doi: 10.1088/1478-3975/7/3/036001.

[8] N. Foloppe and A.D. MacKerell, Jr., "All-atom empirical force field for nucleic acids: 1) Parameter optimization based on small molecule and condensed phase macromolecular target data", Journal of Computational Chemistry, vol. 21(2), 2000, pp. 86–104.

[9] A.D. MacKerell and N.K. Banavali, "All-atom empirical force field for nucleic acids: 2) Application to molecular dynamics simulations of DNA and RNA in solution", Journal of Computational Chemistry, vol. 21(2), 2000, pp. 105–120.

[10] M. Paliy, R. Melnik, and B.A. Shapiro, "Molecular dynamics study of the RNA ring nanostructure: a phenomenon of self-stabilization", Phys. Biol., vol. 6(4), 2009, 046003, doi: 10.1088/1478-3975/6/4/046003.

[11] S.R. Badu, R. Melnik, M. Paliy, S. Prabhakar, A. Sebetci, and B.A. Shapiro, "Modeling of RNA nanotubes using molecular dynamics simulation", Eur. Biophys. J., vol. 43, no. 10-11, 2014, pp. 555–564.

Task Classifying Model based on Data Traits for High Efficiency in Cloud Infrastructure Modeling and Simulation Environment

Sunghwan Moon, Jaekwon Kim, Taeyoung Kim, Jeongseok Choi and Jongsik Lee
Department of Computer and Information Engineering
Inha University
Incheon, South Korea
email: shmoon@inhaian.net, jaekwonkorea@naver.com, silverwild@gmail.com,
jeongseokchoi.korea@gmail.com and jslee@inha.ac.kr

***Abstract*—We proposed task Classifying Model based on Data Traits (CMDT) and conducted experiments using this model. CMDT classifies tasks from user taking account of its own data traits. The classified tasks are allocated to each of the nodes which can process them as fast as possible. In conclusion, CMDT improves a service throughput which is the index of efficiency on cloud.**

Keywords-data traits; task classifying model; CMDT.

I. INTRODUCTION

Raising user-level has led to increase the demand for processing highly complex tasks. Service providers meet their demand using high performance computing which is composed of diverse computing resources on cloud service[1]. Clients and providers contract a Service Level Agreement (SLA) for high performance computing service. According to a SLA, a client pays a specific fee and a provider ensures parameters matching agreement[2]. A low expense for task processing is economic to the client. On the other hand, a high performance for service is profitable to the provider. In cloud Infrastructure as a Service (IaaS)[3], a SLA should be guaranteed by allocating physical computing resources efficiently.

Users request processing tasks which include the data. The data comes in a lot of types such as videos, images, audios, texts, logs, etc. The task including data has a dependency on nodes. The nodes are physical computing resources for processing tasks; their performances are closely related with the efficiency of whole system. If the system classifies the tasks regardless of its own data traits, most of tasks may be processed slowly in a long time[4]. This situation results in breach of a SLA.

In this paper, we propose a task Classifying Model based on Data Traits (CMDT) to increase a resource efficiency on cloud environment. CMDT classifies the requested task with its own data traits. The classified task is allocated to the node which has a dependency on the data. CMDT can increase the efficiency by reducing turnaround time at each node and also ensure a SLA degree for stakeholders.

The rest of this paper is structured as follows: In Section 2, we describe our key idea for task classifying in cloud environment. Section 3 explains the experiment settings and results. Finally, we conclude the paper in Section 4.

II. TASK CLASSIFYING METHOD BASED ON DATA TRAITS

We introduce CMDT in this section. CMDT classifies a task according to its own data traits and allocates the task to highly relevant physical resource. Figure 1 shows a designed architecture of the proposed CMDT.

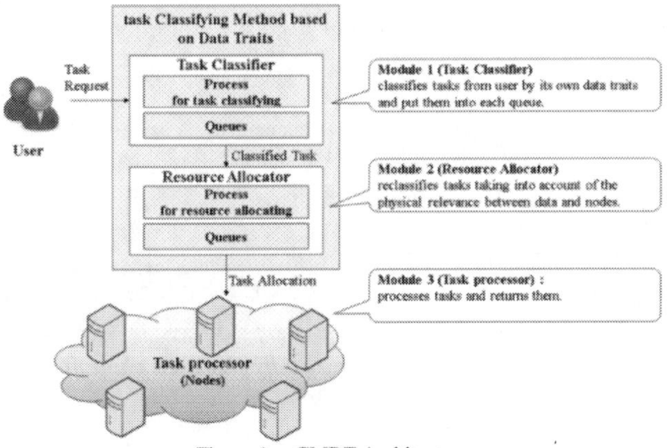

Figure 1. CMDT Architecture

CMDT consists of three modules for resource allocation. These modules take roles as follows. First, Task Classifier stores a requested task from user to each queue according to its own data traits. The data traits depend on the metadata of tasks. Second, Resource Allocator distributes tasks from Task classifiers to each queue according to their physical properties to process efficiently. Third, Task Processor receives tasks from Resource allocators and processes them.

These phases perform on each of the modules as follows:

A. *Task Classifier*

There are various requests in cloud services. Some tasks include complex applications which need high powered computing. Others are just based on web services. Task classifier stores every task with many purposes referring to its own data traits, three roles of which are as follows.

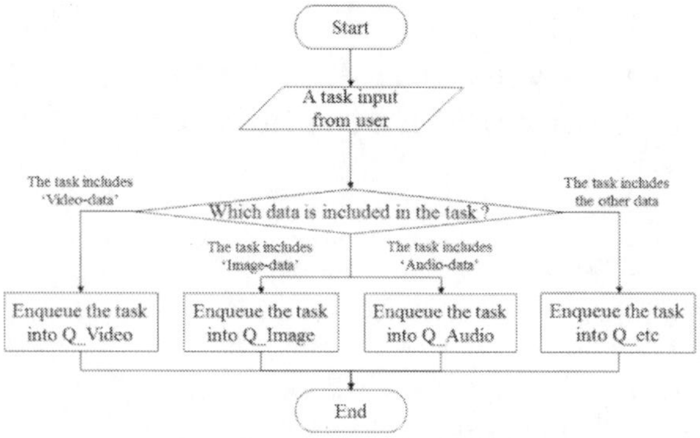

Figure 2. Process for Task Classification

1) As shown in Figure 2, Task classifier stores every task from users in each queue. The tasks is classified by its own data traits. Classified tasks are stored to pre-deployed queues. We use four queues for each trait. Table 1 shows detailed criteria for classification.

TABLE I. QUEUE IN TASK CLASSIFIER MODULE

Queue	Description	Data
Q_Video	Enqueue the User-Request Job including Video-Data	.avi, .mkv, .mp4, .wmv, etc.
Q_Image	Enqueue the User-Request Job including Image-Data	.jpg, .png, .gif, .tif , etc.
Q_Audio	Enqueue the User-Request Job including Audio-Data	.wav, .ogg, .mp3, .wma, etc.
Q_etc	Enqueue the User-Request Job including Other data	.txt, .log, etc.

2) Task classifier sends stored tasks when Resource allocator requests new task as shown in Figure 3. The request occurs when its queue size downs to less than a certain amount. This amount can be adjusted as high or low depending on the maximum length of the queue.

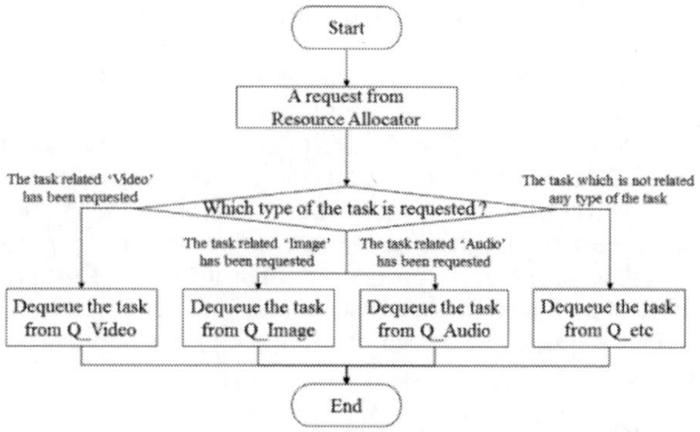

Figure 3. Process for Task Selection

3) Task classifier receives finished tasks from Task processor and returns them to the users. Users can request their tasks if uncompleted.

B. Resource Allocator

Resource allocator manages new tasks taking account of acceptable workloads and throughputs of the computing resource on cloud. Two roles of this module are as follows.

1) Resource allocator receives the task which was classified by its own data traits. These tasks are reclassified in view of the performance ratio of Task processor. A classification criteria is described in the following reasons.

- A task including videos and dynamic images:
  Most of tasks need real-time encoding, decoding and storing for large-scale data. Because of this, CPU utilization is extremely high for these kinds of tasks[5].
- A task including graphics and static images:
  Most of tasks need preview and storing images. RAM utilization is high for these kinds of tasks[6].
- A task including audios and voice speech:
  Most of tasks are streaming service and real-time transmission. These kinds of tasks need minimizing of the network delay[7].

Equation (1) presents a priority rule for allocation of each task to physical computing resource because of the reasons mentioned above.

$$\begin{aligned} &\textit{Video-Data} : Q\_CPU > Q\_NetResp. > Q\_RAM > Q\_All \\ &\textit{Image-Data} : Q\_RAM > Q\_CPU > Q\_NetResp. > Q\_All \\ &\textit{Audio-Data} : Q\_NetResp. > Q\_RAM \geq Q\_CPU > Q\_All \end{aligned} \quad (1)$$

The tasks are allocated into each queue in this module. Resource allocator has four specified queues as described in Table 2.

TABLE II. QUEUE IN RESOURCE ALLOCATOR MODULE

Queue	Description	Property
Q_CPU	Enqueue the Job to be assigned Node which has High-Level CPU	Job including Video-Data
Q_RAM	Enqueue the Job to be assigned Node which has High-Level RAM	Job including Image-Data
Q_NetResp.	Enqueue the Job to be assigned Node which has High-NetResponse	Job including Audio-Data
Q_All	Enqueue the Job to be assigned Node on Low-Load	Job including Other data

2) Resource allocator sends a task according to requests from Task processor. This module estimates how much time Task processors would finish the tasks because the processors have different performances. Resource Allocator operates for allocating the tasks as shown in Figure 4.

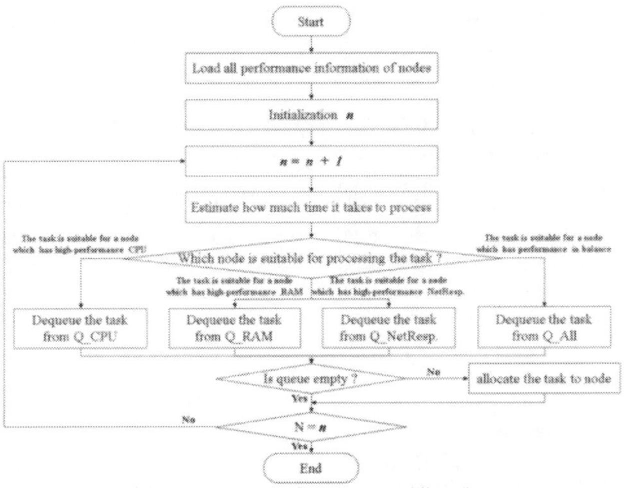

Figure 4. Process for Resource Allocation

C. Task Processor

Task processor, called 'node' on cloud, is a physical computing resource. This module processes the allocated tasks and sends a finished task to Task classifier. Task processor operates for processing the tasks as shown in Figure 5.

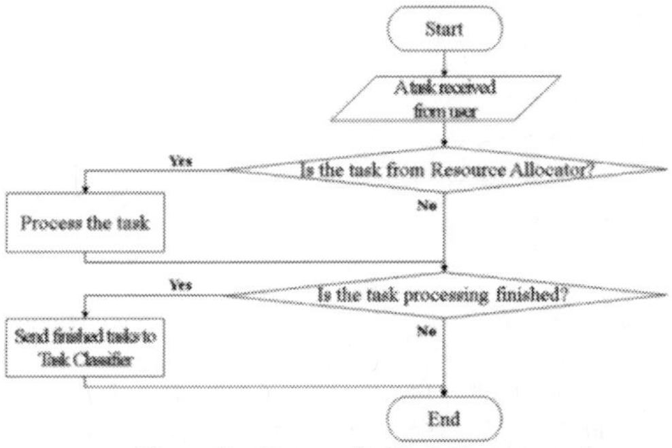

Figure 5. Process for Task Process

III. EXPERIMENT DESIGN AND RESULT

We designed the cloud environments in order to verify a performance of CMDT. This is a virtual distributed environment based on Discrete Event System Specification (DEVS) formalism[8]. We experiment and measure a throughput as a performance index.

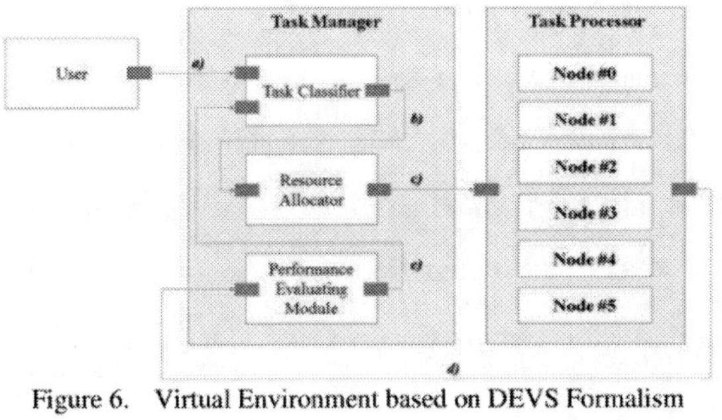

Figure 6. Virtual Environment based on DEVS Formalism

A. Experiment Scenario

In this paper, we build a virtual distributed environment for CMDT using DEVS formalism. This experiment is built to verify the performance of CMDT. Figure 6 shows a test bed and the description is as follows.

1) User generates and requests a task. It also receives a finished task. This module is a generator model.

2) Task Classifier has queues to classify and store a generated task according to its own data traits. This module is a queue model.

3) Resource Allocator reclassifies and allocates each task depending on the computing resource. This module is a queue-processor model.

4) Node processes a task and sends it to Task classifier. This module is a processor model. It is also called a node.

5) Performance Evaluator evaluates a throughput of the task processing. This module is a transducer model.

We define the performance of nodes for our experiment as shown in Table 3. The higher value it is, the better performance it has.

TABLE III. NODE PERFORMANCE

Node	CPU	RAM	NetResp.
Node #0	9	8	8
Node #1	8	9	8
Node #2	8	8	9
Node #3	9	8	6
Node #4	8	9	7
Node #5	7	8	9

In our experiment, we measure a service throughput with increasing 300 to 3000 for finished time. A service throughput is a performance index which is a total amount of services of each model during designated experiment time. This index is calculated by dividing the number of service response to a finished time as given by (2).

Throughput =
The Number of Service Response / Finished Time (2)

We select two algorithms for applying CMDT because CMDT is an adjunctive method which can be applied to all the task scheduling algorithms. First model is a round robin scheduling algorithm (RR)[9]. RR sequentially allocates tasks to all nodes. In other words, the task is allocated in the order of nodes. Finished tasks are also returned in the order. Second model is a minimum load first scheduling algorithm (MLFS)[10]. MLFS allocated tasks to the node which has the minimum number of task among all nodes on cloud. This model has the merit of load balancing. We applied CMDT to those algorithms.

We finally conduct two comparative experiments. One experiment is comparing RR with RR-CMDT. RR means an original round robin scheduling algorithm. RR-CMDT means an improved round robin scheduling algorithm which

CMDT has been applied to. The other experiment is comparing MLFS with MLFS-CMDT. MLFS means an original minimum load first scheduling algorithm. MLFC-CMDT means an improved minimum load first scheduling algorithm which CMDT has been applied to.

B. Experiment Results

We measure the service throughput in order to compare performance between four scheduling algorithms. They are RR, RR-CMDT, MLFS and MLFS-CMDT. In our experiments, the user requests the tasks which have random sizes. The sizes are based on the Amazon Access Samples Data Set [11], which is opened through UCI Machine Learning Repository. The purpose of these experiments are to verify that CMDT ensures a SLA by increasing the service throughput.

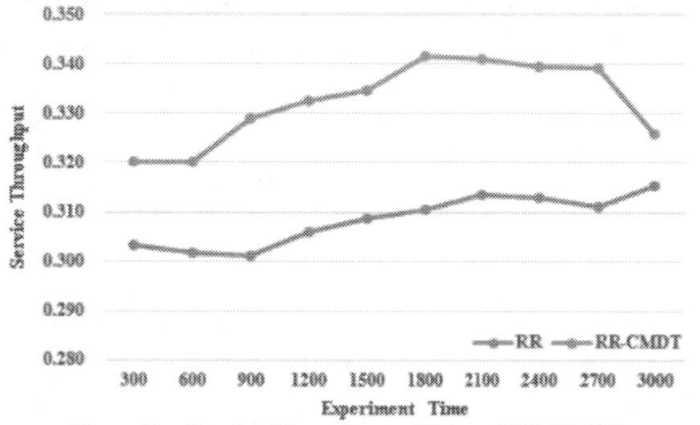

Figure 7. Service Throughput of RR and RR-CMDT

As shown in Figure 7, RR records 0.308 and RR-CMDT records 0.332. This resulting value is an average of the service throughput. It is seen that when CMDT has been applied, a service throughput increased.

RR allocates the requested tasks in order. This method not only classifies the tasks regardless of its own data traits, but it also does not consider the state of nodes. These cause an overload problem at each node. On the contrary, RR-CMDT classifies the tasks taking account of the physical relevance between data and nodes. This method enables the system to process more tasks using limited resources by reducing turnaround time at each node. Service providers can ensure a SLA more easily when the service throughput increases.

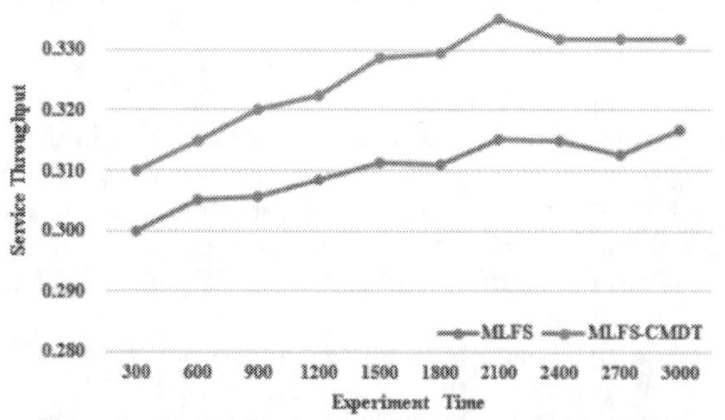

Figure 8. Service Throughput of MLFS and MLFS-CMDT

As shown in Figure 8, MLFS records 0.310 and MLFS-CMDT records 0.326. This resulting value is an average of the service throughput. We see that when CMDT has been applied, a service throughput increased.

MLFS allocates the requested task to the node which has the least number of tasks in its queue. This method balances the load of whole system, but it does not consider the physical relevance between data and nodes like RR. Meanwhile, MLFS-CMDT classifies the tasks taking account of the physical relevance between data and nodes like RR-CMDT. Finally, RR-CMDT and MLFS-CMDT improves the efficiency and ensure a SLA by managing the tasks taking account of the physical relevance between data and nodes.

IV. CONCLUSION

Cloud services provide a high performance computing which can process a large-scale data and complex tasks. There is an outstanding issue ensuring a SLA with the limited resources available on cloud.

We propose a task Classifying Model based on Data Traits (CMDT). This method increases the efficiency of computing resources by applying its own process to the usual scheduling algorithms. CMDT classifies tasks according to its own data traits and allocates tasks depending on relevance between data and physical properties of nodes. It ensures a SLA through improving the service throughput.

Future work will concentrate on applying CMDT to the other task scheduling algorithms. We think CMDT can be applied to more diverse algorithms.

ACKNOWLEDGMENT

This work was supported by Defense Acquisition Program Administration and Agency for Defense Development under the contract UD140022PD, Korea.

REFERENCES

[1] G. Kim, W. Lee, and C. Jeon, "Virtualization Technology for Cloud Computing", Journal of the Korea Society of Computer and Information, Vol. 18, No. 1, 2010, pp. 25-33.

[2] H. Kang, J. Koh, and Y. Kim, "A SLA-based VM Auto-Scaling Method in Hybrid Cloud Computing for Scientific Computational Applications", Journal of KIISE, System and Theory, Vol. 40, No. 6, 2013, pp. 266-273.

[3] J. K. Kim and J. S. Lee, "Fuzzy Logic-driven Virtual Machine Resource Evaluation Method for Cloud Provisioning Service", Journal of the Korea Society for Simulation, Vol. 22, No. 1, 2013, pp. 77-86.

[4] B. S. Kim, S. D. Lee, T. G. Kwon, and S. H. Lee, "Design and Implementation of the Unformatted Data Manager for Multimedia Storage System", Journal of KIISE, Vol. 20, No. 2, 1993, pp. 191-194.

[5] S. J. Lee, E. J. Lee, S. W. Hong, H. N. Choi, and Y. W. Chung, "Secure and Energy-Efficient MPEG Encoding using Multicore Platforms", Journal of the Korea Institute of Information Security and Cryptology, Vol. 20, No. 3, 2010, pp. 113-120.

[6] H. S. Oh, "Tiled Image Compression Method to Reduce the Amount of Memory Needed for Image Processing in Mobile Devices", Journal of Korea Game Society, Vol. 13, No. 6, 2013, pp. 35-42.

[7] B. J. Kim, "Service Quality Criteria for Voice Services over a WiBro Network", The Journal of the Korea Institute of

Electronic Communication Sciences, Vol. 6, No. 6, 2011, pp. 823-829.

[8] Bernard P. Zeigler, H. Praehofer, and T. G. Kim (2000), "Theory of Modeling and Simulation: Integrating Discrete Event and Continuous Complex Dynamic Systems", Academic Press, 2000, pp. 76-96.

[9] S. Pooja and P. Mishra, "Analysis of variants in Round Robin Algorithms for load balancing in Cloud Computing", International Journal of Computer Science and Information Technologies, Vol. 4, No. 3, 2013, pp. 416-419.

[10] T. Janaszka, D. Bursztynowski, and M. Dzida, "On popularity-based load balancing in content networks", Teletraffic Congress (ITC 24), 24th International. IEEE, 2012, pp. 1-8.

[11] Amazon Access Samples Data Set. [Online]. Available from: http://archive.ics.uci.edu/ml/datasets/Amazon+Access+Sampl es
2015.12.17

Research on Optimal Control of Large File Access upon VPDN

Jing Feng, Kunpeng Jing,Yang Wu
Institute of Meteorology and Oceanography
PLA University of Science and Technology
Nanjing, China
e-mail:jfeng@seu.edu.cn

Xiaoxing Yu
Department of Information and Networks
TELECOM ParisTech (ENST)
Paris, France
e-mail:yu@telecom-paristech.fr

Abstract—**Facing the optimal problem of meteorological large data files access upon Virtual Private Dial-up Networks (VPDN), transport back of reliable radar data and optimize retrieval of single-server is studied. Focusing on the requirements and radar data application, such as images split joint of multiple weather radars, the strategies of data division and storage are proposed, and an evaluation model named Quality of Experience based on Reliability and Time (QoE-RT) is presented. Consequently, Adaptive File Access Control (AFAC) algorithm is designed and implement, which is consisted of reliable file transmission, rapid file retrieval, file size adjustment and service quality evaluation. The performance is verified by experiments of the file retrieval and transmission in actual environment, which shows that the file access time is decreased by 20%, transport success rate is more than 95%, and the QoE is significantly improved.**

Keywords-optimal cotrol; file access; VPDN; QoE.

I. Introduction

In the field of meteorological and hydrological information, there are hundred gigabytes (GB) of data collected by satellite, ground observation stations, radar and numerical weather forecasting every day. The size of individual files might be hundreds of megabytes (MB); some raw satellite imagery data is up to a few GB. On the one hand, these data needs to transmit back from the detection/ observation points to the data center, and on the other hand professional users also need to get the national or global meteorological data. For motorized stations and mobile users, Virtual Private Dial-up Networks (VPDN), a mixed network of solid and mobile communication by means of Layer 2 Tunneling Protocol (L2TP) is often used. For such large files like radar mosaic data, satellite images and numerical forecast products, using lossless compression method, even if the compression ratio is 50%, the data size is still around dozens of megabytes, so it is difficult to solve the reliable transmission problems upon VPDN radically. It is necessary to find a new solution, which can conduce to the efficient querying and reliable file transfer.

Although there are many mainstream network storage technologies in large data centers, including Direct Attached Storage (DAS), Storage Area Network (SAN) and Network Attached Storage (NAS), etc.[1], the low-end server clusters are efficient solutions in primary sub-center concerned with space, funds and other conditions. When the network performance and server hardware performance cannot change, the server storage strategy and the setting of maximum file block not only are important factors which affect the Quality of Experience (QoE) of users, but also can be set by user and configurate parameters adaptively with control program. Therefore, how to provide the management efficiency of stand-alone storage is significant for improving server access and cluster configuration.

In general, the optimal control of large file access upon VPDN is rarely mentioned, and how to decide the transmission block size of large file is not explored yet. For example, the user cannot control the partition of file size in FTP, which is not easy to guarantee performance [2]. According to the business requirements, the characteristics of the channel and the network environment, the optimization method is studied for large file transfer by dividing big files into smaller block size.

Analyzing the classic New Technology File System (NTFS), the relationship between access efficiency of its file and directory structure was quantitatively analyzed to obtain the optimal results. File access time and transmission success rate were both the metrics of Quality of Experience based on Reliability and Time (QoE-RT) referring to psychology. Facing the transmission of weather radar data, an Adaptive File Access Control algorithm (AFAC) was developed with the optimal data block segmentation strategy.

The rest of the paper is organized as follows. The background and motivation is described in Section II; the strategies for big file optimal transport and storage are analyzed in Section III considering the influence of NTFS file directory structure and file size; in Section IV, AFAC algorithm is presented and evaluated by QoE-RT. Finally, the conclusion and future work are given in Section V.

II. Background and Motivation

In remote areas with poor communication of terrestrial broadband, deploying meteorological equipment such as automatic weather stations, motorized radar, using wireless network to transmit data back is a convenient and economical way. Although the third-generation (3G) network is able to meet the basic requirements of small quantities of data transmission, it cannot guarantee the weather radar data (dozens or hundreds of megabytes) reliable transmission. The optimal control mechanisms of data transmission and access need to be studied between sub-center and measurement station to improve service abilities in limited condition.

A. *VPDN–based Solid and Mobile Mixed Network*

Motorized radar usually is deployed on demand with around 100KM detection range. Sometimes multiple radars compose an observation network, which requires each radar data must be transmitted to the data center within the stipulated time to split joint images. For this kind of field mobile environments, VPDN is a cost-effective way of transport, which combines solid lease line and public mobile network with designated access point, but data transmission is instability in wireless section.

Adopting tunnel technique, the user data is encapsulated by special layer-2 protocol and transported in VPDN [3]. For example, China Telecom employs L2TP to establish VPDN, and L2TP use the Point to Point Protocol (PPP) link layer protocol unit to load data. It allows the both connection endpoint of the Layer-2 link protocol and PPP serving at different devices via a packet-switched network, e.g., IP network, which extends the PPP model and enables PPP sessions to cross a frame relay network or the Internet [4]. The case of networking is shown in Figure 1.

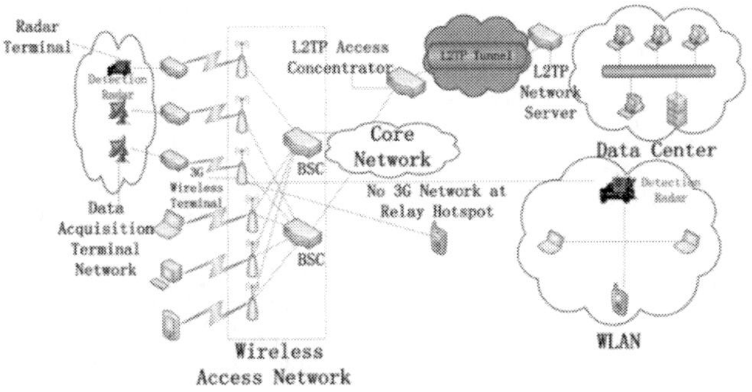

Figure 1. The case of VPDN topology with L2TP

After testing, a phenomenon was found: when the file size exceeds a certain threshold, the transmission failure rate greatly increased upon VPDN. Therefore, autonomous adjustment the size of the data block is the key to improve success transmission rate of big file.

B. *Key Optimal Issues for Retrieval in Single-Server*

In the context of this paper, the radar data is uploaded to the nearest data center/sub-centers, and is stored on the local servers. As valuable data, it will be archived and shared momentarily with the two service ways: Push and Pall. In practical work, we found that when the number of files on the server is more than ten thousand, query retrieval time has increased significantly. Meanwhile, the transport is also very difficult and often fails when the file size is over 1GB upon FTP, even in the LAN environment.

The efficiency of mobile terminals access data center and download big files via VPDN, will directly affect the user experience. If the reading time is denoted by T_s, it can be expressed in (1).

$$T_s = T_1 + T_2 + T_3 \tag{1}$$

T_1 is locating time of root directory that is related with the file system itself; T_2 is the time of traversing the index tree that is concerned with structure of the tree; T_3 concerns with the time of control and disk access related to hardware performance. Under the same file system and hardware, T_1 and T_3 are fixed basically, so T_2 is the only changeable factor that impacts on access efficiency.

III. ACCESS CONTROL ALGORITHM AND OPTIMAL STRATEGIES OF BIG FILE

In this section, the influence factors are analyzed quantitatively from network behavior characteristics and the server's file system.

A. *Ralationship betwween File Transport Success Rate and Data Size upon VPDN*

Investigating VPDN fundamental network protocol, L2TP protocol consists of two components: control messages and data messages. Control messages establish and maintain the tunnel and connection session, and reliable transport is achieved by using flow control and congestion control. Data messages are encapsulated as the UDP packet in unreliable transmission over public networks.

L2TP packet encapsulation structure is shown in Figure 2.

IP header (Public network)	UDP header	L2TP header	PPP header	IP header (Private network)	Data

Figure 2. L2TP PDU format

From the analysis of L2TP, it is known that the user data will be regarded as a transparent load of UDP encapsulated even if it adopts TCP-based application layer protocols (e.g., FTP) over Internet, so once packet loss, the TCP retransmission message will be treated as unreliable transport. PPP sends data units by the order, and has higher loss rate while the data block is too large or the transport rate is too fast. Once the packet loss rate rises, it will lead to retransmission mechanism of TCP failed to achieve. The default number of TCP retransmissions is three, so if there is no acknowledgment message coming back, the TCP connection will be ended after three times of retransmission,

In order to successfully transport big files, the most direct way is to split big files into small pieces. However, dividing and merging the file will increase overhead, so we must find out the maximum size of the file block and have higher transport success rate. In the actual environment, 2G, 3G and 4G networks are mixed, China telecom 3G mobile devices were used in experiment scenario considering most area covered by 2G and 3G networks. China Telecom uses CDMA2000 standard, compatible with GSM, and the basic rate as shown in Table I.

TABLE I. CHINA TELECOM RATE OF 2G AND 3G

Standard	**2G**		**3G**
Technique	***GSM***	***CDMA2000***	***CDMA2000***
Down rate	236 kbps	153 kbps	3.1 Mbps
Up rate	118 kbps	153 kbps	1.8 Mbps

A set of data transport experiments were taken dividing the typical data file of C-band Doppler weather radar (110MB) into different size. The sending end accesses VPDN router (HUAWEI SRG1200) through WLAN router (HUAWEI EC177, supports CDMA2000 2G and 3G), and the VPDN router is located in our lab as a sub-center, which is linked China telecom via the leased line. For different length of data block (e.g., from 1MB, 2MB increase to 21M.) at different signal strength environments. Using FTP command, we tested the success rate by means of Wireshark which is a capture toolkit. The statistic results are shown in Figure.3.

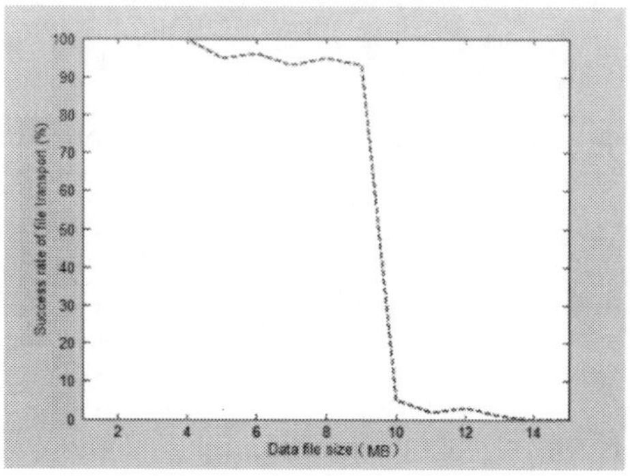

Figure 3. Success rate of different data size upon VPDN

The experimental results indicate that when the data block is less than 4MB, success rate of transport is 100%, and the success rate is more than 90% while the data block is between 4MB and 10MB. Especially, the success rate is less than 3% once the data block exceeds 10MB.

B. *Relationship between NTFS File Directory structure and Query Efficiency*

As described in Section 2-B, user-defined directory structure plays an important role in efficiency of local query access, and there is a large space-optimized for widely used working group server. Mainstream local file systems include NTFS, File Allocation Table (FAT) and Extended File System (EXT). Their main feature is shown in Table II. NTFS file system has maximum data upper limit, minimum index complexity, and is currently the most widely used local file storage system as well.

TABLE II. COMPARISON OF TYPICAL FILE SYSTEMS

Property	NTFS	FAT	EXT2
Cluster size	0.5KB-4KB	4KB-16KB	4KB
Max block	2TB	4GB	2GB
Max partition	2TB	128GB	4TB
Index structure	B+tree	Chained	Chained
complexity	O(logN)	O(N)	O(N)
OS	Windows	DOS, Win 95	Linux

NTFS adopts B+ tree as index structure, and all data structures including directory are considered as file and indexed in the form of database [5]. When the file number is too large, it is necessary to establish multi-level indexing mechanism in order to reduce operation of read blocks and accelerate the speed of queries. In NTFS partition, partition information is stored in the different property files, where the most important file is Master File Table (MFT). It is core file of NTFS partition, which stores and identifies the basic information of all files. It consists of metadata about files, including the creating time, location, length, file name with a fixed length of 1KB.

For the small files and directories of less than 1KB, their content will be stored in MFT. Otherwise, only the location information will be saved in MFT [6]. In the process of reading big files, the file system will frequently visit MFT, so MFT has crucial impact on the access performance of the operating system.

The relationship between files and folders in NTFS is established through the index. If files belong to a same folder, their indexes are record by the property table of the folder's father in MFT. When the number of files within a folder is larger than a certain limit, the file index of the folder forms a B+ tree [7], and the root of the B+ tree is still stored in MFT record of the father directory. The depth of the tree has a crucial impact on the search efficiency, the greater the number of tree's level, the longer the traversal time. The file system has different directory tree structure following the number of files, and then affects the efficiency of retrieval.

For instance, if a big directory tree with three-level B+ tree is completely full according to limit of order, every B+ tree in first level can store 30 entries of index; the one in second level can store 900 entries; the one in third level can store 27930 entries [8]. When the index entries are more than 27,930, it will generate the fourth level's B+ tree. Flat tree structure can achieve the best efficiency of retrieval, so a reasonable directory structure will enable index tree to be balanced and enhance the reading efficiency.

Having retrieval experiments with 10,000 files and 100,000 files respectively, on behalf of the three-level and four-level B+ tree structure, it covers the general application of large directory. By tracking the experimental data and contrasting the results, the best number region of directory and file was estimated. The sample files (about 800KB in size) were put in the N directories averagely, recording its search time. Where, the value of N is set as follows: 5, 10, 20, 50, 100, 200, 500, 1000.The trends of retrieval efficiency are shown in Figure 4.

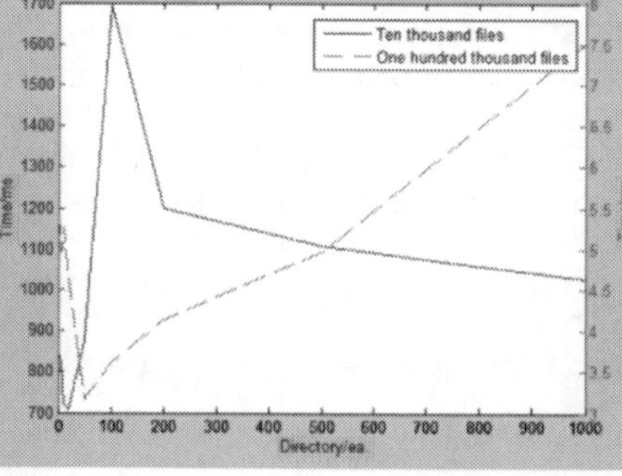

Figure 4. Comparison of file retrieval efficiency

Experiment results say that there is minimum retrieval time for 10,000 files with 20 directories, and for 100,000 files with 50 directories. At this point the B+ tree is balance, and the searching time is least for retrieval the leaf nodes.

C. *Adaptive File Access Control Algorithm*

Considering the reliable transmission of big files upon VPDN and retrieve optimization in single-server, the algorithm for AFAC is designed, which consists of four parts such as application configuration, network recognition, quality control and data transmission, and its components are shown in Figure.5.

1) User applications: provide system parameter setting interface, making it can be dynamically extended;

2) Network recognition: identify network status, or allow user settings, choose modes from CDMA, EVDO, etc.;

3) Quality control: complete data encapsulation and decapsulation, integrity verification and so on;

4) Data transmission: send and receive the data block using TCP mode, adjust file directory and file block size.

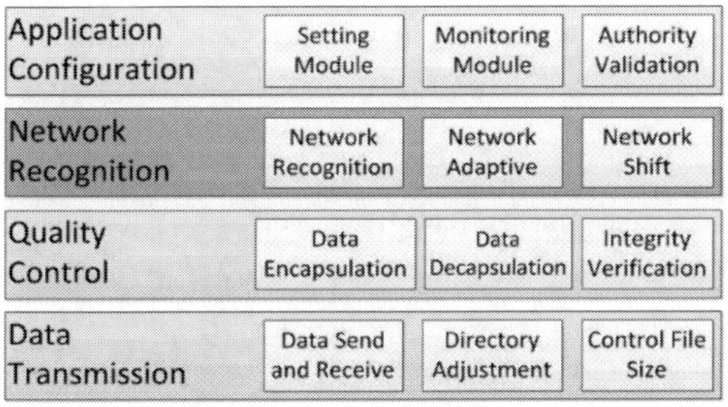

Figure 5. AFAC components

According to the experimental results in Section 3.2, set the initial number of directory is 20, when number of files is more than 10,000, each appending 1000 files with an additional directory. Based on wireless network technique, set the maximum size of the data threshold (the default value is 10240KB), sending data block by using dividing strategy when the threshold of file size is exceeded and merging them at receiving end. For smaller data files, after jointing them to a bigger file within the threshold, send it and decapsulate respectively at the sending and receiving end. Using AFAC for the transport of radar files, make sure the integrity of the layer-scan documents in order to effectively utilize the successful transmission of data blocks.

For example, the volume-scan file of X-band Doppler weather radar is around 9MB including 6 layer-scanned documents, and the volume-scan file of C-band Doppler weather radar is around 110MB including 14 layer-scanned documents. Thus, for X-band radar data, when the network state is good enough, it is transmitted without dividing, but for the C-band radar data, it is almost impossible to successfully complete the data transport without dividing.

Normally, a group of radar data is generated every six minutes, which consists of base data, images and products, occupying total hard disk space approximately 18.11MB (X-band radar). If the radar is on all day, it performs about 260 scans and generates approximately 4.65GB data. In order to optimize storage, a layer-scanned data can be stored as a file in favor of adjusting and optimizing the transport data block.

Definition 1: The data size of guaranteed delivery success rate p is denoted M_p, and the data block size of guaranteed delivery success rate 100% is denoted M_c. In the same network conditions, there is common sense: $M_p > M_c$.

In order to describe the part pseudo code of AFAC accurately, several functions and processes are given as follows:

divide_it(F, N):divide the file F into the size of N data block.
send_it(F):send the file F, and return "0" means fault.
traversal_it(D, N): look for file that size smaller than N in the directory D, and return "0" means no such file otherwise the file names.
merge_it(L,F): merge multiple files L into F.

Assuming the size of file F is x, the part pseudo code of AFAC for data sending module are listed as follows.

```
Data sending (F, x, Mp, Mc)
While (x!=0){
1 if x< Mc then {S=0;goto 5;} // merge the smaller files
2   else if x< Mp then {
        S= send_it(F);
        if S=0 goto 4; //fault, divide F into smaller block
          else x=0; }
  end}
3       else // divide F following Mp
         { F1=divide_it(F, Mp);
           S= send_it(F1);
           if S=0 goto 4;
           else { F=F-F1; x=x-Mp;}
  end}
4       F2=divide_it(F, Mc); // divide F following Mc
         S= send_it(F2);
         if S=0 goto 1;// fault, resend
          else { F=F-F2; x=x- Mc; }
  end}
5 L=traversal_it(D, Mc);
  If L=0 then {
     while( S=0) {S= send_it(F);}// fault, resend
     x=0; end }
   else { merge_it(L,F); goto 1}
  end}
```

Figure 6. The part pseudo code of AFAC

IV. PERFORMANCE EVALUATION BASED QOE-RT

Considering the application background of real-time access to weather radar file, the experience to network Quality of Service (QoS) was investigated, hoping to obtain a comprehensive evaluation for above research results.

A. *QoE Model of File Transport upon VPDN*

There are three main QoE evaluation methods such as statistics [9], artificial intelligence [10] and psychology [11]. The first two of them are suitable for multi-index evaluation system, and need certain expert knowledge. The psychology-based on evaluation method refers to the laws of psychology, and does not need complex training and computing. It can intuitively give the accurate QoE function model related with some QoS parameters. Although it cannot solve the problem affected by multiple factors, it has better effective in some applications.

The complete raw data of weather radar must be transported to information center, and the secondary products can be made. Therefore, the base data has to reach the data center with 6 minutes and no error for the real-time application, e.g., now-casting. For images split joint, the radar data detected by several radars must arrive in the data center within 15 minutes synchronously. In this application mode, the timeliness and correctness are two indicators that are cared by user, and can be used to establish the corresponding evaluation model.

So, the QoE model based on Reliability and Time (QoE-RT) was proposed referencing the psychological principle based on the relative waiting time and reliability factors. Classic Weber - Fechner law is applicative to large-scale range of irritation in middle intensity, which reflecting the relationship between QoE (i.e., the amount of feeling) and physical (e.g., waiting time) is not a simple linear growth: the longer the waiting time, the higher degree of tolerance. This relationship is shown in (2).

$$dp = k\frac{ds}{s} \tag{2}$$

Where dp presents the change of feeling, s indicates the amount of physical stimulus, $\frac{ds}{s}$ expresses the relative change of the physical stimulus, k is a proportion coefficient.

However, in above application scenario, having a smaller waiting time scale and greater irritation, the user experience of time is opposite to Weber - Fechner law: the longer the waiting period, the lower the degree of tolerance.

Definition 2: Let $l = \frac{d}{D}$ represents the relative waiting value, where d denotes the actual data transport time, and D is time-out limit of data transport. QoE-RT is defined in (3).

$$s = (1-\alpha)(1-k) + \alpha l, 0 \le \alpha \le 1, 0 \le k \le 1 \tag{3}$$

Where, s is evaluation scores of QoE-RT, the lower the score, the better the QoE; α is the adjustment coefficient for adjusting the weights that concerns with the contribution of transport success rate and transport time to evaluation score; k is the reliability factor that expresses transport success rate changing with the alteration of the file length.

Fitting the transport success rate curve shown in Figure 3, the function about reliability factor k was obtained in (4), $k = f(m)$, where, m is the file size (unit: MB).

$$f(m) = \begin{cases} 1, m < 4 \\ \beta m + \gamma, 4 \le m < 10 \\ \beta m + \gamma, 10 \le m < 14 \\ 0, m \ge 14 \end{cases} \tag{4}$$

$$\beta = \begin{cases} -0.01, 4 \le m < 10 \\ -0.125, 10 \le m < 14 \end{cases} \qquad \gamma = \begin{cases} 1.04, 4 \le m < 10 \\ 1.75, 10 \le m < 14 \end{cases}$$

According to the experiment data, the maximum waiting time for successfully transport file was the time to transmit 14MB file, which is computed by the expectations as $E(D) = 80$.

According to the result of Figure 3, the file size is related to the success rate of file transport, therefore it impacts on different QoE levels. Analyzing the experimental data by setting four intervals the influence factors α were concluded in (5).

$$\alpha = \begin{cases} 1, m < 4 \\ 0.8, 4 \le m < 10 \\ 0.2, 10 \le m < 14 \\ 0, m \ge 14 \end{cases} \tag{5}$$

In order to enable the user to intuitively get the results of the evaluation, S scores of QoE-RT were graded as five ranks and shown in Table III.

TABLE III. QoE SCORE MAPPING

S	QoE
(0,0.2]	excellent
(0.2,0.4]	good
(0.4,0.6]	medium
(0.6,0.8]	average
(0.8,1)	inferior

B. *Performance Evaluation*

In order to evaluate the performance of AFAC algorithm, two methods were compared for single file transport and multiple files transport with QoE-RT score as follows:

1) Using conventional FTP, files are stored in a directory without any control;

2) Using AFAC algorithm, set the initial directory number as 20.

We chose the 10,000 files with different size: 2MB, 6MB, 12MB, 16MB respectively and took 10 tests, and calculated the average data obtained. The result is shown in Figure 7.

For multiple files transport, the experiment scenario is same as the single file transport, and the result is shown in Figure 8.

Contrasting the Table III, it is found that for the same size file, the score of QoE-RT is similar no matter transmitting single file or multiple files. Whereas compared with FTP, AFAC algorithm has a higher level of QoE, it is shown in Figure 9.

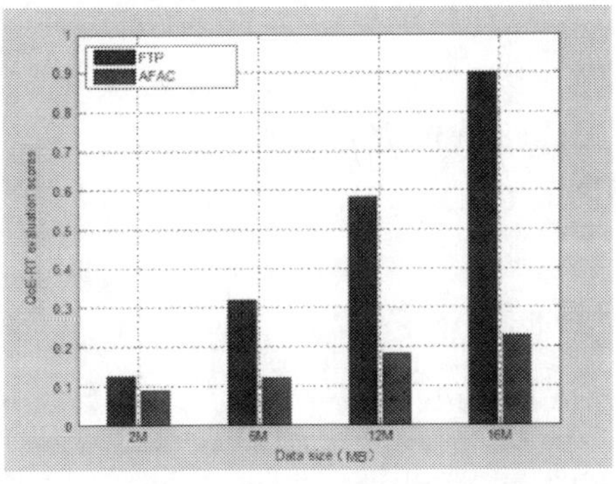

Figure 7. The QoE-RT score of single file access

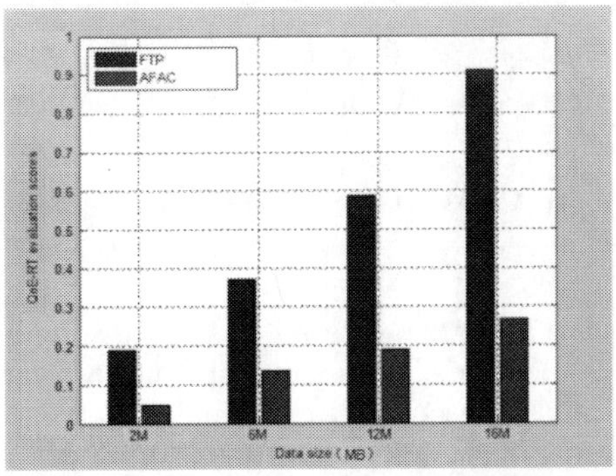

Figure 8. The QoE-RT score of multiple file access

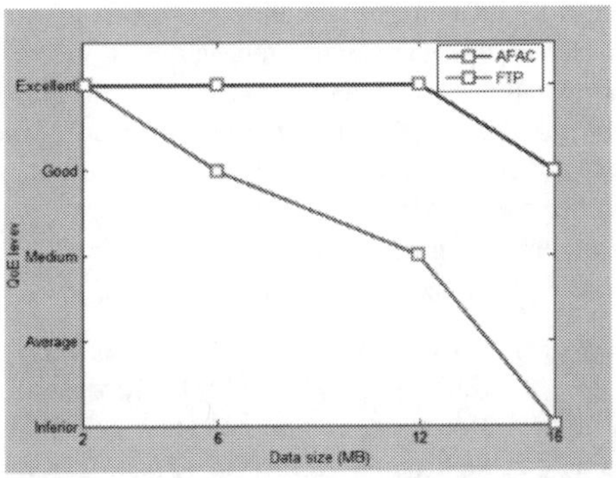

Figure 9. Comparison of both QoE scores FTP and AFAC

V. CONCLUSION AND FUTURE WORK

Facing the efficient real-time transportation and access of meteorological big file in VPDN and NTFS conditions, the optimal control strategy was researched. The AFAC algorithm was put forward based on the initiative dividing big file into several suitable data block and controlling the number of directories and files according to the threshold values shown by experiment results. Referencing psychology QoE evaluation methods, QoE-RT model was established, and made the comparison of performance between AFAC and conventional FTP. The experiment results indicated that AFAC has a better user experience for the condition of weak real-time in weather radar data transport.

In future work, it needs to consider the system overhead of file encapsulation and decapsulation for different network systems, and integrate the algorithm with autonomous network management.

ACKNOWLEDGMENT

The authors thank to the financial support by Nature Fund of Science of China with grant No. 61371119.

REFERENCES

[1] L. Wang, "Mass information resource storage and sharing technology research," Information System Engineering, 2011, pp. 129-131, doi:10.3969/j.issn.1001-2362.2011.11.068 (in Chinese).

[2] Z. Luo, F. Liu, and Y. Xie, "User-Perceived FTP Service QoS Parameters and Measurement" IEEE International Conference on Network Infrastructure and Digital Content, 2009, pp. 69-73, doi: 10.1109/ICNIDC.2009.5360792.

[3] Y. Xu, "Design and Implementation of 3G-based Wireless VPDN Business Network," Environmental Monitoring and Forewarning, 2010, pp. 27-30, doi:10.3969/j.issn.1674-6732.2010.05.009 (in Chinese).

[4] V. Rawat, R.Tio, S. Nanji, and R. Verma, Layer Two Tunneling Protocol. RFC 3070, February 2001. Standards Trackpp.3931L2TPv3,3070,doi:http://dx.doi.org/10.17487/RFC3070.

[5] J. Liang and Y. Zhang, "The main data structure of NTFS file System," Computer Engineering and Design, 2003,pp.116-118,doi:10.3321/j.issn:1002-8331.2003.08.039 (in Chinese).

[6] L. Wang and J. Ju, "Analysis of NTFS file system structure,"Computer Engineering and Design,2006,pp.418-419,doi:10.3969/j.issn.1000-7024.2006.03.019(in Chinese).

[7] Z. Lu and X. Chen, "The optimization of B+ tree index file structure," Computer Engineering and Design, 2000,pp.40-44,doi:10.3969/j.issn.1000-7024.2000.03.008(in Chinese).

[8] W. Wu, K. Liu, D. Jiang, Q. Su, and Z. Chen, "Dynamic analysis of NTFS B+tree big directory structure," Computer Engineering and Design, 2013, pp. 1376-1382, doi:10.3969/j.issn.1000-7024.2013.04.046(in Chinese).

[9] R. Huang and Y. Guan, "Data Statistics Analysis," Beijing:Higher Education Press, 2010(in Chinese).

[10] A. Altuzarra, JM. Moreno-Jiménez, and M. Salvador, "A Bayesian priorization procedure for AHP-group decision making," European Journal of Operational Research, 2007, pp. 367–382,doi:10.1016/j.ejor.2006.07.025.

[11] P. Reichl, S. Egger, R. Schatz, and A. D'Alconzo, "The Logarithmic Nature of QoE and the Role of the Weber-Fechner Law in QoE Assessment," 2010 IEEE International Conference on Communications, ISSN: 1550-3607, ISBN: 978-1-4244-6402-9 doi:10.1109/ICC.2010.5501894.

Fuzzy Weight Representation for Double Inner Dependence Structure in 4 Levels AHP

Shin-ichi Ohnishi , Takahiro Yamanoi
Faculty of Engineering
Hokkai-Gakuen University
Sapporo, Japan
email: {ohnishi, yamanoi}@hgu.jp

Abstract - **The inner dependence Analytic Hierarchy Process (AHP) is useful for the cases in which criteria or/and alternatives are not independent enough and related to modeling and optimization. However, using the original AHP or inner dependence AHP may cause results that cannot have enough reliability because of the inconsistency of the comparison matrix as data. In such cases, fuzzy representation for weighting criteria or/and alternatives using results from sensitivity analysis is useful. In this research, we first define fuzzy local weights of criteria and alternatives. Moreover, via fuzzy sets, overall weights for double inner dependence structure AHP in 4 levels are obtained.**

Keywords - AHP; fuzzy sets; sensitivity analysis.

I. INTRODUCTION

The Analytic Hierarchy Process (AHP) proposed by T.L. Saaty in 1977 [1] is widely used in decision making, because it reflects humans feelings naturally. A normal AHP assumes independence among criteria and alternatives, although it is difficult to choose enough independent elements. The inner dependence method AHP [2] is used to solve this problem even for criteria or alternatives having dependence.

On the other hand, the comparison data matrix may not have enough consistency when AHP is applied because, for instance, a problem may contain too many criteria or alternatives for decision making. It means that answers from decision-makers, i.e., components of the matrix, do not have enough reliability. They may be too ambiguous or too fuzzy [3][5]. To avoid this problem, we usually have to revise again, but it takes a lot of time and costs.

Then, we consider that weights should also have ambiguity or fuzziness. Therefore, it is necessary to represent these weights using fuzzy sets. In our research, we first applied sensitivity analysis to normal AHP to analyze how much the components of a pairwise comparison matrix influence the weight or consistency of a matrix, and proposed new fuzzy weight representation for criteria and alternatives in normal AHP. Then, a representation of criteria weights for inner dependence AHP was proposed using L-R fuzzy numbers [4]. In the next step, we started to deal with double inner dependence structure [6] and their fuzzy weight.

We now consider fuzziness for double inner dependence [7][8] (among actors and criteria, respectively) when a comparison matrix among elements does not have enough consistency in 4 levels problem (object, actors, criteria and alternatives).

In Sections 2 and 3, we introduce the inner dependence AHP, consistency index, and sensitivity analyses for AHP. Then, in Section 4, we define fuzzy weights for double inner dependence structure, and Section 5 is a summary.

II. CONSISTENCY AND INNER DEPENDENCE

A. *Process of Normal AHP*

(Process 1) Representation of structure by a hierarchy. The problem under consideration can be represented in a hierarchical structure. At the middle levels, there are multiple criteria. Alternative elements are put at the lowest level of the hierarchy.

(Process 2) Paired comparison between elements at each level. A pairwise comparison matrix A is created from a decision maker's answers. Let n be the number of elements at a certain level, the upper triangular components of the matrix a_{ij} ($i< j = 1,\dots,n$) are 9, 8, .. , 2, 1, 1/2, ..., or 1/9. These denote intensities of importance from element i to j. The lower triangular components a_{ji} are described with reciprocal numbers, for diagonal elements, let $a_{ii} = 1$.

(Process 3) Calculations of weight at each level. The weights of the elements, which represent grades of importance among each element, are calculated from the pairwise comparison matrix. The eigenvector that corresponds to a positive eigenvalue of the matrix is used in calculations throughout in the paper.

(Process 4) Priority of an alternative by a composition of weights. With repetition of composition of weights, the overall weights of the alternative, which are the priorities of the alternatives with respect to the overall objective, are finally found.

B. *Consistency*

Since components of the comparison matrix are obtained by comparisons between two elements, coherent consistency is not guaranteed. In AHP, the consistency of the comparison matrix A is measured by the following consistency index (C.I.)

$$\text{C.I.} = \frac{\lambda_A - n}{n-1}, \quad (1)$$

where n is the order of comparison matrix A, and λ_A is its maximum eigenvalue (Frobenius root).

If the value of C.I. becomes smaller, then the degree of consistency becomes higher, and vice versa. The comparison matrix is consistent if the following holds.

$$\text{C.I.} \leq 0.1 \quad (2)$$

C. Inner Dependence Structure

The normal AHP ordinarily assumes independence among criteria and alternatives, although it is difficult to choose enough independent elements. The dependency means some kind of interaction among the elements. Inner dependence AHP [2] is used to solve this type of problem even for criteria or alternatives having dependence.

In the method, using a dependency matrix $F=\{ f_{ij} \}$, we can calculate modified weights $\boldsymbol{w}^{(n)}$ as follows,

$$\boldsymbol{w}^{(n)}=F\boldsymbol{w} \quad (3)$$

where $\boldsymbol{w}$ represents weights from independent criteria or alternatives, i.e., normal weights of normal AHP and dependency matrix F is consist of eigenvectors of influence matrices showing dependency among criteria or alternatives.

If there is dependence in both lower levels, i.e., not only among criteria but also among alternatives, we call such kind of structure "double inner dependence". In the double inner dependence structure, we have to calculate modified weights of criteria and alternatives, $\boldsymbol{w}^{(n)}$ and $\boldsymbol{u}_i^{(n)}$. Then we composite these 2 modified weights to obtain overall weights of alternative k, $v_k^{(n)}$ as follow:

$$v_k^{(n)} = \sum_{i}^{m} w_i^{(n)} u_{ik}^{(n)} \quad (4)$$

where m is the number of criteria.

Also, using the same steps again, we can composite weights of "triple inner dependence" structure, in the case when there is dependency in the 3 lower levels, i.e., not only among alternatives and 1 level criteria but also 2 levels of criteria.

III. Sensitivity Analyses

When we use AHP in some applications, it often occurs that a comparison matrix is not consistent or that there is not great difference among the overall weights of the alternatives. In these cases, it is very important to investigate how components of the pairwise comparison matrix influence its consistency or the weights. In this study, we use a method that some of the present authors have proposed before. It evaluates a fluctuation of the consistency index and the weights when the comparison matrix is perturbed. It is useful because it does not change the structure of the data.

Since the pairwise comparison matrix is a positive square matrix, Perron-Frobenius theorem holds. From Perron-Frobenius theorem, the following theorem about a perturbed comparison matrix holds.

Theorem 1 *Let $A = (a_{ij})$, $(i, j = 1, \ldots, n)$ denote a comparison matrix and let $A(\varepsilon) = A + \varepsilon D_A$, $D_A=(a_{ij}d_{ij})$ denote a matrix that has been perturbed. Let λ_A be the Frobenius root of A, $\boldsymbol{w}$ be the eigenvector corresponding to λ_A, and $\boldsymbol{v}$ be the eigenvector corresponding to the Frobenius root of A'. Then, a Frobenius root $\lambda(\varepsilon)$ of $A(\varepsilon)$ and a corresponding eigenvector $\boldsymbol{w}(\varepsilon)$ can be expressed as follows*

$$\lambda(\varepsilon) = \lambda_A + \varepsilon\lambda^{(1)} + o(\varepsilon), \quad (5)$$

$$\boldsymbol{w}(\varepsilon) = \boldsymbol{w} + \varepsilon\boldsymbol{w}^{(1)} + \boldsymbol{o}(\varepsilon), \quad (6)$$

where

$$\lambda^{(1)} = \frac{\boldsymbol{v}' D_A \boldsymbol{w}}{\boldsymbol{v}' \boldsymbol{w}}, \quad (7)$$

$\boldsymbol{w}^{(1)}$ is an n-dimension vector that satisfies

$$(A - \lambda_A I)\boldsymbol{w}^{(1)} = -(D_A - \lambda^{(1)} I)\boldsymbol{w}, \quad (8)$$

where $\boldsymbol{o}(\varepsilon)$ denotes an n-dimension vector in which all components are $o(\varepsilon)$.

About a fluctuation of the consistency index, the following corollaries hold.

Corollary 1 *Using appropriate g_{ij}, we can represent the consistency index C.I.(ε) of the perturbed comparison matrix $A(\varepsilon)$ as follows*

$$\text{C.I.}(\varepsilon) = \text{C.I.} + \varepsilon \sum_{i}^{n} \sum_{j}^{n} g_{ij} d_{ij} + o(\varepsilon). \quad (9)$$

To see g_{ij} in (9) in Corollary 1, we can determine how the components of a comparison matrix impart influence on its consistency.

Corollary 2 *Using appropriate $h_{ij}^{(k)}$, we can represent the fluctuation $\boldsymbol{w}^{(1)}=(w_k^{(1)})$ of the weight (i.e., the eigenvector corresponding to the Frobenius root) as follows*

$$w_k^{(1)} = \sum_{i}^{n} \sum_{j}^{n} h_{ij}^{(k)} d_{ij}. \quad (10)$$

Then, we can evaluate how the components of a comparison matrix impart influence on the weights, to see $h_{ij}^{(k)}$ in (10).

Proofs of these corollaries are shown in [4].

IV. Fuzzy Weights Representations

When a comparison matrix has poor consistency (i.e., 0.1<C.I.<0.2), comparison matrix components are considered to be fuzzy because they are results from human fuzzy judgment. Weights should therefore be treated as fuzzy numbers [5][6].

Definition 1 (fuzzy weight) Let $w_k^{(n)}$ be a crisp weight of criterion or alternative k of inner dependence model, and g_{ij} | $h_{ij}^{(k)}$| denote the coefficients found in Corollary 1 and 2. If 0.1<C.I.<0.2, then a fuzzy weight $\tilde{w}_k$ is defined by

$$\tilde{w}_k = (w_k, \alpha_k, \beta_k)_{LR} \tag{11}$$

$$\alpha_k = \mathrm{C.I.}\sum_i^n \sum_j^n s(-, h_{kij}) g_{ij} \,|\, h_{kij} \,|, \tag{12}$$

$$\beta_k = \mathrm{C.I.}\sum_i^n \sum_j^n s(+, h_{kij}) g_{ij} \,|\, h_{kij} \,|, \tag{13}$$

Then, we assume about double inner dependence structure in 4 levels problem. For example, above of the criteria level there might be actor's level for decision. "Leisure in holiday with family" may have 4 family actors {father, mother, older child A, younger child B}, 4 criteria {popularity, good for rain, fatigue, expense} and 4 alternatives {theme park, indoor theme park, cinema, zoo}. They may have dependency structure at 2 in 4 levels and inconsistency in some levels.

Even in these cases, we can define overall weights of alternatives with fuzzy representation using sensitivity analysis. Let the modified local weight of a actors, $\boldsymbol{x}^{(n)} = (x_i^{(n)})$, $i = 1,\dots,l$, using dependency matrices F_P, modified fuzzy weighs of criteria with only respect to actor i, $\tilde{\boldsymbol{w}}_i^{(n)} = (\tilde{w}_{ij}^{(n)})$, $i = 1,\dots,l$, $j = 1,\dots,m$ using dependency matrix F_C, and weights of alternatives with only respect to criterion j, $\boldsymbol{u}_j = (u_{jk})$, $j = 1,\dots,m$, $k = 1,\dots,m$. We can define the modified fuzzy weight

$$\tilde{w}_j^{(n)} = (w_{ij}^{(n)}, \alpha_{ij}^{(n)}, \beta_{ij}^{(n)})_{LR} \tag{14}$$

$$\boldsymbol{x}^{(n)} = (x_i^{(n)}) = F_P \boldsymbol{x} \tag{15}$$

$$\boldsymbol{w}_i^{(n)} = (w_{ij}^{(n)}) = F_C \boldsymbol{w}_i \tag{16}$$

$\boldsymbol{w}_i$ is crisp weights of criteria with only respect to actor i, and α_{ij}, β_{ij} are calculated from a result of sensitivity analysis (details are shown in [6]).

At last, fuzzy overall weights of alternative k can be calculated as follows:

$$\tilde{v}_k^{(n)} = \sum_i^l \sum_j^m x_i^{(n)} \tilde{w}_{ij}^{(n)} u_{jk} \tag{17}$$

If there is also inconsistency in actor level, using fuzzy weight $\tilde{x}_i^{(n)}$ instead of crisp $x_i^{(n)}$, fuzzy overall weights of alternative k can be calculated as follows:

$$\tilde{v}_k^{(n)} = \sum_i^l \sum_j^m \tilde{x}_i^{(n)} \otimes \tilde{w}_{ij}^{(n)} u_{jk} \tag{18}$$

where $\otimes$ denotes, fuzzy multiplication defined by extension principal.

V. Conclusion and Future Work

There are many cases in which data of AHP does not have enough reliability. For these cases, we propose fuzzy weight representation and compositions for double inner dependence in 4 levels AHP using sensitivity analysis. Our approach can show how to represent weights and is efficient to investigate how the result of AHP has fuzziness even if data are not enough consistent or reliable.

In the next step, we must find better fuzzy multiplication for composition fuzzy weights.

References

[1] T. L. Saaty, The Analytic Hierarchy Process. McGraw-Hill, New York, 1980.

[2] T. L. Saaty, Inner and Outer Dependence in AHP, University of Pittsburgh, 1991

[3] D. Dubois and H. Prade, Possibility Theory An Approach to Computerized Processing of Uncertainty, Plenum Press, New York (1988)

[4] S. Ohnishi, H. Imai, and M. Kawaguchi, "Evaluation of a Stability on Weights of Fuzzy Analytic Hierarchy Process using a sensitivity analysis," J. Japan Soc. for Fuzzy Theory and Sys., 9(1), Jan. 1997, pp.140-147.

[5] S. Ohnishi, D. Dubois, H. Prade, and T. Yamanoi, "A Fuzzy Constraint-based Approach to the Analytic Hierarchy Process," Uncertainty and Intelligent Information Systems, June 2008, pp.217-228.

[6] S. Ohnishi, T. Yamanoi, and H. Imai, "A Fuzzy Weight Representation for Inner Dependence AHP," Journal of Advanced Computational Intelligence and Intelligent Informatics, Vol.15, No.3, June 2011, pp. 329-335.

[7] S. Ohnishi, T. Furukawa, and T. Yamanoi, " Compositions of Fuzzy Weights for Double Inner Dependence AHP," COGNITIVE2013, May 2013, pp. 83-86.

[8] S. Ohnishi and T. Yamanoi, " Applying Fuzzy weights to Triple Inner Dependence AHP," DBKDA2015, June 2015.

AUTHOR INDEX